Web Theory

Web Theory is a comprehensive and critical introduction to the theories of the Internet and the World Wide Web. Robert Burnett and P. David Marshall examine the key debates which surround Internet culture: from issues of globalization, political economy and regulation, to ideas about communication, identity and aesthetics.

Web Theory explores the shifts in society, culture and the media which have been brought about by the growth of the World Wide Web. It identifies significant readings, Web sites and hypertext archive sources that illustrate the critical discussion about the Internet and it mediates these discussions, indicating key positions within each debate and pointing the reader to key texts.

Web Theory includes:

- Chapters showing how specific media have been affected by the Internet
- Boxed case studies and examples
- References, an extensive bibliography and a list of Web sites
- A glossary of key terms with important words highlighted in the text
- A Web theory timeline which details important events
- A comprehensive and regularly updated Web site at www.webtheory.nu with links and support material.

Robert Burnett is Professor of Media and Communication Studies at the University of Karlstad, Sweden. He is the author of *The Global Jukebox*. **P. David Marshall** is the Chair of the Department of Communication Studies at Northeastern University, Boston. He is the author of *Celebrity and Power* and the co-author of *Fame Games*. He is also the founding editor of one of the premier Internet journals, *M/C, a Journal of Media and Culture*.

Web Theory

An introduction

Robert Burnett and P. David Marshall

Routledge
Taylor & Francis Group

LONDON AND NEW YORK

First published 2003
by Routledge
2 Park Square, Milton Park, Abingdon Oxon, OX14 4RN

Simultaneously published in the USA and Canada
by Routledge
270 Madison Avenue, New York, NY 10016

Transferred to Digital Printing 2004

Routledge is an imprint of the Taylor & Francis Group

© 2003 Robert Burnett and P. David Marshall

Typeset in Galliard by
Wearset Ltd, Boldon, Tyne and Wear
Printed and bound by
Antony Rowe Ltd, Chippenham, Wiltshire

British Library Cataloguing in Publication Data
A catalogue record for this book is available from the British Library

Library of Congress Cataloging in Publication Data
Burnett, Robert, 1956–
Web theory : an introduction/Robert Burnett, P. David Marshall.
p. cm.
Includes bibliographical references and index.
1. Internet–Social aspects. 2. World Wide Web–Social aspects. I.
Marshall, P. David. II. Title.
HM851 .B86 2002
303.48'33–dc21

2002011565

ISBN 0–415–23833–1 (hbk)
ISBN 0–415–23834–x (pbk)

To our children

Sara and Jonatan;
Erin, Hannah and Isaac

CONTENTS

TABLES

ACKNOWLEDGEMENTS

Both authors would like to express their thanks to all those who have helped them complete this book. Together they would like to acknowledge the contributions of their editors Rebecca Barden and Christopher Cudmore. They would also like to extend their appreciation to the readers whose valuable reports and criticisms of drafts helped make the book more complete. They also would like to extend their appreciation individually.

A work like this takes on a life of its own and intersects with many different Webs, both professionally and private. The support of Karlstad University, and especially my colleagues, staff and students in the Department of Media and Communication Science has been very important. I wish to particularly thank Steve Gibson and Andreas Kitzmann for their willingness to discuss all things Web connected. My work has benefited from funding by the Swedish Council for Research in the Humanities and the Social Sciences (HSFR) and by the Swedish Knowledge Foundation (KK-Stiftelsen). Most importantly I want to thank my family for putting up with my many long nights on the computer. Thank you Vendela for sharing your life with me, and thank you Sara and Jonatan for being my constant inspiration.

RB

There are many who have contributed to the development of this book. Students in my New Media Culture course at both the University of Queensland and Northeastern University have critically engaged with the material and have aided in its development. My postgraduate students, particularly Axel Bruns, Sherman Young and Nick Caldwell, have provided a wealth of insights as they have developed their own research directions. All those who have been involved in founding and maintaining *M/C – A Journal of Media and Culture* have kept me attuned to how the intellectual currents of contemporary culture have intersected with the Web. Sue Morris, David Jensen and Rumana Faruque all worked at different times as research assistants in the developing stages of the book. My colleagues and staff at the University of Queensland and the Key Centre, particularly Angela Tuohy, Frances Bonner, Tom O'Regan, Gil Woodley and Graeme Turner, and at Northeastern University, particularly Joanne Morreale, Kevin Howley, Bernadette Metrano, Kristen Kilbashian and Alison Hearn have all provided stimulating environments for the exchange of ideas so important for the development of the concept into a book. The financial and institutional support of New York University, Karl-stad University, Northeastern University, University of Queensland, the Media and Cultural Studies Centre, and the Key Centre for Culture and Media Policy over the last three years of the project was essential for its coming to fruition. Finally, I would like to thank my family. A book goes through a rather long gestation period – longer than any member of the animal kingdom. Thank you Louise for your innovations, your support and your energy. And thanks to Erin, Hannah, and Zak – your lives are my Web and my reality check.

PDM

INTRODUCTION

AT THE DAWN of the new millennium the shift to **digital** communication is breaking down the barriers between traditional media industries and the telecommunications sector. The shift to digital transmission of all forms of **data** has been increasing at an accelerated rate for several years now. In the very near future almost all forms of data and **information** could conceivably be produced and stored in digital **bits**. This shift is redefining the way music, film, radio, television, newspapers and books are produced, manufactured, distributed and consumed. Distinctions between 'old media' appear to be eroding as different forms of 'new media' evolve. The name of the game goes by the buzzword **convergence**, the blending of the media, telecommunications and computer industries, and the coming together of all forms of mediated communication in digital form.

There is an abundance of speculation and claims that the **Internet** will replace traditional media and that 'old' media, are dinosaurs on their way to extinction, soon to be replaced with new Web based delivery systems. A proper reading of the history of communication technology tells us a different story. The introduction of new media have rarely caused the elimination of existing media, although audiences and consequently their revenue bases do often shift.

The 1990s saw the rise of the Internet (variously described as the Infobahn, the Information Highway, the Net, the Matrix, or the Web), mostly due to the establishment of the **World Wide Web (WWW)** as the **user** friendly **multimedia** portion of the Internet. The Web part of the Internet, which is the focus of this book, enabled access to increasing amounts of information and data and new possibilities for interaction.

In recent years the number of people with Internet access has increased exponentially. In addition to 'surfing' the Web, many users of the Internet are interacting with others synchronously via **Internet Relay Chat (IRC,**

ICQ), in 'chat rooms' (chatplanet, chatropolis), or Multi-User Domains (**MUDs**) as well as non-synchronously via **e-mail**, and through newsgroups (**Usenet**), and electronic mailing lists (**listserv**). Analysts of online relations often use the term 'community' to describe these **virtual** spaces, conceptualizing them in terms of a good/bad binary. They are either seen as viable replacements for physical communities that rely on face-to-face communication, or they are dismissed as pseudo-communities, enabling a false sense of intimacy and connectedness.

To write about the possibilities and the problems which the Web poses for any form of research, it is necessary to cope with its chameleon-like nature. From the point of view of the media analyst, the Web is just as complex and enigmatic a medley of modes as a John Coltrane jazz composition, for it can be regarded as a kind of postal service, or as a town hall meeting, or even an electronic Hyde Park Speaker's Corner. It is at once a newspaper, a bookstore, a library, a museum, a shopping mall and so forth. It can be superficial, profound, entertaining, boring and a tremendous source of information and tool for communication. It is a media form that subsumes and potentially changes all electronic media.

One problematic aspect of the coming-of-age of the Web as a global, and very likely the future global **communication network**, arises from the way that various electronic technologies are closely linked and can no longer be conceptualized as distinct media and communication forms. Another is how these technologies have impinged upon a privileged notion of speech by creating the possibility for integrated, interactive communication utilizing text, sound and still and moving images. This feature of the Web challenges those historical approaches to modes of communication that have granted a unique, privileged status to speech and print in contradistinction to other modes – whether visual, gestural or kinesthetic or the extensions of these through electronic means. Therefore, the first task that we will have to face in our approach to the Web is to understand the genuine complexity of this new medley of technologies and to anticipate how decisions and policies concerning its potential benefits and dangers could affect its future values to society.

THE PURPOSE OF THIS BOOK

Throughout the book we will be using two developing theses to help the reader understand the Web. Both the **loose Web** and the **Cultural Production Thesis** are new ways of making sense of the societal changes brought on by the growth of the Web and they help us reflect upon the cultural shift and the media shift that identify the convergence of activities, practices and institutions.

The loose Web metaphor acknowledges that there is a great difficulty in writing about the Web as some definable whole. By its very nature, it frustrates any unitary claim about its existence. Yet there is a new convergence in cultural forms that have either developed on the Web or have been successfully adapted to the Web that are linked in different ways than past cultural forms; that form of linkage – whether it involves the immediacy of use, the breakdown in distinctions between cultural consumption and cultural production, the **hypertext** links between sites and texts, or the blending of personal space with sites that are for more public perusal – allows the Web to be generally conceptualized as a media technology that produces a loose Web of interrelated activities. The loose Web is a major object of investigation of this book.

The Cultural Production Thesis refers to the way that the Web implies a greater engagement with the cultural apparatus which differentiates the Web from popular twentieth-century media forms such as television and radio. In contrast to the predominance of a purer reception orientation of an audience with television, the Web actively hails or interpellates its user into a sensation of production. There is with the Web a sense of seamlessness between production and consumption. This sensation is dependent on the accessibility of the technology, not just in terms of being able to 'read' (i.e. classic media literacy) but to actually produce new products, artefacts or texts. The Cultural Production Thesis builds from a model that was generated by cultural studies in their interpretation of the active audience as opposed to the passive public supposedly presumed in earlier propagandistic models of mass media communication.

The Web allows us to see more clearly the operations of cultural production and makes it possible to identify the patterns which have no doubt worked in the development of other media forms. The current stage of the Web could be likened to the early stages of radio where reception and production were not clearly delineated as the technology produced a two-way flow. This model of production quickly transforms with the new technology into a very particular cycle which is access, excess and exclusion.

HOW TO USE THIS BOOK

Web Theory introduces a range of debates and issues pertinent to our move into the **network** or Web society. We identify key sources, in order to illustrate critical debates about the Internet, and to place such debates in relation to broader theoretical discussions. Our aim is to mediate such discussions, indicating key positions within the debates and pointing the reader to core readings, hypertexts and other sources. In some cases, our recommendations are very direct, and we summarize and appraise different critical positions, and point to books and articles in which these positions are prominent. In much of the literature we discuss, clear stances and quite explicit positions in relation to the Web are offered. In other instances, our goal is to draw attention to implicit, underlying assumptions which inform the theoretical stances adopted. The focus is not on the day to day specifics of the Web, as these change rapidly. The perspective is on the underlying phenomena, as a way of understanding the general issues.

Since the purpose of *Web Theory* is to introduce issues and ideas which may not yet be familiar, design elements have been incorporated to aid the reader. Some chapters include specific case studies, and summary tables or charts, which are separated from the main flow of the text. This is so that they can be seen in relation to the main argument, but also considered relatively autonomously. Key references to core readings, and also to hypertext archive sources appear at the end of the book so the reader can follow up the issues and ideas which have been introduced in individual chapters. All references are summarized in an extensive end of book bibliography. We also include a glossary. Terms which may be new to the reader are printed in bold on their first occurrence in each chapter to remind the reader that a glossary definition is available. The reader will also find a Web theory timeline which chronologically highlights important events during the growth of the Web. Other resources are available on the book's Web site: www.webtheory.nu

CHAPTER BY CHAPTER

Chapter 1 takes a different reading of the Web's history. Wedded to the emergence of any new technology is a conceptualization of the technology as having the capacity to transform fundamentally the society. This **technological determinist** perspective is applied to analysing the Web as the chapter engages with media technology theorists to determine the value of the approach in interpreting the Web.

Chapter 2 begins with the concept of information that is generated from **cybernetics** and systems theory and debates its applicability to how the Web in fact runs. It connects also to other conceptualizations of information – the **information society**, the postindustrial society, and to a lesser degree, the Web as postmodern form. The conclusion points to the need to think of information in relation to knowledge and action as opposed to some non-applied and value-free state.

Chapter 3 deals with the use made of the Web in terms of theories of communication derived from linguistics and discourse theory and defining its distinctiveness from media theory that is connected to a broadcast model. E-mail, Usenet newsgroups, listservs, bulletin boards, MUDs and chatgroups all are connected to a different communication paradigm from that of mass media. This requires utilizing techniques and tools of analysis that are drawn from speech acts, conversational analysis and a transformed interpersonal communication. The loose Web of connectivity is introduced here.

Chapter 4 begins with some of the early research on the Web that dealt with the capacity to transform identity. It debates the boundaries of that research with examples of recent research and engages in a more general debate about the formations of **subjectivity** that are generated through the Web. It then advances on the communication approach of Chapter 3 by analysing the difference that the idea of user embodies. The chapter introduces a theorization that is derived from the active audience work of cultural studies approaches and repositions it in terms of the Web's category of the user. What is developed in this chapter is how the 'loose Web' is a loosened construction of cultural power and identifies a shift in cultural production. This chapter elaborates on one of the key themes of the book and its reading of the Internet in what we are calling the Cultural Production Thesis. The Cultural Production Thesis articulates this clear move expressed by the Web around production (the massive proliferation of Web sites and Web design and the engagement in that process of dissemination and display by millions of users) as more significant than the formations of reception.

Chapter 5 uses the tools of textual, historical and **semiotic** analysis to study the formations of meanings that are produced on the Web. The array of images and texts produced on the Web make it difficult to isolate on one style of presentation predominating. Nevertheless, there are distinctive patterns in the look of Web sites and certain graphic shorthands become the fashionable way to present information on the Web. Web designers like fashion designers are acutely aware of what is *au courant* and what is decidedly *passé* in Web aesthetics. Through studies of particular sites in greater depth, the chapter establishes links to magazine and television graphic design and identifies the **graphic Internet stage**, where still images and coloured text/fonts remain the central feature of the Web experience over and above the applications of sound and moving image. The chapter also investigates the hypertext and hyperlink structure of the Internet as an active play in the world of connotations from a production/consumption construction and explains the theory associated with hypertext and the noncoherent subjectivity generated by the Web.

Chapter 6 explores the Web economy and how it intersects with global culture. On one side it has developed from an exchange process that resembles a massive library. Through all the hypertext connections we move between a variety of sources of information and that information is a gift as opposed to a commodity. Prior to the Web's emergence, there were (and still are) massive **databases** of information where individuals and institutions paid for access by the minute or by the word. The Web as a source of relatively 'free' information, challenged this commodification process partly because of its clear affinity with the university research system. On the other side, there are amazing amounts of time and energy put into developing the **'killer application'** of the Web, the one tool that will produce a commodity relationship that has become part of other media forms. The relationship between the free and the desired commodity structure is explored in this chapter as well as a study of the global structures emerging on the Internet as large corporations attempt to create new patterns of hierarchy and exclusion in the content and quality provided.

Chapter 7 looks at cultural policy, regulation and copyright. Regulating the Internet has become the *bête noire* of cultural policy makers. Issues concerning censorship and community standards have led to the most visible attempts at policy work. Part of the argument considers the relative utility of using broadcast regulation models for developing the Web and its uses that are coordinated with national interests and objectives. The chapter investigates the issues surrounding intellectual property and copyright.

Chapter 8 looks at news and the Web. The chapter is an investigation of **informational news** and what that means in a Web context. The development of Web versions of the *Wall Street Journal, USA Today,* or *Time Magazine* are still money losers for most media corporations mainly because the indeterminate structure of the Web audience and the general failure of subscriptions on the Web. Nevertheless, Web versions continue to exist with their relatively limited advertising revenue. This chapter debates the thesis of convergence – that the Web versions of print media will eventually be the single or dominant format – in the context of the developing economies of the Web and the transformations in contemporary culture in how they use print media for different purposes (related to identity formation) than in the past (news and information for engagement in a public sphere).

Chapter 9 focuses on entertainment and more specifically popular music on the Web. The digitization of the information generated by sound and image has produced the evident convergence of media forms. From developments such as **Web radio** to the transforming music industry's integration of MP3 and the **streaming** of video and audio, media convergence now has a certain inevitability. This chapter develops its discussion of convergence from the way that new kinds of networks and new formations of entertainment are in their genesis and how and where media corporations are fitting into these new culture and industry Webs.

Our concluding chapter discusses the two overarching concepts that have been developed through the book. One is the concept of a loose Web, which describes the different institutional and social networks, forms of identity and forms of cultural commodities that the Web has allowed to flourish. The other is the cultural production thesis which expresses that the Web is much more about the expansion and proliferation of cultural production than previous media forms such as television.

Chapter 1

WEB OF TECHNOLOGY

Information Technology is friendly; it offers a helping hand; it should be embraced. We should think of it more like ET than IT.

Margaret Thatcher, 1982,
quoted in Robins and Webster (1999: 74)

Nicholas Negroponte opened his popular book *Being Digital* with a peculiar list of the near future and how **digital** technology will get us there:

> Early in the next millennium your right and left cuff links or earrings may communicate with each other by low-orbiting satellites and have more computer power than your present PC. Your telephone won't ring indiscriminately, it will receive, sort, and perhaps respond to your incoming calls like a well-trained English butler. Mass Media will be redefined by systems for transmitting and receiving personalized information and entertainment. Schools will change to become more like museums and playgrounds for children to assemble ideas and socialise with other children all over the world ... Twenty years from now, when you look out a window, what you see may be five thousand miles and six times zones away ...
>
> (Negroponte 1995: 6–7)

THIS KIND OF reading of the future through technology has a long history and a very large popular impact on how we receive any current generation of technology such as the Web. In the past World Expositions such as the New York World's Fair of 1932 would be a magical site of what the future would be like and help stimulate the cultural imagination.

Aerodynamic cars racing above the surface, sleek angular buildings and the prevalence of modern conveniences for the home were all part of the imagined future provided by corporations that participated in that exposition. At the beginning of the twentieth century the skyscraper provided the image of both progress and the future. The dizzying heights were monuments of human achievement, power and ultimately an expression of the triumph of modernity and civilization. The continuing race to have the tallest building (Kuala Lumpur's Twin Towers) or freestanding structure in the world (CN Tower) is a testament to how technology expresses the future in its present forms.

In a similar vein, the introduction of home computers in the early 1980s produced a series of magazine articles and book chapters that celebrated telecommuting culminating in the 'microcomputer' becoming *Time* Magazine 'Person of the Year' for 1982 (Dyer-Witheford 1999: 21): instead of coming into the smog-filled city, the new worker managed to produce their intellectual labour at their cottage by the lake. A real cottage industry that resembled the production of crafts was heralded for the digital age. Where the industrial revolution produced problems, the post-industrial revolution promised through **information** and computer technology a path to what could be called a new traditionalism. In the 1985 film *Brainstorm*, there was a depiction of this new idyllic life that was connected to high technology. Although the lead character was producing a sophisticated **virtual reality** device, he casually and pleasantly rode on a sophisticated tricycle to and from work, where work was part of both the home and the office.

Past media forms have provided similar depictions of the future. When radio was first developed and introduced it was generally believed to offer a path to a better future. Education and the more general desire for human betterment accompanied the emergence of radio and a similar range of desires were placed on television as it emerged in the 1930s and 1940s. (Douglas 1987; Winston 1998: 81; McChesney 1990).

With this long history of presenting technology in utopian terms, it seems natural and inevitable that the Web was presented as offering a future paradise for users as it emerged as a generally available platform in the 1990s. Writers such as Rheingold (1994) in his influential book, *The Virtual Community* underlined the communitarian qualities of the Web. Communities could be developed without the past restrictions of spatial constraints. In a blending of new age philosophy with **computer-mediated communications**, the **Internet** provided the means to make a more active and engaged public that would allow a new era of truer and greater democracy. The Web offered a wide array of dimensions that promised a better world: e-commerce provided better business solutions; the massive amount of information on the Web meant it was ultimately the most interesting and diverse library available for education; and its transnational quality allowed for greater global communication and – the generally implied – understanding than could be imagined through past media forms.

When one reads the ruminations on the future from George Gilder (1994), Bill Gates (1996) or a host of what we can group as futurologists a coordinated description of the power and value of the Web is painted. In perfect synergy, the newspaper supplements of the mid-1990s that focused on the Web provided a general discourse of wonder and urgency that everyone should come online.

The Web's introduction in its close parallel with the introduction of other technologies identifies that there has been an **ideology of technology** operating in contemporary culture. What we mean by ideology is a framework of representations that makes whatever is current appear to be completely normal, natural and appropriate. An ideology that is concerned with technology therefore makes any new technology not only natural and normal for the culture but also what is needed to make the society better. In other words, an ideology of technology creates a desire for the cultural transformation promised by technology. It serves to reduce public debate about the technology and shifts most discussion to a functional level of how to expand, implement and integrate the new technology into our everyday lives. Critics have called this ideology a form of 'technological rationality' (Marcuse 1964; Habermas 1975) or 'instrumental reason' (Horkheimer and Adorno 1987) where there is a simple means-end approach to its implementation. For the Web, debate might be reduced to how do we get greater numbers of people online rather than what kind of content or structures will be available online. Or perhaps it leads to a continuing and spiralling drive to technical perfectionism on the Web, where the current version is perpetually obsolete and technologically unsophisticated and we are encouraged to purchase the latest computer and load the latest software to participate in, for example, new versions of video and audio **streaming** or other forms of virtuality. In an ideology of technology we have accepted the speed of technological obsolescence and have naturalized our consumer desires that we cannot really be happy without the latest model. For many of us, this ideology of technology is a cultural reality that shapes our everyday lives. Many Web and computer-related corporations depend on that ideology to continue to operate as a constitutive element of contemporary society and to produce what Webster and Robins (1999: 2–3) describe as 'technoculture'.

In media and communication studies, the concept of **technological determinism** is generally used to describe this power of technology over a culture and is very useful in understanding the current power of the Web and where that power originates. McQuail (1994: 107) defines technological determinism as 'the links between the dominant communication technology of an age and the key features of society'. To make the definition complete there are some other elements of technological determinism that need to be identified:

Technological determinism often highlights an inevitability around technological change

There is a resignation about the nature of change in a culture because of the power of the dominant technology to determine how people interact. From a technological determinist perspective, we as a society often are *reacting* to technological change. Past technologies such as television produced a certain kind of culture: in its broadcast form it may have privileged the nation state and national identities in the twentieth century. The Web, if it is in fact becoming the dominant communication technology of this century, produces a non-broadcast structure and potentially a non-national structure.

Technological determinism as an approach has produced a dialectic of utopian and dystopian views of technology in culture

As much as there has been a celebration of technology by the futurologists that we have described above, there is an antithetical relationship to its value in culture. For instance, popular cultural forms such as novels and films often dance between the utopian and dystopian. William Gibson's cyberpunk novels such as the original *Neuromancer* (1984) present a stark and bleak world as people jack-in to a parallel **cyberspace** that occasionally transforms them ('their wetware') irrevocably. In the film *The Matrix*, we learn that the future world is entirely simulation as humans are used as an energy source to power a machine world. Clearly these and other representations of the future, including the *Terminator* films, *Blade Runner*, and countless others, present a negative and dystopian future through technology. But in an odd paradox their various special effects are celebrated as technological breakthroughs in the various promotion and publicity campaigns that surround these films. As filmgoers, the film narrative contradicts the very reason and the kinds of pleasures we derive from a film that relies on new technology: we go to enjoy the technological effects even as we view the dystopian future that is produced by the technology.

The dystopian technological determinism has a couple of variations that intersect with the emergence of the Web. For instance, Alvin Toffler's general approach as a futurologist is a scare tactic: the speed of technological change will leave you behind and so he entreats you to act on what is about to change around you. Toffler (1970, 1980) maintains an inevitability about technological change that is dangerous if not heeded. Fundamentally, the Web implies a new information-driven society that implies different kinds of work and forms of knowledge.

Popular journalism and some psychological studies have linked Web technology to a form of addiction that indicates that the technology itself has the capacity to transform human behaviour at an almost physiological level by its very nature. This form of technological determinism is not necessarily new – television has long been written about as an addiction (Winn 1977) – but it has been adapted to several features of the Web. For instance, many articles have been written about individuals addicted to **Internet Relay Chat** programs or to what is often called virtual sex on the Web. A particular panic developed around the early **MUDs** which operated as interactive role-playing games that were perceived to absorb completely adolescent boys. This fear of the power of Web technology continues to be a source of new news stories; even consultancies have sprung up which help you or someone you know lose their addiction to the Internet.

Technological determinism is generally a term used to critique the various approaches specifically because of the reduction of historical, social and cultural processes to one causal factor

Technological determinism is used as a critical analytical tool to group a certain generalizable approach to the relationship between technology and society. It would be rare to see one of the writers we have isolated here as describing him or herself as a technological determinist. The critique of technological determinism is that it is a reductionist reading of the contemporary or future world. There is a complex interplay of social, economic, governmental and cultural needs that help determine the successful adoption of a technology such as the Web. For example, if we look at the history of the Web it developed from very specific but intricate institutional connections. (See the Web Theory timeline in the Appendix for greater detail.) Its original US military origins as a system that would have no centre so that communication could be maintained despite the most apocalyptic nuclear attack on any individual centre allowed for the development of the multiple nodes of **CERN** and **ARPAnet**. The *network of networks* structure of the Internet has built from these origins but advanced in its application as a research **network** that became wedded to university research. However, the original intention of the network was military information and research, while the Internet's connection to universities presented a different kind of institutional direction. For example, research is often exchanged freely between different researchers in order to advance a certain kind of knowledge. Informal networks of researchers then used the Internet for these exchanges of information. This kind of university culture with its accessible libraries, its general direction of dissemination of information and knowledge is fundamentally different from the military's desire for control and regulation of the flows of information for usually highly specific and often classified, national security reasons. When the exchanges between university researchers began to diverge from their research and into more interpersonal and recreational communication exchanges, elements of how we see the Web today began emerging in earnest. Computer pictures – sometimes pornographic – were exchanged. Personal details and relationships were tagged on to the end of correspondences, and computer games began circulating. For instance, one of the most popular computer games in the 1970s was a game of skill requiring the **user**/player to land the lunar module on the Moon (Poole 2000: 29–30). Other information began being deposited and available via the Internet. Systems such as the University of Minnesota's **Gopher** allowed one to search categories of material that were made available by other researchers. In conjunction with these developments, the expansion of telephone connections via **modem** technology to this emerging Internet allowed for its use to move outside the research institutions and into people's homes. Parallel networks developed that were more closely connected to people's hobbies rather than their research and a rapid proliferation of bulletin boards developed for exchanges of information. Because the early users of the Internet were more computer literate there was a tendency for these early bulletin boards to have a science fiction or fantasy focus that paralleled the computer culture's interests. Thus sites devoted to *Star Trek* or *Dr Who* or particular science fiction authors, films and novels were some of the most popular bulletin boards that eventually came to be called usegroups and newsgroups.

What one should notice about this history of the Web is its unravelling of the original technological intention: the military purpose seems almost incidental. Because of the variety of institutions that were connected to the Internet and the emergence of the Web, it cannot be reduced to simple causal factors. The Web that we see today has relied on a government connection that has produced a quasi-public service quality to the Web even as it has been commercialized throughout the 1990s. The result: continuing tension between its public role and the desires to make it increasingly commercial. Technological determinism oversimplifies the process of social use of a technology that transforms the technology and the institutional web of power that also shapes any cultural technology.

Nonetheless, a number of writers and thinkers that can be grouped as technological determinists have produced some interesting insights around the emergence of new technologies. And although their approach should always be treated with limited applicability it is worthwhile detailing what they have tried to explain in their work. Part of understanding the Web's current presence can be elucidated through people such as H.A. Innis (1950, 1951), Marshall McLuhan (1962, 1965), and Lewis Mumford (1963) and more recent writers who have used their insights to make sense of contemporary technologies such as the Web. Our objective here is to highlight their utility in studying the Web by isolating on what theoretical insights they have provided in their work.

THE BIAS OF COMMUNICATION

One of the richest resources for studying the emergence of new technologies is a Canadian political economic historian H.A. Innis. Most of his early writings dealt with detailed economic histories of staple industries which shaped the relationships between colonies and empires (Innis 1940). The long and intricate history of the fur trade between Canada and Europe helped Innis develop a very interesting model of exchange and communication that he expanded in his work just before his death (Innis 1956). Although others have elaborated on his approach with other metaphors, Innis established the concept of centre – peripheral economic relations which helped shape the very transport and communication routes that were established in perceived-to-be-new territories such as Canada. For Innis, transport and communication were not so clearly separated and were very much conceptualized on a related continuum. Thus a road served not only as part of a transport system; it also verged on the quality of a communication medium in its promotion of exchange and, both by its use and physical presence, a relationship to the centre's power. What fundamentally linked transport and communication in Innis's innovative ponderings was their relationship to another continuum that he conceptualized in two polar extremes: space and time (Innis 1951).

Innis developed a grand theory of history that tried to demarcate the relationship a particular culture had to space and time. The key defining causal factor according to Innis was related to the dominant form of communication. Each communication technology betrayed a bias towards either spatial or temporal concerns. That particular bias of communication would shape the nature of that society and, like an Achilles heel, would lead to its inevitable decline or its inherent limitation. A medium of communication was either concerned with a preservation of information (time-biased) or capacity for wide distribution (space-biased). With past civilizations Innis's approach is revealing (Innis 1951).

An oral-based culture, Innis considered to be one that worked on the maintenance of traditions, rituals of life, death and ancestry – in other words a bias towards linking the present with the past. Because of its oral communication form, the actual size of the culture is inherently limited: messages had to be passed interpersonally and knowledge also had to be relayed verbally. Memory of the explanatory tales and legends served as the guides for future generations' actions and were kept by a limited number of high priests(esses) or oracles as they were called in ancient Greece. Extensions of time-biased communication forms might be the communication medium of writing on clay tablets or conveying one's culture through the depictions of temple architecture: both of these examples indicate the relative immobility of the dominant communication media and therefore bias towards the maintenance of temporal continuities. Time-biased societies tended to be

more insular and clearly less open to exchange with other cultures and traditions and therefore ultimately conservative in their sustenance through
establishing the flow from ancestors to descendents.

In contrast, a space-biased culture, worked with communication technologies that allowed for much wider dissemination and exchange. If stone
and clay tablets made it difficult to move messages around, the development
of papyrus – the precursor of paper – permitted the ability to transfer commands, orders and general information much further. Paper in conjunction
with a relatively simple script of characters in written form like the alphanu-
meric system, allowed the capacity to dominate greater and greater territories. Innis's example of the Roman Empire's form of communication that
only worked with a transport network that also was spatially biased allowed
control to be exercised from the Roman centre to the barbaric limits of the
empire like Hadrian's Wall on the border between Scotland and England.
The sentinel system of passing written messages ensured a rapid distribution
and thereby also ensured a consistency of the message that could not be
altered by memory or an individual's failings. The spatial bias of communication describes most accurately the development of Empires (Innis 1950).

Innis's own plaint for the contemporary era was some sort of balance
between spatial and temporal biases of communication. And his fear was
that the essential nature of contemporary communication technology was
space-biased and facilitated the continued territorial forms of expansion that
were part of the Roman Empire as much as they were part of the British
Empire in the eighteenth and nineteenth centuries. Although most of
Innis's communications writings were completed in the late 1940s and early
1950s, they provide useful metaphors for the understanding of the Web's
biases.

How can we characterize the Web in terms of this spectrum? Does it
present the possibility of spatial control or does it present the bias of time in
its infinite archival structure? As an emerging 'bias' of communication, it is
worthwhile thinking how it may produce particular forms of social structures (Burnett 1997).

Certainly, the Web elucidates an active play with space and time. Like
television it presents an instantaneity over space that may indicate the
potential power of the technology to be space biased. But can we accurately
identify the centre of the Web? If a president or prime minister wants to
focus the nation, the Web is less effective at producing the simultaneous
impact that a national television broadcast would achieve. The Web has a
greater reach than terrestrial broadcast television, but its message is diffused.
Although it can be simultaneous for an audience, there still remains a fair
bit of activity for the user of the Web to locate at a given site at a given time
that makes the remote control of television a greater technology of instantaneous connection.

On the other hand, the Web has further accentuated the power of the

English language and advanced the centralization of power in imperial, Innis-like ways as the language of the Web is dominated by English and dwarfs any other language in use. Partly because of the Web's emergence in North America and its proliferation through English-language defence and research institutes, the model of communication of the empire is reinforced through the Web.

Another interesting question arises from the insights of Innis. How is space in fact defined through the Web? As we are aware, the metaphor cyberspace implies a different relationship to territoriality. Its virtuality makes the Web discontinuous with the material world of countries and geopolitics. Does the control of virtual space actually generate a control of geographical space? What the Web does emphasize is that there may be new divides that cross geographical boundaries in grouping activities and inter- ests. These groupings may relate to power – in other words, the Web now helps isolate on the 'symbol workers' or an 'information' elite that is engaged in the communication form. Their alliances may not be coordinated with the interests of empires unless we alter that notion to include multinational conglomerates that would not be different from Innis's earlier descriptions of companies such as the Hudson Bay Company. Although we will deal with these issues more in Chapter 6 on the Web economy, it is worthwhile also noting that there are efforts by these large firms to exercise greater control over the use of the Web and through this control we see the expansions of cyberspatial control which have repercus- sions in the international geopolitics of work, economy and cultural life.

There is also a great deal of thinking and writing on the virtuality of space, that the dwelling in cyberspace actually becomes experientially as significant for its users as real space. Certainly cyberspace gives the sensation of movement and therefore connection over great expanses of territory. However, the use of this space is not necessarily coordinated into expres- sions of power by its users. The virtual world of cyberspace often represents an imaginary domain that actually removes heavy users from the exigencies of everyday life. Thus the Web is as much a tool for the coordination of ter- ritorial expansion as it is for the loss of self into the pleasures and entertain- ment of 'surfing' the Web. It must be remembered that porn sites and games are some of the most popular and intensively used sites in cyberspace and their connection to productive pursuits of power cannot be adequately dealt with in Innis's theorization although they may express a gendered power differential rearticulated from the social world into the cyberworld.

Pondering the temporal dimension of the Web and questioning whether the Web produces a time-biased culture seems less supportable. The deterri- torialization of space that the Internet promises and delivers makes it diffi- cult to read the contemporary embrace of the Web as anything that implies a static and enduring structure for culture. Yet the Web is a massive archive of material and some claim it is an elaborate library of documents that dwarfs the Library of Congress, the largest library in the world. The Web through its computer technology is organized around memory and storage. The succession of storage technologies moving from bytes to gigabytes on personal computers over the last twenty years is replicated exponentially by the storage capacities of **servers** that act as the memory hubs of the Internet.

Ultimately, however, the Web is fundamentally a movement towards a more rapid transfer of information spatially. Its instantaneity is one factor in identifying the space bias of the technology. Along with the infinite mutability of Web sites – that is, the capacity to continuously change the presence of any document, the disappearance of sites without any overseeing supervision, and the movement through the Web via hyperlinks – the Web produces ultimately a fluid and unstable reflection of culture that does not support the tradition-based kind of culture that Innis referred to in his study of time-biased communication technologies.

McLUHAN: THE MEDIUM, THE GLOBAL VILLAGE AND THE ELECTRONIC COLLECTIVE CONSCIOUSNESS

No non-contemporary thinker and writer has been celebrated more with the emergence of the Internet than Marshall McLuhan. McLuhan, a Canadian academic derided for his undeveloped ideas for over twenty years by many in communication studies, was a popular media icon and 'guru' of the 1960s and early 1970s. Although he died in 1980 before the emergence of the personal computer, many of his ideas seemed particularly prescient less in relationship to the technologies of television and print that he studied but with a much greater correlation with the emerging computer-related technologies. Writers such as Levinson (1999) have been central in this reinterpretation of McLuhan and his recuperation as an important visionary.

Innis and McLuhan's approaches have been linked in a number of different directions not only by McLuhan himself but also most writers that have attempted to read the McLuhan enigma. But there are certain approaches by McLuhan that are less related to the technological determinism of Innis. These large sweeping insights have been applied to the Web as if they are self-evident. McLuhan worked in aphorisms that produced an interesting dialectic. His thinking appeared superficial and yet his ideas were appropriated and debated widely (Marshall 2000).

The medium

The central insight of McLuhan (1965) was that 'the medium is the message'. McLuhan argued that the content actually confuses our reading of the technology and its likely future. For instance, the dominant content of film was novels and plays; likewise television became organized around the content of movies or replicating movie structures. As a general rule, the content of the new medium is filled with the forms of the past medium and takes a period of time to establish its own reorganization of content (1965: 32). Although certainly not claimed by McLuhan, but possibly a McLuhanesque reading was that the first truly televisual form was in fact the 1980s music video. McLuhan adds to this insight the concept of hot and cool media, which is a transformation of Innis' bias of communication. Using the argot of the 1960s, McLuhan considered print a very hot medium because it was too complete and did not permit a great deal of interaction. Television, in contrast with its less developed visual quality, demanded a kind of audience completion and therefore was a 'cooler' medium. Orality allowed for more interchange with the content being less fixed; print's lack of dynamism was seen as dangerous in its production of an overheated culture (1965: 36–44).

The 'digitizing' of McLuhan for his applicability to the Web and digital technology has been done very completely by Levinson (1999). However, it must be realized that Levinson has been an enthusiastic acolyte of McLuhan for most of his professional writing life and his celebration of McLuhan's metaphors needs some tempering. Our analysis here acknowledges Levinson's work without a wholesale endorsement.

Thinking of the medium of the Internet as opposed to the myriad content patterns that have emerged is a very useful insight that McLuhan has generated. It places in perspective the incredible desires of media corporations to reproduce television, radio and popular music on the Internet. It also situates the Web's development in a longer historical trajectory than the supposed rapid revolutionary metaphors that populate the current generation of futurists on the Internet. The longer-term effects of the Web are derived from understanding the way that the technology reorganises society. From a McLuhan perspective, the technology produces a Web of interaction and exchange that resembles the way he imagined the technological sensorium to emerge from television and earlier electronic communication technologies. **Interactivity** for McLuhan was positive in its transformation of the rigidities of a heated up print culture. Although print and text predominate the Web experience, the mutability of the content and the dynamic nature of the changes to the Web must be read as being similar to an oral culture. Television when it is redistributed as a phenomenon on the Web has the potential to generate things like jennycam (www.jennycam.org) and other **Webcam**era sites (www.camcentral.com) that redistribute the idea of the structured and hierarchical order of broadcast television. As a medium, the Web at least presents itself as non-hierarchical and, although McLuhan cannot lay claim to conceptualizing this distinctive quality of computer-networked communication, his directive to concentrate on the technological implications of the medium points us in the right direction. The interchange of the Internet is built from the network of networks that form its technological structure. Distinctive from telephony, the Web implicates a production component, that is, where content is developed and enhanced beyond its original orality (think of any conversation and its unpredictable flow) into some combination of visual, textual and graphic structure. The Web, when thought of as a medium is a hybrid that invokes the sensation of orality and contingency with the guided structure of a book or magazine. Its hypertextual links shift the linearity of print into something that implicates other sources of information. Hence any text on the Web is often part of, or linked to, networks of related texts and the people who have generated those other texts.

Global village

The interconnections that McLuhan saw in the expansion of television and other communication technology internationally led him to coin the term **global village** (1962: 43). Although inaccurate as a definition of what television and radio produce internationally, for it could be argued that at least for the first 80 years of broadcasting, television and radio were very effective at reproducing strongly national and sometimes nationalistic cultures, McLuhan did identify a 'structure of feeling' (Williams 1965: 64–88) transformation in contemporary culture. An awareness of other parts of the world became possible. And in some instances, international media events and internationally popular series such as Dallas in the 1980s or the Kennedy assassination in 1963 produced a sense of interconnection and conversation epicentres that produced *communication* similarities across continents. These forms of exchange certainly did not construct a new sense of community that would have resembled the way that a village relied on interpersonal knowledge and orality to make sense of itself.

Reading the Web from this perspective also does not lead one to conclude that there is a new global village. The Web is part of a trajectory of **globalization** that makes it possible to move information instantaneously around the world. Globalization, however, is much more an economic imperative that has enveloped the Internet rather than the result of the technology itself leading to such transformations. The unitary global village may not make sense, but McLuhan's insight of village or community that is maintained transnationally through the medium of the Web is more evident from current patterns of Internet use. The community structure of exchange occurs at the level of transnational interest communities who maintain their linkages through the Internet in a variety of ways that we explore further. In an incremental way, the Web provides another channel for the establishment of international virtual connections and thereby weakening the hold of the traditional geographically defined conception of the village.

Electronic collective consciousness

There was something particularly apocalyptic about McLuhan's thinking that believed that the various technologies were the outering or the 'extension' of the senses (1965: 35). His close affinity with the electronic technologies is that he saw them as having the closest affinity to the outer ring of the central nervous system. Where other technologies such as film have emphasized one sense and allowed for us all metaphorically to see things from great distances, his utopian reach for the future is the combinatory reading of the senses by the brain itself. In extrapolating McLuhan's belief in an eventual outering of the mind into the electronic technology, Levinson has considered the contemporary Internet as expressing that interconnection into a global mind better than the technologies that generated McLuhan's thinking (Levinson 1999: 65–80). The complex networking of the Internet resembles the patterns of electric transfer that McLuhan imagined the central nervous system to produce from dendrites to neurons, from memory to action.

McLuhan's thinking on the power of technology to merge, in a sense, with the individual and be the path to a collective mind is not entirely new. The French Catholic techno-mystic priest Teilhard de Chardin (1965) posed a similar future of collective consciousness through technology in the middle of the twentieth century. Even Marx's reading of industrialization was partly connected to a liberating collective class consciousness and the withering away of the state with a workers' utopia emerging in its place (Marx 1978: 197). The latest proponent of a collective consciousness derived from communication technology is Pierre Levy (1995, 1997), a French writer who has managed to coin a whole new lexicon around his ideas of **collective intelligence** built from cyberspace.

It is relatively easy to dismiss the utopian claims of these approaches; but there remains some worthwhile smaller ideas that have come from reading the Web and the Internet as the channel to collective consciousness. First of all, there is an insight about a collective knowledge base that has transformed the way we have conceptualized learning. In early twentieth-century schools in Western societies, there was still a strong emphasis on rote learning through memorization of poems, facts and history. What seems to be emerging partly from the Internet's accessibility to information is that learning has become the ability to retrieve the information and transform it into knowledge and action. The vast expanse of information that is now on the Web makes this the focus of learning from high school onwards. However, the increasing commercialization of the Web is making the issue the actual maintenance of this collective information **database** that is so extraordinarily cross-referenced.

One can also develop a slightly different reading of the relationship between technology and the individual and the *social* through using the collective consciousness metaphor in a limited way. It is worthwhile to ponder the interaction between a technological form and the individual as a form of transformation. Certainly Donna Haraway's (1991) work on the **cyborg** as a form of human and gender liberation acknowledges the way that technology allows our identity to shift and the lines of what constitutes human and non-human to not be so clearly defined. Our point here is that technologies shape our behaviour in particular ways so that we often become unified with the technology. Think of driving a car or riding a bicycle. To do it well, the processes of steering and the processes of gear changing and reading traffic conditions have to become automatic and almost part of our autonomic system. The position of the signalling system in a car is situated so that it is indeed an extension of the arm and is conveniently located to flick upwards or downwards.

We can think of computer-mediated forms in a similar way. The Web, computer games, and other forms of computer activity first appear to be quite distant from the user and there are a series of foreign commands. In fact, the pre-icon and windows computer demanded a familiarity with non-intuitive commands to allow even simple word-processing. The graphic development of the computer screen and the progressive familiarity with the use of the computer leads to the idea that the computer is an extension of certain human activities and forms of creativity. We will explore the human-computer interface in the next chapter; but it needs to be said that the Web, as most technologies, cannot be separated from the human functions from which they arise. Lewis Mumford (1963) – an advocate of human-focused technology and the need for greater control of the technological society – made the interesting remark that tools were not the defining feature of humanity and thereby one of the components that separated their activities from animals. What separated us from the rest of the animal kingdom was the imagination which conceptualized the tool. For Mumford and later Langdon Winner (1977) technology had become autonomous or out-of-control; the question that needs to be posed is: 'Does the Web embody a technology that is out of human control and thereby a channel for the expression of further centralization of power or does the Web express an extension of general human interest and a democratizing relationship to knowledge and power? On an individual level, the question could be reformed: is the Web intuitively an extension of the self into a kind of collective network of knowledge/information? Or, does the Web absorb our thinking to produce the technological rationality that does not allow us to examine the system we are using? Neither of these questions has a simple answer and the next chapter begins to develop the kind of information and knowledge that is generated by our **Web culture**.

CONCLUSION

It must be reiterated that although there are insights that can be derived from McLuhan, Innis or the expanding array of technoutopians, the technological determinist perspective produces a limited causal connection to what has made the Internet and the Web what they are today. Technology may appear to operate autonomously and thereby shape human activities, but it is nevertheless connected to particular institutions and powers. It is appropriated into contexts and some existing social patterns. It may accentuate those patterns because of its structure of use and its basic technology; but the technology becomes recessed behind its use and function. For instance, fewer and fewer people are aware of how computer codes and computers operate; layers upon layers of graphics have distanced us from the nature of the technology itself. We begin to think of the Web as instances of particular forms – a source of news and information, a technique for shopping and home delivery, a divertissement of connected interesting sites, or a place for presenting images that are important to the self. Moreover, technologies become integrated into the everyday and through that process lose their former 'transcendent' and transforming capacity and become mundane. Toasters, microwaves, refrigerators, television, transistor radios have all lost that lustre as transformative technologies (Marshall 1998). But all these technologies have benefited from a continuing narrative in Western culture that we defined as an ideology of technology. The Web is part of that trajectory and has benefited from the power of that ideology to proliferate as an important and significant means of communication for the twenty-first century.

The 'history' we have presented here has been developed to make us think about how the Web has been structured into particular narratives and one of the dominant tropes of those narratives has been the revolutionary transformation story. A parallel story needs to be developed and that is the way the Web has actually built on and intensified many existing institutions, social needs and expressions of desires. One of the clear dialectics of any new technology is how it integrates the past with the present and the future. Contained within the Web, we can see its institutional past (its connection to the military and also its connection to research and universities and its public origins), its media past (in the re-presentation of newspapers, journals and magazines as well as film and television and advertising), and its technological past (as an inheritor of the transformation of space for instantaneous transaction in the tradition of the telegraph and the telephone). To represent its present and future and the distinctive difference it engenders in our relationship to technology the Web attempts to encompass so much and so comprehensively. In other words, it is not defined as other technologies as very use-specific like a toaster or a dishwasher. The Web, in contrast, is the channel through which greater and greater portions of our lives are carried out through its various Internet manifestations. This may not be revolutionary; but it does describe how an applied technology – the loose Web as we have identified it – integrates its way into our present and future everyday lives and insinuates its presence into more and more elements of those daily routines.

Chapter 2

INFORMATION AND NETWORKS

[T]he new communication system radically transforms space and time, the fundamental dimensions of human life. Localities become disembodied from their cultural, historical, geographic meaning, and reintegrated into functional networks, or into image collages, inducing a space of flows that substitutes for the space of places. Time is erased in the new communication system when past, present, and future can be programmed to interact with each other in the same message. The space of flows and timeless time are the material foundations of a new culture, that transcends and includes the diversity of historically transmitted systems of representation: the culture of real virtuality where make-believe is belief in the making.

(Manuel Castells 1996: 357)

A S MUCH AS the history of the emergence of the Web has been linked to a major technological shift, it has also been connected to clear changes in the way we conceptualize **information** and how we think about the concept of the **network**. This chapter unravels the way that theories of information and theories of the network and **network society** can help elucidate the social and cultural changes that are part of **Web culture**.

There is a popular sense that contemporary culture has an overload of information that is counterproductive at both the individual and society level. The **Internet**'s burgeoning supply of information has often become the current shorthand for this information overload. Part of the problem is that it is difficult to determine the relative value of any piece of information and there seems to be fewer means to check the validity of the facts, figures, and arguments that are produced on the Web. In other words, the Web produces a massive surplus of content that may not actually be useable as information. When we use the Web, one of the principal frustrations is getting to a source that may advertise itself through a keyword that in the end has used that word purely to attract Web traffic via the **search engines**. If one of the advantages/values of the current Web is its connection to 'information', we need to think through what 'information' actually is and, from that vantage point, we can assess the kinds of information that are produced by the Internet and its elaborate Web of content.

DEFINING INFORMATION: BINARY CODES

The development of computer technology has been closely associated with very particular meanings of information that are not necessarily the way that information is generally understood. For instance, the basic coding of content that is transmitted by computers is a reduction of everything to binary codes. A binary code is expressed in a series of ones and zeroes, where the most complex form of information is a longer string of those ones and zeroes. To get to a basic understanding of binary codes is to think of their 'meaning' in terms of their difference. Thus it can be thought of as equivalent to a code for switching on and off a light: each '1' represents switching the light on and each '0' represents turning the light off. In series you develop a long version of semaphore-like codes. The ones and zeroes on their own represent no information and it is only the relationship to each other and the pattern that produces some kind of information when it is finally decoded and represented. Each character stroke on the keyboard represents a binary code. For ultimate complexity, the human genome project that is charting all of the various DNA patterns that make up human life represents incredibly long and complex versions of these same binary codes. The length of these series and the patterns of their numbering have demanded the capacity of computers to help establish and store these variations.

This capacity to restructure everything into binary codes is usually called digitalization. The value of digitalization is only partially realized now; but fundamentally it means that past forms such as television, radio, or recorded music can be reread digitally and either stored or retransmitted with greater ease because of the conversion of that original displayed **analogue** information into binary codes. It allows for greater manipulation, non-linear editing, and ultimately a **convergence** of forms through this computerization of their content into the same **digital** language. In a sense, what the computer as a technology has permitted is the reduction of the content and information of images/texts/sounds into the same numerical form; the form is devoid of meaning until codes that explain how it should be interpreted are operated or run on the numerical list.

CYBERNETICS AND INFORMATION

This idea of the reduction of information/content to allow for its storage, conversion, and transmission is derived from a particular approach to the concept of information. Although there are other sources of innovation for the emergence of computers, the concept of **cybernetics** is critical and is very much connected to the digital binary. Of all the possible terms used to describe this new converged digital and Web-based culture, the prefix cyber seems to be ubiquitous. Partially emerging from the William Gibson's *Neuromancer* (1984) the idea of **cyberspace** has proliferated into neologisms such as *cyber*culture, *cyber*café, *cyber*future, *cyber*world, *cy*borg and so on. What does this prefix, cyber, actually indicate and why is it so prevalently used in relation to the emerging Internet culture and the Web?

Cyber comes from the Greek which means 'to steer'. Kubernetes, its Greek root, literally means 'steersman' (OED 1989) When the word is transformed into cybernetics it refers to the science of self-steering or to put in a dictionary definition it is the 'science of systems of control and communications in animals and machines' (OED 1989). There have been several intellectual trajectories that have taken up this concept of self-steering. Norbert Wiener (1948) integrated it into ballistic science research and may have coined the term while what became known as the Palo Alto School under Gregory Bateson (1972) developed cybernetics into an approach for human systems. Ecology, that more radical branch of biological science, has also embraced the system structure of cybernetics to explain something like a natural ecosystem and concept of balance. Indeed, systems theory is often used as a synonym for cybernetics.

The actual concept of cybernetics is quite simple. It is worth using the different examples that have emerged from ballistics science and systems theory to elucidate how information is thought of specifically in cybernetics. Wiener's original problem was the enormous failure rate of trained artillery crews in the Second World War who were unable to have a great success rate at hitting enemy aeroplanes (1948). Once an enemy plane engaged in evasive manoeuvres it easily dodged the trajectory of the missile/bullet from the ground. Wiener's great conceptual leap was to think of the gunner, the missile, and the enemy not in terms of the categories and the idea of a target but as a unitary *system* that had a central objective: the meeting of bullet/missile and aeroplane. Every time an aeroplane shifted its direction, the bullet/missile would adjust its course to match that new trajectory. Wiener's novel approach led to the production of what is often called a self-guiding missile which essentially means that through some technique the missile is linked through *information* to its target so that it is a part of this single system. The method of that linkage was to power the projectile and to make a mechanism that was able to adjust the missile's use of its own engine solely in terms of the target. Missiles guided by the heat of the target, or the shape/size of an image of the target are two means of generating a cybernetic system for ballistic missiles. In military parlance, once a target such as a tank was 'locked in' it indicated that the tank and the missile were now informationally linked and therefore locked into the system's objective of tank destruction (see Galison 1994: 228–66).

In cybernetic thinking, information is always a form of constraint. To exemplify this idea of information as constraint we can think of the room thermostat, one of the simplest cybernetic devices which is composed of two metals strips layered together of different tensile levels. The thermostat's objective is to maintain a particular temperature for the room. Depending on the effect of temperature change, the dual metal strip bends towards completing a circuit and thereby switching on a heater or it does not complete the circuit. What we have is a very basic binary system of either on or off. When the temperature remains at the set temperature, there is *no information* generated by the system and nothing changes in the system; but when there is a deviation from the set temperature, there is information produced by the system. The information constrains the system back to its norm and ideal temperature. Cybernetically speaking, no information represents the ideal; when information is generated it is always negating change to bring the system back to an equilibrium.

The significance of the 'cybernetic explanation', to use Gregory Bateson's expression (1972), is that it highlights two fundamental elements of current computer networked culture: first, the reliance on multiple layers of programming for the Web that are first and foremost cybernetically organized; and second, in a very Orwellian sense, that this general cybernetic system that is the ground of Web-related culture works to incorporate the human into the goal of its system and its objectives.

Let us deal with the first fundamental element: cybernetics' description of information provides the simplicity for the generation of very complex switching devices that are the basis of computer software and hardware along with a host of other technologies. Rudimentary programming for computers entails a series of sequences and feedback loops that are emulations of the cybernetic system. Basic, a program language which is the most accessible to non-technical people, sets up these series and loops of phrases such as

> if this, then goto line 4
> or
> if not this, goto line 12

Although these are not exact basic coding language phrases, they identify how more complex structures that are part of computer functions are built from a cybernetic system. New information, in cybernetic thinking, then leads to deviations from set paths and the requirement for feedback loops to bring the deviation back to the goals of the system. In a positive sense, what cybernetics leads to is what are often called smart machines and the Web represents some of the cutting edge qualities of smart programs for these machines. The idea of a machine being smart is that it exhibits elements of automation, where a series of decisions are made without human intervention. The missiles that can find their target, then integrate the target into their system and complete the explosive objective are often called smart bombs. Appliances such as toasters or microwave ovens that can fulfil their tasks without being watched are primitive forms of **smart technology** that cybernetic thinking has generated. In fact, cybernetics is the father of the field of artificial intelligence. The feedback loops, the binaristic structures, and the complex systems are ways to systematize into clear patterns of information how our minds come up with decisions and take specific courses of action. Although we rarely acknowledge all of the steps taken to make any decision, the layers upon layers of feedback loops and sequences that we automatically employ are what can be coded into computer programs. The more intricate and case-specific the feedback loops, the smarter the program is to respond to variations and changes. Cybernetics, in its structuring of information into the control of systems, has been the foundation for the graphic layering of windows and **icons** that are part of the contemporary computer screen and have formed the basic structural organization of the Web itself.

To understand this cybernetic explanation of the Web, we can begin by looking at the meaning of the icons that are constructed on our computer screens. This can best be explained through recalling the transformation of Microsoft's Disk Operating System, generally known as MS-DOS, to the generationally updated Microsoft Windows systems. The icons chosen to make a directory or to move a file from one location to another may have required several steps to complete through MS-DOS commands; but with Windows the commands are grouped in series under the icon. The more complex the operation, the more layers of commands and codes are embedded in the icon. When we produce a simple macro command to change all sentences with the word 'mud' in a document to the word 'dud', we are once again employing a cybernetically developed way of structuring information through feedback loops. Likewise searches on our personal computers for a particular file or someone's name in a massive **e-mail** folder are dealing with these large blocks of codes of letters and numbers to find the correct sequence to the elimination of all others. The simple process sets up a system, an objective and, through its execution of the elimination of all other patterns, it achieves an equilibrium in this particular system by giving one the location of the occurrence of the file or name.

The cybernetic approach has to be seen as something that has proliferated throughout our culture as both a means of explanation and a clear pattern for innovating new applications (Hayles 1999: 107–12). When we think of cybernetics' explanatory power we can see it operating dramatically at both the macro and micro level in our everyday lives. Our general understanding of our own health in contemporary culture is influenced by cybernetics/systems theories. We try to achieve a homeostasis both psychologically and physically. Think of how dieting is a cybernetic system that constrains the individual to fitting into the idealization of body-type which on certain occasions pushes the individual to harmful ends. Social problems are also thought of in systems approaches as are economic issues. We again aspire for some sort of equilibrium and balance between social and business needs. What is sometimes lost in this cybernetic world for which the Web as a technology acts, at the very least, as a supporting frame, is that we can change the objective of the system. When we exist in a system, it is difficult to imagine other objectives and ultimately other systems; we are reduced to what we referred to as a means-end rationality and instrumental reason that both Habermas (1975, 1984) and Marcuse (1964) have developed in their writings. As we have seen information is used in cybernetic terms to restrain and contain and pull everything back to the norms of the system itself. It is worth thinking about this general value of a cybernetically defined world, where information is not directed towards new freedom and liberation but rather a form of repression. Cybernetic thinking may be useful in driving a car, where the human is integrated into the circuit of the system of car operation and traffic flows; but cybernetics may be too constraining in dealing with larger social, economic, and health problems within a culture. From the Marcusean perspective, the instrumental reason that has allowed for the development of the wonders of the Web has created a culture that cannot see the very limitations of the system it has created for itself; that culture may have become so patterned within the objectives of the system that it cannot integrate new information to challenge that system.

There is a seductive quality in this reading of cybernetics as a system that produces restraint, control, and repression in a culture; sadly it is too simple a critique and not entirely where social blame and responsibility should rest. Closer to reality is that cybernetics produces a tension or dialectic of constraint *and* innovation. The **World Wide Web** may be one of the best locations to observe this strange dialectic in operation. It is a system that has entirely built from the digital binary that is essentially cybernetic in its control and its capacity to create elaborate feedback loops that we have described in other systems. From that basis, the Web has developed not only the graphic architecture of point and double-click from one Web page to another, but also the hypertextual interconnections of Web pages. The powerful search engines such as Lycos, Alta Vista, and Google provide the powers to do searches of material throughout the Web. The Web has transformed the personal computer into a smarter machine. The personal computer now has the capacity to seek out and through a combination of automated and human-led interventions arrive at particular points where one can find very specific material. The search technologies, which have been instrumental in connecting the wide array of Web sites, have gained in sophistication over time through essentially cybernetic techniques. The Boolean search, where searches of **databases** link the occurrence of one word or phrase with another and then display those sources that have both of these elements in their contents, is at the base of the Web search engines. The wondrous quality of the Web is this new power to search and find and, of course, enjoy and use what you have been able to locate. With the exponential growth of Web sites, the capacity to search the entire Web has made the search engines some of the nodal hubs of the entire Web – in essence weigh-stations for Web traffic. Moreover, the capacity to digitalize all contents which works within the binary framework of cybernetic information, and then redisplay these various codes has permitted the Web to encompass most media and communication forms. The packet switching that moves these digital signals from one **server** to another and then on to personal computers has also permitted the possibility that any site could have thousands of visitors if not more (all of this depending on the network's **bandwidth**). Innovation on the Web continues to be derived from cybernetic thinking as different sites strive harder to connect their **users** and 'service' their needs.

The wonder of the Web's power as a system that can produce a steady stream of innovation and services, however, needs to be tempered by the dialectical tension of control that is part of cybernetic systems. On a very basic level, the user of the Web has to negotiate an interface with the Web through their computer that launches the user into an implicit and intuitive inculcation in cybernetic thinking. Just as driving a car positions the driver into a coordinated relationship with the vehicle, the computer user must conform to some of the rules of the computer and Web as technologies. On a different level, because the Web is an entire system for both the display *and* the collection of information, the user is cybernetically part of that information flow and feedback. In other words, the individual as Web **browser** becomes translated into a form of information. With the massive storage capacity of this digital world, information about the individual is constantly being manufactured in the form of **cookies**: as s/he surfs the Web, digital identification traces or crumbs are left on the personal computer and on the Web site which identify where the person has been. In addition, one of the key functions of any Web site that provides information to individuals is to have them provide information as a form of access to the site. Passwords and sign-ons are often that starting point for individuals to provide further demographic information and details of interest areas.

A few examples of how this information feedback loop about the user of the Web is employed will elucidate the Web's inherent cybernetic structure. Many users are drawn to free e-mail accounts offered by indexers such as Yahoo! or software providers such as Microsoft. With Yahoo.com, the new e-mail account personalises their use of Yahoo!'s search engine devices; in setting up that account you are asked to indicate your age, occupation, address, previous e-mail account, income and gender along with other details of how you like to use the Internet. These questions are couched in the language of marketing but are expressed in terms of a service to the user in order to better match the user's needs. With Yahoo!, the service moves beyond the provision of e-mail to helping set up a 'personalized' homepage that provides links to the user's requested areas of interest. The new home-page is thus composed of these categories that appear simply to connect to the user's interests; but they are linked to specific, allied Web sites for information, news and weather with which Yahoo! has developed content deals. The home Web page that is personalized also integrates the Web user into the circuit of information that is provided through Yahoo! Instead of surfing the Web completely through a variety of search engines, the home-page simplifies the circuit of information and use so that each Websurf may begin and end within this display of information and news. The openness of the Web is packaged and patterned and constrained partially through the information provided by the user to Yahoo! in setting up their personal home page (My Yahoo!). Although the user is free to move to the wider Web and other search engines, the presented space and information helps hold the user into a pattern of use. This constructing of a controlled space was pioneered by America Online, where content and surfing the net were more or less organized into a closed network. It is not surprising that this safer suburban, family construction of the Web has become one of the more profitable Web corporations. We will deal more with profit and capital on the Web in Chapter 6; here what needs to be emphasized is that the objec-tive of setting up pre-structured, yet personalized, home pages by different Web companies has been expanding for the last five years.

Bonzi.com provides an interesting variation of how parts of the Web draw one into a particular circuit of use. Through offering a free download-able version of a surfboarding, talking purple **virtual** gorilla called Bonzi (although the site does not indicate how this should be pronounced), they attempt to provide a seamless connection to their particular structure of the Web (Bonzi.com). Bonzi hangs out on the computer screen and tells jokes, talks directly to the user, sings a repertoire of songs and provides trivia and information. Once downloaded, he addresses the user spontaneously every few minutes, literally hanging out on the screen no matter what software is employed. Embedded into Bonzi's general cuteness and innocuousness is regular information about how to surf the Web and how to improve surfing through **downloading** particular software. Like Yahoo! and many other ser-vices, Bonzi's registration demanded the release of a great deal of demo-graphic detail. That detail, particularly the age and gender of the user may be instrumental in determining what kind of information, perhaps even what kind of jokes and trivia, that Bonzi speaks about to the user. Bonzi regularly requests to be upgraded from his homesite, bonzi.com, which indicates that Bonzi's capabilities in providing a form of interactive Web surfing can also be increased as the programmers develop more sophisticated techniques of connecting the user to particular parts of the Web. What Bonzi represents besides a sophisticated voice and word recognizer (which are the 'hooks' which get the user to download the software) is a very specific form of **interactivity** that the Web promises. Interactivity itself implies an elaborate system of feedbacks that can respond to the requests and decisions of any user. Bonzi at this stage is massively preprogrammed with only a few binary questions asked of the user which when answered by either 'yes' or 'no' move one to search the Web in particular ways. Nonetheless, Bonzi represents a cybernetic oracle to the Web that can structure any user's use. Bonzi is clearly a direct descendant of the original Eliza computer program designed in the 1970s as an automated psychotherapist who would sympathetically ask questions based on the user's comments. Both are versions of smart and interactive devices that reach for artificial intelligence. In the human–Web interface, this amounts to the user fitting into the specific system provided. Bonzi's world may be intriguing and interesting; but it is always structured towards a particular objective of making a sale. Despite all its sincerity of friendship in its repertoire of remarks, it obsequiously reconstructs the user into a consumer in this system.

A CYBERNETIC/DIGITAL INFORMATION SUMMARY

In order to summarize this cybernetic reading of the Web and its production of information, there are several important points to reiterate:

1   First, that the reduction of all manner of content into binary systems, what is called digitalization, is essential to understanding not only the Web but computer technology and the flowing convergence of many cultural forms into one accessible pool. The Web serves as the manifestation and the articulation of this digital convergence; the only caveat of the Web's structure of being the repository of this digital reconstruction of culture is the speed at which it can present certain forms. The complexity of the digitalization for moving images can occupy massive amounts of memory and this limits the accessibility of certain video productions to certain Web users because of bandwidth limitations of phone lines and other Internet connections; nevertheless feature films, documentaries, music and computer games are downloaded from Web sites. The reduction of information to a digital representation has allowed for this convergence through the Web.

2   Second, the conceptual insight of cybernetics has powered the massive

proliferation of applications that are the essential features of the Web, from its graphic construction of **applets** and **avatar**s to the development of **hypertext**, from its computer base to its sophisticated techniques of 'knowing' its users.

3   Third, that the concept of information from cybernetics is that information is a form of constraint of the system which makes the gathering of information an essential feature and capability of the Web. The Web is as much about finding information as generating information. The generation of information tends to be focused on finding out about its users and using that information to include those users into a particular version of the Web – a system.

INFORMATION, VALUE AND KNOWLEDGE

Although cybernetics is essential for understanding the Web and its computer origins, it is not the only way to think of information in the context of the Internet. It is important to realize that information has been thought of as the basis of our contemporary economy and culture. Manuel Castells, in his three volume study *The Information Age* (1996, 1997, 1998) identifies that there is a fundamental shift underway globally. Whereas a past society was called regularly and accurately industrial, Castells invites us to think that because information is at the core of both our economy and culture that we should call the current era 'the informational society'. The economic dimension of this informational society will be investigated in the Chapter 6. In this section concerning information and the Web it is worthwhile to analyse critically the Web's production of information.

Information as a category implies a neutrality that it should be acknowledged is never absolute. In its pure form, information is believed to be factual and this pure ideal has emerged from scientific inquiry and the quantification of the universe. However, it becomes evident when studying the Web that the factual truth of the information available is always under suspicion. Whereas disciplines such as chemistry have built on years of scientific experimentation, a system of peer evaluation, and multiple proofs before any claimed fact/information about chemistry is acknowledged as true, the same cannot be said of the sources of information that are present on the Web.

It is best to think of information as it is often represented on the Web as a raw material rather than a finished product. Both the sheer quantity of Web sites and the diversity of sources has produced this effect. Although the Web can and does absorb the best writing and research from a number of disciplines, it is not adjudicated by any system that accredits value universally. The forms of gate-keeping that have developed in book publishing or scientific journal publication are just not in operation on the Web. It is an unusual repository; unlike a library archive, the Web can change its representation while appearing to be as it was before. A Web site can be updated and amended. These changes may or may not be acknowledged, but they do indicate that information is *dynamically* conveyed and *malleable* in form; that is, that information possesses a greater temporality on the Web than it would possess in printed form. Another extreme is also possible: Web sites that are no longer updated present static information that is orphaned from its original source and its form of validation.

With information as raw material, the Web performs different functions in our culture than previous information sources. As we developed in Chapter 1, the Web has constructed a free relationship to its sources and that surfing the Web is an expression of both the access to its burgeoning content and a representation of liberation from the structures and patterns of past institutions and past media forms. Although he was predominantly looking through the world of contemporary television, Hartley (1996) has identified a postmodern public sphere where there is a greater search for identity from information sources than the purity of information and facts that worked in a modern public sphere. The Web, instead of providing only the singular authoritative version of information, actually presents multiples of information sources. The individual surfer produces clusters of related information and connection through the links to various Web sources, not so much for the production of knowledge but for the production of identity. With identity in greater flux in contemporary culture and less defined by nation and community – key features of this postmodern public sphere – the Web allows for the building of identities through a diverse range of investments and forms of interpersonal communication.

The dynamism of the Web's structure of information leads to a new instability that breaks down what Gaye Tuchman labelled as the 'Web of facticity' (1978) that undergirded the production of information on television or in newspapers. Even though there are powerfully backed attempts at establishing the key sources for information on the Web – from CNN.com to Salon.com – these are not as clearly positioned as authorities in the cacophony of the Web and can be unseated by new generations of users that are not attached to these pre-existing media patterns and do not necessarily consider the single powerful source as the final end point of their search for information. Thinking of information as raw material allows us to think of the Web as a place for the debate about the value of information more directly and regularly. The concept of the source of information suddenly moves to the pivotal point in everyone's use of the Internet as opposed to its recessed and hidden status in the reception of television news. One has to acknowledge that this debate about the value of information is not being carried out by all users; nonetheless users are generally conscious of the unstable, less clearly legitimated, and often less geographically grounded sources of their production of knowledge and identity through the Web.

The Web's different production of information produces certain effects that we can now summarize:

1   It is a dynamic archive that mixes a variety of registers of sources. By register, we mean that the Web can be the source of very well recognized sources of information that rely on past media hierarchies (which is clearly one register) rubbing shoulders with the relatively unknown personal sources (a different register) and newly created Web-centred sources of information (a third register somewhere positioned between these two registers). Fansites would appear in a search for information about *Buffy the Vampire Slayer* as much as Time Warner Communications, the distributor of the television series, and condensed information produced by entertainment-oriented newsites produced by America Online. The number of distinct registers clustering around the production of information is also never fixed. Newsgroups and chatrooms linked to all three of these registers listed above may provide another level of register that shifts the production of information away from the more constructed quality of the Web site into the interpersonal correspondence register of gossip and expressions of emotional investment.

2   The use of the Web as information source may be a reflection of a postmodern public sphere. The Web becomes the raw material for the formation of identity as opposed to a simple presentation of facts. Information is used for quite different ends and part of the development of the Web's diversity reflects this different use of what McLuhan labelled as 'extensions of our senses' (1965). The Web both reflects and services this shifted mode of connection and interconnection in contemporary culture.

3   The Web as a principal source of information puts into flux past naturalized conceptions of cultural value and significance. In its linked structure, the Web places the production of knowledge itself under scrutiny and investigation continuously. In many ways, the Web foregrounds a contemporary legitimation crisis around the production of knowledge from information.

4   The Web presents an overabundance of information. Estimates by some researchers indicate that any search engine only covers less than 20 per cent of the Web's content (Bergman 2000). In fact, because of the similar nature of the search engines there is massive overlap with each of the search engines which means that most of the Web is not easily accessible as an information source. The implication of this plenitude of sources is that the Web begins to represent an entity that is uncontrollable and never completely catalogued. The massive content of the Web maintains a perpetual instability.

THE CONCEPT OF THE NETWORK

In this chapter we are investigating the Web on two levels. So far we have analysed the Web in terms of its content that we can label as the first level. What we discovered was that to understand the Web's content we needed to think of the various ways that it is a manifestation of information theory and a presentation of information. We now want to move on to the second level of our investigation where we study the Web in terms of its form. What is the architectural structure of the Web and what are the consequences of such a form?

At the technological base of such an enquiry is that the Web is fundamentally a network. Van Dijk simplifies the concept of the network for us by making it generally applicable: 'A network is a connection between at least three elements, points or units' (Van Dijk 1999: 28). There are different kinds of networks that needed to be distinguished and compared to the Web, but it is useful to isolate on this simple chain relationship of network structure. A network's technical base may be as simple as telephone wires and telephone transmitters and receivers or it may be even the simpler network defined by the proximity of at least three houses in a particular neighbourhood. The key point here is that a network implies some relayed exchange among its elements. The content of that exchange as we have investigated in this chapter is information. As Castells' (1996) work underlines investigating networks is to look at the processes and flows of information that develop through these networks. The Web constitutes a new organization of flows and processes of information which are servicing a different social structure. Castells (1996), who has done a great deal of research into the new patterns that are developing from information technology like the Internet, has labelled this shifted culture the 'network society' and links these new flows to the **globalization** of economy, information and culture. The unique element of the network society is that there is an increased traffic and trade beyond goods into the movement of information itself. The Web both services these flows and is one of the key representations of the network society.

CONVERGENCE AND NETWORKS: CONNECTIONS OVER TIME AND SPACE

There are two further dimensions to the concept of the network that need to be investigated. There is a spatial dimension, in other words, how the network works over geographical areas and a temporal dimension, that is, the kind of timeframe made possible by the network and how the relationship to time shapes the network's use. The Web's particular relationship to time and space is derived from its emergence from the converging technologies of computers and telecommunications. The physical network of the

Web is a combination of cables, phone lines and, to a lesser degree, satellite linkages. The hub of the Web is composed of those sites that are cabled to each other through the original and expanded defence and research networks that emerged from **ARPA** in the United States and were expanded (and are still expanding) internationally through a grid of universities and research centres. This kind of connection to the Internet is usually called **ethernet** that implies a direct cabled access to the World Wide Web. The tentacles of the Web have broadened through phone and **modem** connections to millions of households as **Internet Service Providers** (**ISPs**) have provided the connection directly to the hub of the Internet. In a fundamental sense, the Web is part of this elaborate network of networks – the Internet as it is generally known. The technical antecedent of the Internet and the World Wide Web was the national and international telephone system that is also a network of networks. The technical innovation of the Internet that permitted the Web to have multiple users of any site simultaneously and thus change the predominant telecommunications paradigm of one-to-one communication was the **packet switching** of digital information. Sites could be downloaded on individual personal computers in packages of digital information which could switch to download others. Because of the digital form, greater amounts of information could be downloaded relatively quickly to each user and the speed of the download procedure was determined by the capacity of the phone or cable line and the capacity of the modem. The Web has become a mass communications technology that permits the collapse of time and space for its audience of users and browsers. Although there are limits to the size of the mass audience that any site can handle, it is clear that the system allows that group of users at any one time to be geographically diverse. As a communications technology, the Web provides the possibility for very large audiences, but also interpersonal, group and one-to-one forms of communication. The Web is thus a convergence of communication forms through its particular display of the network of networks called the Internet.

All networks have different relationships to the dimensions of time and space. With the Web's capacity to technologically reconstruct different kinds of networks it is worthwhile perusing these other networks in order to make sense of how the Web may transform their place and operation in contemporary culture.

In the loop: networks as elites and the play of interpersonal communication

How a network is organized can vary greatly. Business networks within any industry are often the linkages of power that are not necessarily organized in the same way as the administrative or management structures of corporations. The connection between people where information is exchanged may take place in different settings. Thus, the cliché of joining a golf club to advance a business career is often a correct reading of the way that a social network intersects with a business network outside normal hierarchies. Networks operating at this interpersonal level are means of inclusion and exclusion and pattern the way that information/communication moves through social organizations. The Los Angeles term of 'networking' highlights the need to link business interests with social interests in order to stay close to the pulse of the entertainment industry. It is important to realize that these forms of inclusion are not always related to economic or political power even though these locations are where networks are referred to the most. Interpersonal networks of information occur with fan groups for television series or popular music groups as much as the power networking that may occur at exclusive clubs. The similarity between these levels is that there is an informal and formal system of information exchange that is dependent on specific locations and/or specific technologies.

The Web as a network can change the patterns of interpersonal networks. Because of its potential wide distribution of information through Web sites and the ease at which interpersonal communication can be established through e-mail or chat groups, the Web is a channel for the geographical dispersion of the intimacy of interpersonal networks. The Web itself is not the means for the maintenance of interpersonal networks; but rather the place where information about interpersonal networks is discovered. For example a Web site that is devoted to celebrating David Duchovny of *X-files* fame may be a nodal point for the formation of a network of like-minded fans. Newsgroups and e-mail lists may be announced on the Web site. The Web site can serve to broadcast the existence of these ways of corresponding and building a particular network of interest. The Web as a network is not exclusionary in itself; but because the number of Web sites is not limited or controlled, it allows for Web sites to be very specific in terms of interest areas. The exclusionary element to the Web as a network is that there is a dispersion of users to more isolated pockets of interest.

Business to business communication can also develop through the Web and serves the very particular needs of the network society. The construction of **firewalls** to control what sites are part of a particular network is generally working against the relative open structure of the Web. Nonetheless, business intranetworks are growing rapidly and new forms of exclusion and techniques for protecting and controlling information are being developed through parallel technologies to the Web.

Broadcast networks: the one way flow and common culture

Prior to the development of the Internet, the concept of the network was most closely associated with broadcast television and radio. These networks represent a counterpoint to the organization of the Web as a network. The original form of the broadcast network can be linked to very specific origins that are related to consumer capitalism and nationalism. In the American setting, the Columbia Broadcasting System (CBS) developed the radio network at the end of the 1920s that became the template for most of the major networks to follow. Through a system of affiliates, William Paley's CBS was able to guarantee the simultaneous broadcasting of a particular programme across the United States. Through this guarantee of time, Paley was able to ensure consistently large, national audiences for advertisers and thereby garner sponsorship arrangements with companies that had national distribution and sales. National brand names were solidified for toothpaste, cars, soaps, detergents and cigarettes through this structure of the network. In a similar fashion, broadcasting that emerged from government departments and regulators was intent on ensuring national audiences and made sure that their signals were relayed through transmitters to the geographical borders of the country. The network was a further guarantor of national sovereignty through its provision of the same or similar programmes across regions and intranational diversity. In both the commercial and the government broadcast structures the result of this networking was the development of a common culture. The same entertainment programmes as much as the same news broadcasts worked their way into the everyday lives of the nation's citizens to produce a sense of national consciousness. In countries with a predominantly commercial system, all stations and their networks were licensed by the government and through that license had to strive for some element of public service.

Although there have been some means for the audience to participate in programming through feedback and marketing efforts, fundamentally broadcasting networks were and are centralized distributors. The network continues to be a means to centralize that process of distribution of content and information to the widest possible audience for the greatest possible effect. While the desired objectives of this distribution system may alter from producing consumers to producing citizens, it is fundamentally a network system that brought production, distribution and exhibition into clearly structured patterns. With the development of satellite distribution, cable retransmission and the associated multichannel structure of contemporary broadcasting some of this structured unity of a common culture has been lost. The old style network that Paley had perfected demanded a geographical presence – a station – in each area to carry network programming. The new satellite networks actually ensure an even more centralized structure of control even as they produce a diversity of content. What is remarkable about current television is the generic similarity in channels between countries and their cable/satellite television systems. A transnational company such as Rupert Murdoch's News Corporation, one of the key international satellite television distributors, has been very successful at distributing the same material across international boundaries with great economic success.

The Web as a network has emerged in this latter stage of broadcasting networks. There continues to be the strong presence of national networked broadcasters, but their ability to provide this common culture has been fractured by transnationally structured forms of satellite and pay/cable television. Nevertheless, television as an internationally networked system can produce truly phenomenal audiences and common cultural moments. World Cup soccer broadcasts worldwide easily and regularly surpasses more than a billion viewers. Likewise Olympic coverage produces the same overwhelming audience sizes. There continue to be regular national political, entertainment and sporting programmes that produce the same blanket audience within each individual country. What still distinguishes television as a network is its capacity to produce uniquely live events from one locale that can be disseminated economically and easily through transmitters and satellites to wherever an audience congregates.

Because of the timing of the Web's emergence as a network that similarly traverses borders and passes through those borders (yet much more quietly than satellite television), its influence is often compared to television. The Web's network works in a fundamentally different structure, but it does have points of comparison with television. The making of a television audience is built from domestic viewing in millions of homes and therefore there are isolated experiences of small groups or individuals that are cumulatively built into the large audiences that are sold to advertisers. The Web experience as a media form is similarly isolated in either its use at home or at work predominantly on computer screens but increasingly through television itself through **Web-TV**. Perhaps the key difference here is how the Web becomes an acceptable part of certain business environments that would rarely accept the intrusive play of television. The Web's network is not so clearly defined in terms of its content in the generic reduction of television to predominantly entertainment. The Web maintains a stronger relationship to information than the broadcast network partly because of the individual control over the perusal of content. A Web site is a continuous entity that is not so temporally defined as a broadcast news bulletin. In the same vein, a Web site allows for greater manipulation of its content if so desired into personal files, while a television programme can be recorded but not so easily 'sampled' into smaller citations and personal usages.

There are great efforts to make the Web like television and its network structure. There are Webcasts that attempt to make an event and a particular moment so that a large audience can be built simultaneously. A specific chat-time with a popular music performer may be organized on a Web site, or perhaps a world premiere of a film or movie may be Webcast at a particular moment. Most of these Webcasts highlight the value of television for live events and the inadequacy of the Web to produce similar mass phenomena.

The Web's network does not naturally produce mass audiences, though many Web sites have enough '**hits**' per day to rival a major television network in terms of apparent audience size. The Web does not produce a network that highlights a communal telesthetic (seen at a distance) experience the way that television regularly produces and routinizes as 'third nature' (Wark 1994: 10, 84–6). In contrast, the Web produces flows of users across Web spaces and those flows of users – even on the same Web site – may navigate the site quite differently. For instance, the IBM-sponsored Wimbledon Web site had hundreds of millions of visitors on its site and would be deemed a phenomenal success (**http**://championships. wimbledon.org/). But the use made of the Web site was not for viewing matches: it was divided into users looking at Wimbledon archives, others **streaming** audio and video interviews of players, playing 'Wimbledon radio' as ambient sound while traversing other Web sites, or just checking current results. What we can learn about this particular site is that the Web as a network is very much like its digital technology: there are 'packets' of users. A well-financed site can handle the traffic of these packets better than other sites; but nevertheless there is not the same sense of unity in the users as they work their way through a Web site. As an audience produced by the Web they may be characterized as a **loose-audience**: they may be attached to the particular event and drawn to the Web coverage of the event, but the nature of the Web's **navigation** is that users are clicking and engaging in the process of making their entertainment or their news or whatever else they may be perusing somewhat idiosyncratically. Having made all these distinctions between television and the Web, it is important to realize that the experience of the Web as television or more generally as a common event is still limited by the technology of the network. With limited bandwidth and more severely varying home computer technology, it is impossible to identify that the experience is identical for all those browsing a particular location.

Finally, another key difference between television as a network and the Web as a network arises from their relationship to new media. Van Dijk (1999: 9) establishes clear benchmarks for the definition of new media that separates our media forms precisely: new media express forms that *integrate* past communication technologies into their structure and possess noticeable advances on forms of interactivity. Where television provides one possible form of interaction, the Web provides that form along with several other forms of communication including voice and text. The Web has integrated the technology of telecommunications networks, the patterns of computing, the forms of newspapers, radio, film and television into a **multimedia** network. Moreover, the networked Web's other clear separation from older media networks is its changeability. The continuous online nature of the Web makes it fit into the definition of new media. It is a much more transformable entity than the older media that have a quality of static products/objects associated with their content. Older media tend to produce the distinct commodity; while new media networks such as the Web present a service of a continuously updating commodity.

The network society and the Web

We have mentioned a conception of the network expressing a larger social phenomenon than what we have described in the above two examples. When Castells uses the notion of the network society, he is implying something that envelops areas beyond even the nation state to express something truly global in its reach and impact. In his conclusion to the *Rise of the Network Society*, Castells explains the pervasiveness and significance of the network:

> Networks constitute the new social morphology of our societies, and the diffusion of networking logic substantially modifies the operation and outcomes in processes of production, experience, power, and culture. While the networking form of social organisation has existed in other times and spaces, the information technology paradigm provides the material basis for its pervasive expansion through the entire social structure.
>
> (Castells 1996: 469)

He goes on to explain that this network structure places more significance and ultimately power on the flows of information than the flow of power. The implications of the network society for Castells are monumental. It has led to transformations in work and has allowed for the expansion of the capitalist economy as the nature of the network is the exchange of information to reshape any form of production, be that cultural or material. It has produced new relationships to space – where geographical connections that are no longer grounded in physical communities but are connected through the flows of information weaken the patterns of the formerly spatially constructed communities and societies. In his second volume on identities, Castells remarks on how the network society's focus on processes and flows has led to a destabilization of patterns of identity formation globally and a reaction to these flows at the local level. Efforts to search for concrete identities in terms of nationalism merely put in relief the operation and pervasive challenge to social structures that the network society has produced globally.

The concept of the network society is not entirely new, although Castells' work has moved it to a clearly new level of understanding of interpenetrating relationships produced by the flows of information. Daniel Bell (1973) and Alain Touraine (1971) both indicated the emergence of the post-industrial society, where the exchange of information formed a new layer over the industrialization process that has occurred in Western countries over the last 150 years. Jacques Ellul (1965) provided a slight variation of this understanding of a fundamental shift in global structure under his term, the technological society. Other writers, contemporaneous with Castells, have also developed parallel arguments to the emergent network society. Mark Poster (1990) through his study of the predominant mediatization of culture, links the current new media structures to what has been called postmodernity. Van Dijk (1999), although disagreeing with Castells on the pervasiveness of the network structure to transform the *social*, also has highlighted the network society as a key to understanding contemporary culture, from work to government, from recreation to education.

What can be gleaned from these various writings is that the Web has to be seen as an exemplification of the network society. What the Web 'produces' are examples of the conditions that have been described by Castells and others as fundamentally transforming the patterns of industrial society. If we can downgrade the network society to what the Web produces – we can call this Web culture – we can begin to see where the Web fits into these theorizations of the informational/postindustrial/network/postmodern society.

The Web culture represents a new concentration on information and its directional flow

The network society has developed from movements of information for the needs of large scale interconnected organizations to operate. For instance, the complexity of contemporary shoe manufacturing is produced by the flows of information about shoe design from one part of the world – say Nike's headquarters in Eugene, Oregon – for their production in yet another part of the world, say, the Philippines or Thailand (Klein 2000). The digitalization of that information and the physical networks that allow that information to move instantaneously establish these different spatial/temporal relationships. The informational world has produced consequences of employment and consumption along whole new and shifted patterns. These flows of information that change work and culture are not the result of the Web; rather the Web is a result of these information flows. The expansion of the Web to the point that we can call it a Web culture indicates the way that greater numbers of people (at this stage particularly those from affluent parts of the world) have taken on the significance of a network society and the way that information is part of that new shifted world-view. Web culture is about both the proliferation or production of information and its accessibility to be viewed and read. Organizations and individuals participate massively in making and reading Web sites in this dual directive of the network society and thus dovetail into the general needs of the movement of information. The Web is an expression of the conscious celebration in both work and leisure of the value of the network society. The Web's versatility at providing both information and entertainment operates as the cultural connective tissue that works to sustain the ideological value of the network society.

The Web culture can produce dislocations of identity and community

In Castells terminology the network society produces the possibility of unstable and shifting patterns of identity, where the different identities produced by industrialization (often linked to class and class fractions) are no longer seen as central. They are subject to shifts as the needs of the networked world demand a more changeable kind of worker and work. In a parallel vein, the Web presents flows of information that are not geographically centred for the user and a kind of identity that is similarly detached from traditions and past patterns of engagement with the culture. And through regular access to the Web, the user develops particular patterns which can shift the structure of connection to others and identity to be displaced from culture to a Web culture. For instance, access to news and information may be gleaned not from a geographically defined daily newspaper but from a range of news sources that in traditional media would resemble edited wire services. These kinds of dislocations are not complete, for the experience of using the Web is still grounded in its place of use at work or at home. The displacement of **subjectivity** often associated with the postmodern is therefore only partially produced by the network of the Web. With the decline in use and access to newspapers, television and radio, the Web's differing cluster of sources and resources can produce a flow-on effect for self-identity, away from the nation-state or community and towards interest areas. The connection to the network society and postmodernity is that new identity is less fixed and in many ways also less stable.

Web culture facilitates the flow of information for the objectives of globalization

Globalization has become a virtual synonym for the network society. Globalization has to be understood not as some unifying force such as a United Nations-style world government but rather as a very specific characterization of the interconnection of the world. More or less, globalization is connected to an economic imperative which Castells correctly links with the expansion and success of capitalism as a universal economic model. Web culture fits into this general imperative in two primary ways. First, the Web is a virtual template of world power relations – it is a skewed map of the world in terms of its users and yet it 'simulates' the expanses and diversities of the world through its seemingly infinitesimal Web sites. It is an example of diversity within this distorted global map. Second, because of the Web's network structure it is difficult to control within any of the old boundaries of nations. Its unregulatability – except on a global scale – also provides a simulation of the movements of capital through the trans(cendant)national corporation. Web culture, like capitalism, feeds on deregulation of societies for its growth. Web culture is the myth of the benefits of globalization that goes hand in hand with the exigencies of the contemporary 'informational' capitalism.

CONCLUSION: THE WEB AS INFORMATION NETWORK

We have identified two important elements of the Web in this chapter. The Web is constituted by information and it is made significant because of that distribution of information into a network. The digital form of that information permits the dialectical tension that is ever present in the network quality of the Web. On one side of the dialectical divide, digitalization's reduction of all information to binary codes permits the infinite expansion of the Web as it absorbs past media forms from telephony, magazines and newspapers to popular music, radio and television. However, on the other side, digitalization structures the information into a cybernetic system of control and potential surveillance. Its network structure makes the centre harder to determine; yet there are clear directions in the flows of information that both replicate and represent existing power structures that are part of both globalization and what has been labelled as the network society.

Chapter 3

THE WEB AS COMMUNICATION

MANY FORMS OF our communication are mediated through technology. This chapter charts how the Web is challenging many of our models of communication. Through a comparative investigation, we establish the key characteristics of **Internet** communication. One of the central realities of the Web is that it converges different media forms into **networks** and simultaneously different modes of communication. To understand this peculiar form of **convergence** of both technology and communication, the chapter concludes with a discussion of the meaning of these many types of interlinkages and how they can be understood as exemplifying the operation of the **loose Web** of communication.

Media and communication researchers have until recently overlooked not only the Internet but the entire field of computer-mediated communication, staying instead with the traditional forms of media that fit more conveniently into models for appropriate research agendas and theories of mass communication. However, one can argue as Morris and Ogan (1996: 1):

> that if mass communications researchers continue to largely disregard the research potential of the Internet, their theories about communication will become less useful. Not only will the discipline be left behind, it will also miss an opportunity to explore and rethink answers to some of the central questions of mass communications research, questions that go to the heart of the model of source-message-receiver with which the field has struggled.

They urge us to rethink our ideas of what constitutes a mass audience and a mediating technology with the promise that studying 'the computer as a new communication technology opens a space for scholars to rethink assumptions and categories, and perhaps even to find new insights into traditional communication technologies' (Ibid: 1).

THE INTERNET

The word Internet is a combination of the prefix *inter*, meaning 'between or among the other', and the suffix *net*, short for 'network', defined as an interconnecting pattern or system. An inter-network or Internet, can refer to any 'network of networks' or to any 'network of computers' (Yahoo! Dictionary Online 1999). The Internet is the specific name of the **communication network** that is comprised of millions of interconnected computers that freely exchange **information** with each other worldwide.

A key to the success and understanding of the Internet are two fundamental elements – a new way of looking at computers and a decentralized communication system. Computers are now routinely viewed as communications devices rather than just computational ones; witness the fact that **e-mail** has become the most popular use of the network. In addition, the purpose of the decentralized communication system was to provide the network the capability to survive a nuclear attack. Rheingold (1993: 7) explains the impact of this approach:

> Information can take so many alternative routes when one of the nodes of the network is removed that the Net is almost immortally flexible. It is this flexibility that CMC telecom pioneer John Gilmore referred to when he said, 'The Net interprets censorship as damage and routes around it.' This invention of distributed conversation that flows around obstacles – a grassroots adaptation of a technology originally designed as a doomsday weapon – might turn out to be as important in the long run as the hardware and software inventions that made it possible.

The world's first computer network was a US government-funded network called the **ARPAnet** that was developed in the late 1960s and grew slowly through the 1970s. In the early 1980s the ARPAnet was split into two separate networks. Some of its computers were linked together to form a new network called MILNET (a non-classified military network) and the remaining machines stayed together as ARPAnet (Rheingold 1993).

After the split, a computer that was part of one network could still exchange information with a computer that was part of the other network by routing it through a gateway computer. So in addition to connecting together individual computers to form a network, entire networks of computers were connected. In short, a network of networks was created.

A new term was coined to describe this notion: an internetwork –

meaning an interconnected set of networks. The term became shortened to Internet, and this particular internet became known as the Internet and was spelt with a capital 'I' to distinguish it from any other internet. By the mid-1980s the US National Science Foundation (NSF) decided to fund the Internet in order to increase the number of US universities that had computers connected to it, and it was at this time that the Internet's phenomenal growth began (Rheingold 1993).

The Internet as we know it today, includes *informational* services such as file transfer (**FTP**), remote login (**telnet**), location and retrieval (**gopher**) and the **World Wide Web**. The Internet also includes *communication* services such as **electronic mail** (e-mail), mailing lists (**listserv**), **Internet relay chat** (**IRC**) and **multi-user domains** (**MUDs**).

COMMUNICATION MODELS AND THE WEB

How are we to make sense of Internet communication? A good place to start is to compare Internet interaction with traditional levels of communication. Most communication models define four aspects of communication – a sender, a message, a channel and a receiver. Different models emphasize different aspects of the communication act, often concentrating on the role of sender and receiver at the expense of the message and channel.

The 'one-to-one' model of communication refers to when one person communicates to another. Having a conversation face to face is the most common form of one-to-one communication, but telephone calls, letters, and e-mail are usually one-to-one forms of interpersonal communication.

Traditional mass media follow a 'one-to-many' model of communication. In this model one source sends a message through one channel to many receivers, in essence a mass audience. Normally a media conglomerate is the sender and the channel takes the form of a television station, radio station, newspaper, magazine, book or film. Messages sent through these media are often designed to appeal to as many as possible and attract a mass audience.

Computer-mediated communication is often 'one-to-many' but also takes the form of 'many-to-one' communication. This 'many-to-one' model of communication is a hybrid between mass communication and interpersonal communication. Computers, **database** systems and the Internet allow for the storage of large amounts of **data** from various sources that can be retrieved in turn by individuals at random who select only the information that interests them.

The Web's easy to navigate **graphic user interface** (**GUI**) presents us with a fourth communication mode, a 'many-to-many' model of communication. The Web allows anyone to be a sender or a receiver, anyone can send or receive personal or mass messages, and information can be provided by many and accessed by many as a mass audience or stored for individuals to select or retrieve.

The Internet plays with the boundaries that have traditionally delineated three modes of communication: interpersonal (one-to-one), mass (one-to-many) and computing (many-to-one). The Internet allows for all three types of communication, as well as a fourth, many-to-many, mode of communication. It is a new form of communication that allows for different forms and styles of communication.

INTERPERSONAL COMMUNICATION AND THE WEB

An approach developed by Rogers (1986) has three levels of communication: face-to-face (FtF) interpersonal communication, interactive machine-assisted interpersonal communication and mass media. FtF interpersonal communication is one-to-few with the potential for equal control of the communication. The interactive machine-assisted interpersonal communication is characterized as many-to-many (M-M) with the potential for equal control of the communication. Mass media is one-to-many (1-M) with little control of the message by the receivers.

Littlejohn (1996) builds upon this approach and categorizes communication in four levels – interpersonal, group, organizational and mass communication. Interpersonal communication is private, face-to-face (FtF) interaction. Group communication is small group interaction usually in decision-making settings. Organizational communication occurs in large networks with definable structure and function. Mass communication involves a complex institutional organization sending a message from a source to a large audience. Littlejohn stresses that these are not mutually exclusive types of communication but merely convenient mechanisms for organizing communication theory.

The interpersonal communication services of the Internet can be classified using the traditional levels of communication although none of the interaction is FtF. Using the Littlejohn model, (Table 3.1) e-mail is private, interpersonal communication; while IRC, MUDs and listservs are group interactions. Corporate **intranets** would be organizational communication, where as **Webportals** would be mass communication. While **Usenet newsgroups** often feel like small groups with social interaction amongst individuals, many have large numbers of participants and more closely resemble organizational communication. Usenet is therefore difficult to place in any one level and is a hybrid of several levels. As this model ignores any time, space or channel effect on interaction, it is not fully satisfactory in describing Internet communication.

Another way of comparing Internet interactions is to analyse types of conversation. Shank (1994) defines the traditional types of conversation as monologue, dialogue and discussion. In this classification a monologue consists of one sender, one or more passive receivers and a message that

Table 3.1 Levels vs aspects of communication

	Interpersonal	*Group*	*Organizational*	*Mass*
Sender	one	one	one or more	one, maintains control
Receiver	one	few, may take turns	large audience	mass audience
Channel	FtF or mediated	FtF or mediated	FtF or mediated	mediated
Examples	FtF, letters, telephone, e-mail	lecture, discussion, listserv, IRC	corporate, networks, intranets	TV, radio, books, Webportals

Source: Adapted from Rogers 1986 and Littlejohn 1996

may be delivered FtF or via mass media. A dialogue contains a sender and an active receiver taking turns with the sender; traditional dialogue can be oral or written messages. In a discussion, one person starts as the sender with multiple receivers who take turns as senders, but the initial sender retains control of the conversation. Shank adds the category of multilogue for Internet conversation with an initial sender, multiple receivers who take turns as senders, but with loss of control of the conversation.

Internet communication can be categorized using Shank's conversation model (Table 3.2) although none of the interaction is FtF. E-mail is usually dialogue but if messages are ignored, it is a monologue. Listservs or Usenet newsgroups may be monologues if they are moderated and if the moderator allows only a single source to produce the messages. Rafaeli and Sudweeks (1998) show that moderated groups usually become discussions, although interruptibility and turn-taking have different meanings from the FtF model. Unmoderated listservs and newsgroups are generally multilogues as are IRC and MUDs. This conversational model is also limited in that it ignores any time, space or channel effect on the conversation and does not fully describe the differences in types of communication.

A third model of classification developed by Ellis *et al.* (1993) uses a time/place taxonomy, which was originally used to classify groupware systems. This approach emphasizes the messages as well as the people involved. The four categories are FtF, asynchronous, synchronous distributed and asynchronous distributed interactions. If the sender and receiver are in the same place and the message is received at the same time it is sent, then the interaction is FtF and synchronous. If the sender and receiver are

Table 3.2 Type of conversation vs aspects of communication

	Monologue	Dialogue	Discussion	Multilogue
Sender	one	one	initially one, maintains control	initially one, no control
Receiver	one or more, passive	one, active	one or more, active	one or more, active
Channel	FtF, mass media, other mediation	FtF or mediated	FtF or mediated	computer-mediated
Examples	lecture, TV, books, radio, mailing list	FtF, letters, telephone, e-mail	FtF, moderated groups	IRC, MUDs, newsgroups, listserv

Source: Adapted from Shank 1993

in the same place but the message is received at some later time than it was sent, then the interaction is called asynchronous. If the sender and receiver are in different places yet the message is received at the same time it is sent, then the interaction is synchronous distributed. A telephone conversation is synchronous distributed interaction. Leaving a note on the door for someone is asynchronous interaction. If the sender and receiver are in different places and the message is received at some later time than it was sent, (a message on an answering machine) then the interaction is called asynchronous distributed. As can be seen in Table 3.3 sending and receiving a letter is also asynchronous distributed interaction.

No computer-mediated communication is FtF. E-mail, listservs and newsgroups are asynchronous distributed interactions; the senders and receivers are in different places and messages are delivered some time after they are sent. According to the model, and considering the sender's and receiver's physical locations and the real-time delivery of messages, IRC and MUDs are synchronous distributed interactions.

A fourth way of examining Internet communication is a socio-visibility taxonomy that looks at the number of senders and receivers and whether the interaction is public or private. Paterson (1996) uses the term *dialogue* for 1-1 communication; *broadcast* for one-to-many (1-M) and *multicast* for many-to-many (M-M). Public and private interaction refers to the reception of a message. If a message is only received by one person, then it is private. If the message is displayed or made available to an audience other than the sender and receiver, then it is public. A conversation between two people

Table 3.3 Time/space taxonomy

	Same time	Different times
Same place	synchronous (FtF)	asynchronous (note)
Different places	synchronous distributed (telephone)	asynchronous distributed (letter)

Source: Adapted from Ellis *et al*. 1993

on the street is a public dialogue; while a telephone conversation is usually a private dialogue. Radio and television are public broadcasts; an advertisement pamphlet in your mailbox is a private broadcast.

In this model of interaction (see Table 3.4), different relationships are possible. E-mail is usually a private dialogue, but if sent to several mailboxes, such as colleagues at work, it becomes a private broadcast interaction. In a listserv multiple people send messages that are delivered to the e-mail boxes of multiple receivers, therefore listservs are private **multicasts**. Because the multiple messages of newsgroups, IRC and MUDs are publicly viewable, these interactions are classified as public multicasts.

In an attempt at providing and establishing norms for detailed units of analysis for the study of computer-mediated communication, December (1996) argues that protocol, time, distribution scheme and media type be included in distinguishing characteristics of Internet communication. In December's schema the types of distribution include point to point, point to multipoint, point to **server** broadcast, point to server **narrowcast**, server broadcast and server narrowcast. In point to point distribution a single sender transmits a message to a single receiver. In point to multipoint a single sender or application sends a message to many receivers. In point to server broadcast, a single sender or server transmits a message to a server which makes the message available to other servers or to receivers with the appropriate client software. In point to server narrowcast the message is available only to a specific group of receivers, identified with passwords and/or Ids. In the server broadcast scheme, the server has stored information that is available to anyone for retrieval with an appropriate client; the server narrowcast scheme again restricts the information to an authorized set of **users** (December 1996). Media type includes text, sound, graphics, images, video, executable files, **hypertext** and **hypermedia**. E-mail uses a point-to-point distribution scheme; listserv and e-mail distribution lists, point to multipoint schemes. IRC and Usenet use the point to server broadcast and MUDs use point to server narrowcast. The dominant media type used in all of these services is ASCII text.

An essential category for comparison of Internet communication is

Table 3.4 Socio-visibility taxonomy

	1-1 dialogue	*1-M broadcast*	*M-M multicast*
Public	conversation on the street	political speech	Usenet, MUD, IRC
Private	telephone, e-mail	distribution list	listserv

Source: Adapted from Paterson 1996

interactivity. Rafaeli and Sudweeks (1998) investigate the degree of inter-activity among participants in computer mediated newsgroups. The degree of interactivity with its emphasis on the message is in contrast to the other categories that emphasize the relation between sender and receiver. Inter-activity is a process-related construct about communication that describes the extent to which messages are related to each other. Rafaeli and Sud-weeks (1995) argue that interactivity is a continuum–declarative or one-way communication on one end, fully interactive communication at the other end, and reactive or two-way communication somewhere in between. The focus on interactivity also supports their argument that FtF conversation is not to be used as the standard of comparison for group computer-mediated communication. One-way declarative communication has unrelated messages relayed from a source to an audience. Two-way reactive communication is similar to a dialogue with the sender and receiver taking turns, but the new message is in response to the previous one. In full interactivity later messages in any sequence not only take into account the previous messages but also the reactive manner of the previous messages. Thus for Rafaeli and Sudweeks all communication falls short of full interactivity.

None of the above models fully describe the differences among the inter-actions in Internet-based communication; therefore additional character-istics need to be specified. Paterson (1996) argues that the form of messages, the skill level required for full participation, the environment and the metaphors used in these types of communication provide further insights to the types of interactions. The form of a message may be encapsu-lated, fragmentary or operative. An encapsulated message resembles a letter or traditional written communication, is asynchronous and uses contextual support mechanisms such as address spaces and subject line. A fragmentary message is delivered in pieces, resembles traditional spoken communication, is synchronous and has no contextual support other than the screen display. An operative message is a message that carries out some action and is accomplished via a program (Paterson 1996).

EMOTICONS

Emoticons (emotional **icons**) are used to compensate for the inability to convey voice inflections, facial expressions and bodily gestures in written communication. Some emoticons are better known as 'smileys'. Emoticons can be very effective towards avoiding misinterpretation of the writer's intents. While there are no standard definitions for the following emoticons, we have supplied their most usual meanings. Most emoticons will look like a face (eyes, nose and mouth) when rotated 90 degrees clockwise. Skill with the use of emoticons is highly valued in online forms of communication from e-mail to chatrooms and its use and misuse betrays the newbie from the seasoned geek.

:) or :-)	Expresses happiness, sarcasm, or joke
:(or :-(	Expresses unhappiness
:] or :-]	Expresses jovial happiness
:[or :-[	Expresses despondent unhappiness
:D or :-D	Expresses jovial happiness
:I or :-I	Expresses indifference
:-/ or :-\	Indicates undecided, confused or skeptical. Also :/ or :\.
:Q or :-Q	Expresses confusion
:S or :-S	Expresses incoherence or loss of words
:@ or :-@	Expresses shock or screaming
:O or :-O	Indicates surprise, yelling or realization of an error ('uh oh!')

Persons:	Description:
~(_:(l)	Simpson, Homer
(_8^(l)	Simpson, Homer
888888888:-)	Simpson, Marge
:~.)	Crawford, Cindy
=:-)	Cyberpunk
C:\> or D:\>	MS-DOS Programmer
<|-)	Chinese
>8=[...	Alien / Martian
+O:-)	I'm the Pope
<]:^)	A clown
*<||:o) o o o	Santa
{ :-~[]	Smoker
@:-§	Russian Folk Dancer
:[~	Vampire
=):-)	Abraham Lincoln
'8^)	Dilbert
<|:~,	A witch
8(:-)	Mickey Mouse

Source: www.pb.org/emoticon

These different characteristics presented in the various models help complete the descriptions of the types of communication available on the Internet. Internet communication skill levels can vary from low to high. An example of low skill requirements is basic editing skills with few commands. High skill levels require programming expertise. E-mail, listserv, and newsgroups have encapsulated messages, while IRC and MUDs have fragmentary messages. MUDs have operative messages that construct the environment and provide actions for the participants. E-mail, listserv and newsgroups require only basic editing skills and only a few commands for reading, sending and replying, so they have low skill requirements. IRC has talk functions and multiple commands for emoting, movement between rooms, reading and posting messages to a message board, locating people, creating channels and removing people from channels. Depending on the commands used, the skill level for IRC ranges from low to moderate.

MUDs have conversation and additional programming components to build the environment, to construct agents and to structure the action. Depending on the set of commands used, the skill level for MUDs ranges from moderate to high. The MUDs environments are usually constructed by the users, while the other services use the existing standardized setting provided.

Different metaphors for Internet communication are also of some usefulness for categorization purposes. The underlying metaphors, and the structure of the interaction provided by the software, differ widely. E-mail and listserv use a postal service metaphor; IRC uses a room metaphor; Usenet is a discussion or a conversation, and the constructed environments of MUDs provide fantasy worlds. The hybrid nature of the Web make a singular metaphor less satisfactory, but town square, shopping mall and library all fit to some extent. Table 3.5 presents a summary of the characteristics of Internet communication.

The Web is often seen as the site where different modes of communication come together resulting in the convergence of the mass media. Convergence has been defined by Pavlik (1996: 132) as the 'coming together of all forms of mediated communication in an electronic, **digital** form, driven by computers'. The Web facilitates this convergence of different modes of communication. The Internet as seen in Table 3.5 can be a one-to-one medium (e-mail), a one-to-many medium (discussion groups and listservs), a many-to-one medium (selection of stored information) and a many-to-many medium (commercial Web sites).

One could argue in many ways that the technologies and cultural practices developed around MUDs, listservs, Usenet, IRC, etc. belong to what can be called the Old Internet (Tetzlaff 2000: 99), the pre-Web era. This Old Internet form focused highly on interactivity and user involvement.

ACRONYMS

Speed is often a factor in online communication. Chatroom aficionados ensure that their line of communication is confined to short bursts in order to maintain the conversational connection. Along with emoticons, users have developed a shorthand through acronyms that quickly summarize a state of being, an action or a common turn of phrase. Acronyms are used throughout all forms of online communication including MUDs, chatrooms and e-mail and like emoticons are a form that separates the veteran users from the newbies. Acronyms are now used extensively by seasoned SMS users on their mobile telephones where textual brevity is a key to communication.

AAMOF	as a matter of fact	MGB	may God bless
BBFN	bye bye for now	MHOTY	my hat's off to
BFN	bye for now		you
BTW	by the way	NRN	no reply necessary
BYKT	but you knew that	OIC	oh, I see
CMIIW	correct me if I'm	OTOH	on the other hand
	wrong	ROF	rolling on the
EOL	end of lecture		floor
FAQ	frequently asked	ROFL	rolling on the
	question(s)		floor laughing
FITB	fill in the blank	ROTFL	rolling on the
FWIW	for what it's worth		floor laughing
FYI	for your information	RSN	real soon now
HTH	hope this helps	SITD	still in the dark
IAC	in any case	TIA	thanks in advance
IAE	in any event	TIC	tongue in cheek
ICL	in Christian love	TTYL	talk to you later
IMCO	in my considered	TYVM	thank you very
	opinion		much
IMHO	in my humble opinion	WYSIWYG	what you see is
IMNSHO	in my not so humble		what you get
	opinion	<G>	Grinning
IMO	in my opinion	<J>	Joking
IOW	in other words	<L>	Laughing
LOL	lots of luck or	<S>	Smiling
	laughing out loud	<Y>	Yawning

Source: www.pb.org/acronym

Table 3.5 Characteristics of Internet communication services

	e-mail	listserv	IRC	MUD	Usenet	WWW
Level	inter-personal	group	group	group	hybrid	hybrid
Conver-sation	usually dialogue	monologue, discussion	multilogue	multilogue	monologue, discussion, multilogue	multi-logue
Source	one	many	many	many	many	many
Receiver	one	many	many	many	many	many
Channel	computer	computer	computer	computer	computer	computer
Distribution	point to point	point to point multipoint	point to server broadcast	point to server narrowcast	point to server broadcast	point to server broadcast
Media type	text	text	text	text, executable	text	multi-media
Message	encapsulated	encapsulated	fragmentary	fragmentary operative	encapsulated	encap-sulated
Temporal	asynchronous	asynchronous	synchronous	synchronous	asynchronous	asynchro-nous
Spatial	distributed	distributed	distributed	distributed	distributed	distributed
Sociality	dialogue	multicast, can be broadcast	multicast	multicast	multicast	multicast
Visibility	private	private	public	public	public	public
Interactive	usually reactive	ranges	usually reactive	usually reactive	ranges	ranges
Skill	low	low	low to moderate	moderate to high	low	low
Environment	existing	existing	existing	constructed	existing	existing
Metaphor	postal	postal	room	fantasy world	discussion, conversation	town square/ shopping mall

Source: Adapted from December 1996 and Paterson 1996

The Web era of new media does not necessarily extend this involvement, and may well have more in common with traditional old media forms of user patterns.

The Web blurs the boundaries that traditionally distinguish one medium from another. Text, graphics, video and audio can be presented via the Web. Some Internet resources are asynchronous, while others are synchronous. We argue that the Web has evolved into a new interactive medium. It is the convergence of many of the features of traditional media merged together into something new, a unique medium for communication.

Will traditional media be eliminated by the Internet and the plethora of new electronic delivery systems available? The history of communication technology provides us with some clues. Through history, new media have not caused the demise of existing media. Radio did not replace newspapers, and television did not replace radio. New media have eroded existing media audiences and thus their revenue bases. For traditional media to survive, they have to continually adapt to the new competitive environment. Adaptive strategies often include narrowcasting to **niche audiences**, increasing services and recycling existing content into new formats (Pavlik 1996). Traditional media are trying to adapt to the Internet by providing their content online. The Internet is a means for media to market their brand, to extend their existing services, to add new services, and to repackage old content. As we shall see in Chapters 8 and 9, the Internet can thus be said to augment existing media rather than replacing them.

FROM NETWORKS TO A LOOSE WEB

Today one can agree with Castells (1996) that 'networks' or as we prefer to argue 'Webs' are on their way to becoming the defining metaphors of our time. This has to do directly with the explosion of digital technology. Think about two of our most important modern technologies, gene technology and information technology. We can talk about a Web of chromosomes or a computer network. Both express new ways of seeing the world and our role in it. Digital technology combines 0s and 1s, into a world wide network or Web, a **virtual** room where we can communicate. Gene technology lets us experiment with our biological network, weaving new Webs, as the much-celebrated Human Genome Project has taught us. Seeing the world as a Web of connections has consequences for the way we live and the decisions we make.

Tim Berners-Lee, the man credited with 'inventing' the World Wide Web, explains his vision of the Web of connections:

> The Web is more a social creation than a technical one. I designed it for a social effect – to help people work together – and not as a technical toy. The ultimate goal of the Web is to

support and improve our Weblike existence in the world. We clump into families, associations and companies. We develop trust across the miles and distrust around the corner. What we believe, endorse, agree with and depend on is representable and, increasingly, represented on the Web.

(Berners-Lee 1999: 133)

Berners-Lee has a two-part vision for the future of the Web. In the first part, the Web becomes a much more powerful means for collaboration between people: 'the dream of people-to-people communication through shared knowledge must be possible for groups of all sizes, interacting electronically with as much ease as they do now in person.' In the second part, collaborations extend to computers creating what he calls a 'Semantic Web'. It is at this stage that 'Machines become capable of analysing all the data on the Web – the content, links and transactions between people and computers' (Berners-Lee 1999: 169).

Indeed the driving force for Berners-Lee was communication through shared knowledge, and the driving 'market' for it was collaboration among people at work and at home. By building a hypertext Web, a group of people of whatever size could easily express themselves, quickly acquire and convey knowledge, overcome misunderstandings and reduce duplication of effort. This would give people in a group new tools and a new power to build something together.

He further explains that:

my definition of interactive includes not just the ability to choose, but also the ability to create. We ought to be able not only to find any kind of document on the Web, but also to create any kind of document, easily. We should be able not only to follow links, but to create them – between all sorts of media. We should be able not only to interact with other people, but to create with other people. Intercreativity is the process of making things or solving problems together. If interactivity is not just sitting there passively in front of a display screen, then intercreativity is not just sitting there in front of something 'interactive'.

(Berners-Lee 1999: 182)

The key in reaching this vision is that concepts become linked together. By linking things together we build Webs of relationships from which it is hoped that we can move forward towards creating common understanding.

In a similar vein, Wellman and Hampton (1999) make a strong case that we are living in a paradigm shift in the way we perceive society, but especially in the way people and institutions are connected. They see a shift from living in isolated groups, or 'bowling alone' in the words of Robert Putnam

(2000), to living in networked relationships. If people often view the world in terms of groups, they function increasingly in networks. They describe that in networked societies: 'boundaries are more permeable, interactions are with diverse others, linkages switch between multiple networks, and hierarchies (when they exist) are flatter and more recursive' (Wellman and Hampton 1999: 1).

The Web both fosters the proliferation of weak ties and holds together spatially distant ties in place when face-to-face meetings are lacking. The Web is 'especially useful for maintaining contact with "weak ties": persons and groups with whom one does not have strong relationships of work, kinship, sociability, support, or information exchange' (Wellman and Hampton 1999: 1). Weak ties are seen as more socially heterogeneous than strong ties, thus they connect people to diverse social milieus and provide wider ranges of information. Wellman and Hampton conclude that connectivity has reduced the identity and pressures of belonging to groups while increasing opportunity, contingency, globalization and uncertainty through participation in social networks.

CONCLUSION: THE LOOSE WEB

At the very core of the meaning of the Web is linkage and connection: it is fundamentally about modes of communication and presenting possibilities about how those modes might intersect. Thus the Web is simultaneously a mass-mediated *and* one-to-one form of communication. It is a site of incredible cultural consumption *and* cultural production and makes it harder to establish the boundary between these two activities. Whether one is referring to the immediacy of use, the **multimedia** play, the hypertext links between sites and texts, or the blending of personal space with sites that are for more public perusal, the Web and the Internet can be conceptualized as a media technology that produces a loose Web of interrelated activities. In this chapter we have highlighted the varied levels and forms of communication that interlink, converge and criss-cross the Internet and form the backbone of Web-based engagement and investment.

The metaphor of the loose Web recognizes that with these varied forms of communication, the user's connection to the Web is qualitatively different than with traditional media. User engagement with the Web draws on traditional media but is not fully defined by them. There is an elastic quality to the Web as the network is never fully defined, being on a shifting continuum from the very simple (personal home page) to the very sophisticated (corporate Web sites). Moreover, the Web often is a promotional network, often implying things not there, but that are at least possible to aspire to.

The significance of the Web is in more general terms associated with exchange, but in more specific terms it is fundamentally defined by links and linkages. Links are the lifeblood of the Web and the Web experience. When sites are connected, they are not defining each other's content; rather they are indicating that there is correlation between the sites. No location on the Web stands on its own because of this massive system of interlinkages. Like-wise, the use of the various communication forms possible via the Internet, from e-mail and newsgroups to chatrooms and discussion forums, become the way that any particular Web site both expands its own content and con-nects with its users to provide a rich form of interactivity and engagement.

The Web brings into clear relief the significance of certain boundaries: as a technology it highlights whether these boundaries need to be shifted or whether the distinctions between one side and the other should be trans-formed. The Web plays between the public and the private, the broadcast form and the conversation, the notion of public access and private property, and the author and the reader to name the most prominent dichotomies. As a loose Web, it cannot be defined as on one or other side of these various dichotomies of contemporary culture. It is much more the place for the debate and discussion and perhaps, through the linkages that are so essen-tial to the practice of the Web, a location that incites a continuous exchange across these boundaries. What is produced by the loose Web is a spectrum of engagement that expresses a new media form. The loose Web is an inter-connected media and communication mix that produces simultaneously audiences, community, conversation and connection.

Chapter 4

WEBS OF IDENTITY

> we are moving from modernist calculation to postmodernist simulation, where the self is a multiple, distributed system
>
> (Turkle 1996: 148)

INFORMATION AND COMMUNICATION technology shapes our perceptions, distributes our pictures of the world to one another, and constructs different forms of control over the cultural stories that shape our sense of who we are and our world. The instant we develop a new technology of communication – talking drums, papyrus scrolls, books, telegraph, radios, televisions, computers, mobile phones – we at least partially reconstruct the self and its world, creating new opportunities for reflection, perception, and social experience.

The technologies of **information** and communication – 'media' in the broad sense of the term – are technocultural hybrids (Davis 1998). Information technology often transcends its status as a thing. In enabling a new interface between the self, the other and the world beyond, media technologies become part of the self, the other and the world beyond. As Davis (1998: 4) explains, 'they form the building blocks, and even in some sense the foundation, for what we now increasingly think of as the "social construction" of reality'. Different forms of communication – oral, writing, print, television, **e-mail** – shape social and individual consciousness along specific lines, creating unique networks of perceptions, experiences, and interpersonal possibilities that help shape the social construction of reality. As Godwin (1997a) puts it, the Net 'is the first medium that combines all the powers to reach a large audience that you see in broadcasting and newspapers with all the intimacy and multi-directional flow of information that you see in telephone calls. It is both intimate and powerful'. It is this conjunction of power and intimacy that reveals the complex nature of the Web.

In this chapter, we will attempt to conceptualize the **user** in what we identify as the 'Web of identity'. The Web of identity refers to the role that the **Internet** now plays in the construction of contemporary identities. We do not argue that the Internet's role eliminates other social constructions of identity, but like other media forms it is implicated in the process. What the Web does underline is the identity of the 'user' which, although it has similarities to the role of the media audience member, is a significant qualitative shift in perspective and activity. To understand the shift away from audience to user that occurs through Internet usage, it is useful to map out the various early readings of identity in **cybercultural theory**. From that basis, the chapter surveys the more recent empirical readings of the social aspects of the Internet as a counterpoint to earlier efforts to explain contemporary identity through postmodern theory. We then develop an approach through the concept of the user of how the Web allows a particular presentation of the self through personal Web sites. From that perspective, the chapter concludes with a discussion of how cultural production on the Web differs from other media forms precisely because of the heightened role of the user.

CYBERCULTURE THEORY

Much of the early research that dealt with aspects of Web identity can be grouped under the term cyberculture theory. In that research, authors such as Turkle and Stone, argued that the Web led to a radical deconstructive effect on both identity and culture (Stone 1996; Turkle 1995). Their arguments were closely linked to postmodern theory and the Web became yet another new phenomenon that was fragmenting modernity's project very similar to the interpretation of music video heralded the postmodern dimension of television in the 1980s (see Goodwin, 1992). As Stone claims:

> The identities that emerge from these [Internet] interactions –
> fragmented, complex, diffracted through the lenses of techno-
> logy, culture and new technocultural formations – seem to be
> ... more visible as the critters we ourselves are in the process of
> becoming, here at the close of the mechanical age.
>
> (Stone 1996: 36)

Stone's work like much of Turkle's scholarship mostly concerns the '**virtual persona**'. Her examples have been drawn to a large extent from online subcultures in **multi-user domains** (**MUDs**):

> In the story of constructing identity in the culture of simulation,
> experiences on the Internet figure prominently, but these experi-
> ences can only be understood as part of a larger cultural context.

That context is the story of eroding boundaries between the real and the virtual, the animate and the inanimate, the unitary and the multiple self, which is occurring both in advanced scientific fields of research and in the patterns of everyday life. From scientists trying to create artificial life to children 'morphing' through a series of virtual personae, we shall see evidence of fundamental shifts in the way we create and experience human identity. But it is on the Internet that our confrontations with technology as it collides with our sense of human identity are fresh, even raw. In the real-time communities of **cyberspace**, we are dwellers on the threshold between the real and the virtual, unsure of our footing, inventing ourselves as we go along.

(Turkle 1995: 10)

An often made postmodern claim is that the Internet provides people the opportunity to abandon the confines of a limiting self. For example, Stone outlines the self as a politically constructed and locatable entity which is open to social control.

The individual societal actor becomes fixed in respect to geographical coordinates that determine physical locus ... by a metaphysics of presence I mean that a (living) body implies the presence within the body of a socially articulated self that is the true site of agency. It is this coupling, rather than the presence of the body alone, that privileges the body as the site of political authentication ... Tactics of discipline and control are meant to manage the coupled self with which agency and consequent political authenticity have been constructed to reside.

(Stone 1996: 91)

Stone argues that the Web has the liberating effect of making more freedom available to generate interpretations that suit the participant. This reflects another postmodern writer, Poster (1990: 6) who claims that in cyberspace, 'the self is decentered, dispersed, and multiplied in continuous instability'. These ideas have been with originality argued by Haraway (1991) whose construct of the **cyborg** relates to the possibility of radically altered bodies and conceptions of identity that can be 'postgendered'.

Hayles (1999) explains that although virtuality is clearly related to postmodernism it has distinctive features that 'seriate' from the postmodern. Hayles's description of the difference between postmodernism and virtuality which is expressed through the Web and other computer mediated cultural forms can be represented in Table 4.1:

Table 4.1 A comparison of Postmodernism and Virtuality

	Postmodernism	*Virtuality*
Declining dialectic	Presence/absence	Pattern/randomness
Integration into capitalism	Possession	Access
Psychological crisis	Castration	Mutation
Theoretical inversion formalism	Deconstruction	Maximum entropy
Creation of narrative	(De)construction of origin	(De)construction of chaos

Source: (Hayles 1999: 79)

Although Hayles uses these characterizations to analyse the transformations of cultural forms in virtuality, her analysis implies a shifted constitution of identity in the era of the Web. One of the key differences that Hayles's reading of the virtual emphasises is that **subjectivity** is organized out of randomness and no longer out of the negation of the past which identifies a partial transcendence of the postmodern condition.

As we have indicated, much of cyberculture theory writing is derived from small subcultural experiences on the Web and then wedded to postmodern thinking. It has a utility in identifying a shifted subjectivity but lacks an ability to encompass a wider range of experiences and identities formed through the Web and the Internet. The critique of cyberculture theory has been expressed by Wynn and Katz (1998) who explain:

> The departure from social theory in attempting to explain social phenomena, in Turkle's case, leads to a theoretical radicalism based in deconstructivist philosophy, Lacanian psychoanalytic theory, and neural nets. The work of Stone parallels this line of thinking using additional sources and concerns. Both claim to base their views in social science but in fact use contemporary psychological and literary theories as a primary basis of argument. The **data** used in these accounts come from within the target community of computer users that most exemplify the extremes of behavior upheld as social trends. Without social theory and more grounded methods, the Internet is plausibly portrayed as fantastic and unreal rather than practical, effective and socially constructed.
>
> (1998: 299)

This critique emerges from the social sciences where there are common ideas of self or identity that involve a definition of the individual in relationship to others, not just a singular presentation but occurring as an artifact of dyads, settings, and groups. Social scientists share an emphasis on negotiation and co-construction as central to any definition of identity or self. The point to be made is that the idea of self as varied is not new but a feature of mainstream social theory (Wynn and Katz 1998). One could take issue with the idea that the self is discontinuous and a creation of the individual, as this has consequences for any notion that selfhood can be changed in nature by social interaction with an electronic medium such as the Web. Well known writings that discuss identity as an artifact of social context are seminal works by Simmel (Wolff 1950), Mead (Miller 1973), Schutz (1970), and Berger and Luckmann (1967). All view selfhood as a product and process of social forces, whether it be in the context of everyday interaction, negotiations over meaning and manners, or struggles for social dominance.

RESEARCH ON THE SOCIAL EFFECTS OF THE INTERNET

The impact of the Web on our lives is often depicted as a contested space. Will the Internet unite us or further divide us? Utopian (see Katz and Aspden 1997) and dystopian (see Kraut *et al.* 1998) visions abound. The most common fear has been that the more time spent online decreases the amount and quality of time spent offline. In his influential book *Bowling Alone*, Putnam (2000) makes the argument that we are increasingly becoming suburban hermits, seldom leaving the comfort of our homes to engage in other civic and or social activities. A highly publicized study of the Internet and society (Nie and Erbring 2000), concluded that 'the more hours people use the Internet, the less time they spend with real human beings'.

What does the research to date have to say about the Internet and the possible tranformation of the self? Is there empirical evidence to back up the postmodern claims about a shifted identity that is now less grounded in past constructions of social identity and cohesion? To date there have been two major stances on the Internet's social effects that reveal two quite distinctive interpretations of the Internet's effect on one's identity and integration into the larger social world: one that the Internet is positive, and the other that the Internet is harmful (Baym, Zhang and Lin 2001). Now it must be made clear that these studies use different methodologies, ask different questions, and draw widely differing conclusions. Nevertheless, together they demonstrate the major concerns regarding interpersonal Internet use, the range of arguments debated, and the assumptions often taken for granted.

NEGATIVE

The dominating position that provides the mainstream media immediate and regular headlines is that the Internet has negative consequences on the offline, real lives of those who use it. There is an ever expanding literature making this stance with regard to the effect of online life on offline life of Internet users. The Homenet study (Kraut *et al.* 1998) and the Internet and society study of Nie and Erbring (2000) can serve as examples of the concerns raised from this perspective. The Homenet study follows 256 socially engaged members of ninety-three Pittsburgh families from their first introduction to the Internet through their first year online. Measures of Internet use were obtained through capture programs on the subjects' computers. The Nie and Erbring study consists of a random sample survey of 4,112 people in 2,700 households. Together, these two studies argue that use of the Internet challenges traditional relationships, lessens total social involvement, increases loneliness, and increases depression. Kraut *et al.* found that greater Internet use was associated with subsequent declines in family communication, while Nie and Erbring found that people reported spending less time with or on the phone with family and friends after gaining access to the Internet. Kraut *et al.* found that greater use of the Internet was associated with declines in the size of both local and distant social circles. Nie and Erbring found that people reported spending less time in social activities after going online, while Kraut *et al.* also found that people who were online subsequently reported increases in loneliness and depression.

Kraut *et al.* (1998) theorize that these negative effects might be attributed to two processes. Poorer quality, weak tie, Internet social relationships were substituted for face-to-face relationships, or time spent online is time in which people would be forming strong face-to-face ties were they offline. Thus the Internet is seen as either replacing existing strong ties or as interfering with the development of new strong ties. Nie in the much quoted press release accompanying the Internet and Society study states that heavy Internet users, 'lose touch with the social environment' and as more people go online, there are, 'more people at home, alone, and anonymous'. Both of these studies were headline news in both the *New York Times* and *CNN*, which is indicative of the extent to which the findings struck a responsive chord in the media food chain.

POSITIVE

There have been several reports that suggest that the Internet may indeed enhance and enrich offline social life. The UCLA Center for Communication Policy (2000) surveyed 2,096 American households comparing Internet users and non-users. The study reports that 92 per cent of Internet users report spending the same amount or more time with family members since going online. The respondents reported no difference in their socializing with friends or on their children's time spent with friends since going online. They also report that people are less likely to feel ignored because of a household member using the Internet than by one using the television. Internet users and non-users reported essentially the same amount of friends outside their household. An interesting finding was that they found that compared to non-users, Internet users spend more time with clubs and volunteer organizations.

Another large scale survey study from the Pew Project on the Internet and American Life (2000) found that Internet users were more socially active than non-users. The study also suggests that the Internet is enhancing traditional relationships and that the specific application of e-mail has increased contact in and improved strong tie relationships. The Pew study (2000: 20) states that, 'significant majorities of online Americans say their use of e-mail has increased the amount of contact they have with key family members and friends'. The Pew study (ibid: 7) found that women, and men in lesser numbers, 'have used e-mail to enrich their important relationships and enlarge their networks'. In the same vein the UCLA study found that Internet use slightly increased the number of people with whom subjects stayed in contact, especially family, friends and professional colleagues. Dimmick *et al.* (2000) found that among the appeals of e-mail are that it takes so little time, that it is inexpensive, that it is easy to fit into one's schedule, and that it minimizes the communicative relevance of time zones. Similarly Stafford *et al.* (1999) concluded that e-mail is being used to support and maintain meaningful relationships.

Some studies have argued that Internet use may improve emotional well being rather than creating loneliness and depression. La Rose *et al.* (2001) argue that, 'internet communication with people we know can alleviate depression, at least among socially isolated and moderately depressed populations such as college students, who may tend to rely on social technologies to obtain social support'.

A study by White *et al.* (1999) found that those who used the Internet in a retirement community tended towards decreased loneliness. The UCLA Internet Report (2000) found that Internet users reported slightly lower levels of life dissatisfaction, interaction anxiety, powerlessness and loneliness than non-users.

MAKING SENSE: THE LIMITS OF CURRENT RESEARCH

The research reviewed share a series of issues such as the ways in which the Internet affects our daily affairs, our relationships with others, our engagement in social activities, as well as our psychological health. The negative view argues that the Internet threatens traditional relationships, lessens social involvement and has negative psychological effects on its users. The positive view sees the Internet as rather integrated into daily social life instead of being in opposition to it. Instead of threatening traditional relationships, the Internet is seen to simply extend and often enhance them.

It must be remembered that comparing these studies is problematic as they almost always use different questions, use different measures and are most often based upon large scale survey research in the United States. These surveys are based upon self-reported measures of Internet use and its estimated effect on other activities. What are lacking are studies of actual social Internet use as it occurs in the context of daily activity. We need to know more about how the Internet is used across the full range of social interactions, how it fits in and compares to these interactions and ultimately what meanings and significances are generated by these new configurations. Although certainly not in their intentions as researchers, the results of the research around the negative effects of the Internet support in many ways the cyberculture theory approach to the Web and its constitution of identity. Social ties are weakened, and community and family structures are challenged. This is a negative outcome of the integration of the Internet into everyday life. In contrast, postmodern thinkers consider these less stable identity formations a sign of liberation and freedom. Nonetheless, this apparent concurrence of research does not indicate that we understand how people use the Internet: rather, it indicates that a great deal more research must be developed to contextualize the use of the Internet in our daily lives.

HOME PAGES AND THE PRESENTATION OF SELF IN EVERYDAY LIFE

Deciphering the uses made of the Web can also be explored through what people invest in developing for dissemination via the Web. An interesting way to enter into that world of production that is closely connected to identity formation is through a study of personal Web sites and how they represent a new form of communication about the self. Dominick (1999: 647) points out that, 'prior to Web pages, only the privileged – celebrities, politicians, media magnates, advertisers – had access to the mass audience'. Personal Web page publishing is quickly becoming a popular type of Internet use, especially amongst younger users. Can the ways personal home pages are constructed as a presentation of self tell us anything about the individual use and interaction with the Web?

Today there are an array of online companies such as Yahoo! Geocities, which offer free online space for personal Web pages in exchange for advertising banners, making the creation and maintainence of personal Web pages relatively convenient and affordable. An interesting question is why people maintain personal Web pages and how they use them to represent themselves.

People are increasingly using the Web to create virtual homes and online communities. Dominick (1999) points out that personal Web pages present us with a unique opportunity to study the audience as producers of media content rather than just as consumers. Personal Web pages are an important component of the production of culture thesis, in that they allow individuals to become producers of media content, with the possibility of access to a mass audience that they normally would be unable to reach.

While the presentation of self online is a rather new research topic, self presentation in general is certainly not. Goffman's (1959) seminal *The Presentation of Self in Everday Life*, remains uncannily current. For Goffman the presentation of self is a daily ongoing process of negotiation and information management, whereby the individual is constantly trying to influence the impression others develop, as a way of influencing others' attitudes and ultimately, behaviour. Goffman makes a distinction between the expression the individual 'gives' and the expression 'given off', acknowledging that expressions given off are more theatrical and contextual, usually non-verbal, and presumably unintentional, while the expressions an individual gives are easier to manipulate. Thus the individual sets the stage for a never ending, daily 'information game', whereby the impressions formed are a result of the 'performance'.

Web pages offer a new setting for Goffman's 'information game'. The important difference is that online self presentation provides a level of information control that is not normal in real life interaction. The Web as realized in the personal home page is possibly seen by some as providing a fairly safe and secure environment for self-disclosure.

For example, Dominick's (1999) content analysis of personal home pages found that the strategies employed on personal pages were similar to interpersonal strategies of self-presentation. People used links on their home pages as a means of social association, so that by providing a set of links to other sites, people indirectly defined themselves by listing their interests. Web page hosts also often sought positive reinforcement for the work they put into constructing the site through inviting visitors to e-mail them or sign their 'guestbooks'.

In a similar study, Smith (1998) identified a taxonomy of Web-based invitational strategies, identifying the following: feedback mechanisms (e-mail, guestbook), vertical hierachies (the position of items on the page, from top to bottom), personal expertise, external validation (awards), direct address and personality. People used these strategies to project their identities and to try to connect with online audiences.

Papacharissi (2001), underlined the social dimensions of home pages, and questioned the use of a real/virtual life dichotomy when researching the social consequences of new media technologies. She found that the most frequently encountered reasons for hosting a personal home page were entertainment and information. Communication with friends and family and self-expression presented more novel, yet popular motives that reflected some of the unique capabilities the medium provides for communication. Respondents pointed out that compared to other entertainment and pastime options, home page production was much more productive and filled them with a sense of accomplishment.

Papacharissi (2001) found an interesting paradox. Her subjects made use of home pages to extend their social networks, channel their creativity, express themselves, for entertainment, to fill time, or to obtain and display information. This led to more time spent online, perhaps at the expense of off-line activities. She warns us that drawing conclusions on media effects based on the number of hours spent on or off-line is simplistic, and that we must focus on the quality of the interaction, rather than the time spent online.

Several studies, including Baym (2000), Papacharissi (2001), and Sveningsson (2001), reveal people who meet, socialize, express themselves, and are creative online. Knowing the workings of current media logic and the focus on 'bad news' we run the danger of stigmatizing the social uses of the Internet. It is important to acknowledge the community building going on and the social potential of the Internet, before the media condemn it for promoting social isolation. People do encounter and communicate with real people online; it is one of the primary appeals of the Internet. Time spent online is not necessarily time spent apart from other people. All too many researchers have allowed themselves to be trapped by a false real/virtual world dichotomy.

CONCEPTUALIZING THE USER

The refraction and formation of identity through the Web is without a doubt a complex process to understand and, as we have discovered, to research. The range of uses of the Web by individuals makes it difficult to come up with a unifying paradigm that would express a definitive subjectivity produced through one's interactions with this media form. Subjectivity has been explored in the critical study of other media forms such as film and television. In those studies, subjectivity is often concerned with projections of the self or debates about the passivity or activity of the audience and we have intersected with those approaches somewhat in our review of cyberculture theory and postmodernism earlier in this chapter. Although it is useful to adapt those approaches to the study of the Web, they do not fully capture the sense or even the structure of experience of its use. Audience, consumer, reader and listener are the usual ways of identifying the subjective experience of other media and cultural forms and, though they relate to the experience of the Web, they do not express its essential difference. In order to advance on understanding the Web of identity, it is the different subjectivity of the user that has to be explored. To organize that interpretation of the user and how it relates to but differentiates itself from how people use traditional media, we have called this interpretation the **cultural production thesis**. What follows is an explanation of the user through an elaboration of this thesis of why production is so central to the meaning and use of the Web.

The cultural production thesis

What we are defining as the cultural production thesis for understanding the Web derives from a reinterpretation of one strain of the long tradition of media and communication studies that can be grouped as effects studies. Effects research emerged from an intuitive reading of the dominant communication technologies of the twentieth century. In its early incarnations, effects research was a study of propaganda (Lasswell 1971): the broadcasting form of radio and television led to the continuous assessment of its ultimate influence and power over a populace. In the twists and turns of research traditions, effects research has led to three related traditions that can serve as quite different but useful starting points for interpreting the Web as media form:

- the propaganda tradition in a discontinuous line has reformed in contemporary thinking through **cybernetics** and its significance in new media and **computer mediated communication** as we have discussed in Chapter 2. The tradition thus emphasizes and makes us think about what the media do to people.
- effects research has become a study of media functionalism and uses and gratifications; these studies highlight either the power of the audience or the power of the individual to control their use of the media for their own interests (Blumler and Katz 1974). In Web-related terms, functionalism celebrates the capacity of the user to choose their sources and provides a natural extension of the approach's study of television. This research approach emphasizes what people do with media.
- the active audience tradition developed through cultural studies is a celebration of the power of the audience in negotiating the meaning of any media text. It is a recognition of the interplay that media forms play between a dominant culture and subordinate cultures who reinterpret and remake the messages to fit into their everyday lives (Abercrombie and Longhurst 1998; Fiske 1994). In its focus on the remaking of meaning and a form of active engagement, the active audience approach comes close to making sense of the level of engagement that the Web implies in its 'audiences'. This tradition emphasises how people negotiate and remake media.

These traditions all highlight a media architecture which is both centralized and patterned to be distributed from the top downwards. Their utility in analysing the Web is thus limited to their ability to accommodate the dispersed patterns of the Web's distribution of texts. More critically, their adaptation to Web analysis is severely constrained because one of the essential features of this shifted and dispersed hierarchy of sources is that production itself is at the core of participating/using the Web. Although effects research may be the focus of studies that try to determine the dangers of the Web because of its lack of regulation of who can connect to and see particular sites (the development of 1996 Communication Decency Act in the United States as well as Internet censorship attempts in a variety of countries are results of effects-like research around pornography in particular), the key feature of the Web is that what is often conceptualized as the 'audience' of the media form has a much greater role as user and ultimately producer of the content itself as much as observer/viewer.

Of these three traditions, the cultural studies approach, despite its focus on the audience, actually addresses the issues of activity and by implication the idea of production best. The cultural production thesis is an adaptation of the cultural studies' approaches by shifting the focus on to the cultural politics of production on the Web while maintaining the insights derived from celebrating the activity of the populace in making meaning. This new thesis is the fundamental reorientation of cultural studies from reception to production in order to make sense of the Web.

To further develop the cultural production thesis, it is useful to think of the basic different experience of the Web from other media forms. Various monikers have been employed by journalists to describe people's engagement with the Web. A common early term was that people 'surfed' the Net, which embodied a surface gliding from site to site as well as expressing a particular attachment to youth cultural experience. Surfing the Net is one form of modality of engagement, but it does not encompass the range of activities that the Web permits; surfing the Web is derived from its television precursor of channel surfing. Web surfing acknowledges the sensation of perpetual linkage as it privileges an audience conception of the experience and a limitation with the level of engagement.

Netscape, Internet Explorer and other **search engines** have characterized the movements around the Web as browsing and hence the idea of the Web **browser** as both person and search engine/software overlay is also commonly used to demarcate Web activity. Metaphorically, the browser is linked to the activities of the flaneur who would stroll through shops, streets, markets and parks idly observing the trades and practices of other people. A browser is also associated with less goal directed activities, where the browser is searching generally to find something – an article of clothing, a book in a library, or a particular corner of a park – without a completely purposive-rational and linear approach. Although there is a quality of engagement that borders on a kind of disinterested **interactivity** that browsing expresses, it again represents a modality of Web use rather than encompassing the full range of experiences and practices.

The concept of the user comes closest to expressing the range of possible modalities of engagement that the Web implicates. Perhaps the most common use of user outside of the realm of computer mediated communication, has been to describe the use of illicit drugs. Even this usually pejorative sense intersects with Web activity: the Web user often goes beyond the passive engagement of the surfer or the disinterested play of the browser and into a form of immersion into the Web and what it promises. User implies a kind of active exchange that is central to the Web experience. Because of its multidirectional network structure, the Web is centrally about communicative exchange. This idea of multidirectional exchange and involvement has led many to think that the defining feature of the Web is its greater fulfilment of the promise of interactivity than any past media form. Within Web sites certainly there is a range of choices for links and directions that involve the user centrally in the construction of their experience of the Web.

The term 'user' also captures another clear defining characteristic of the Web: it is as much about looking, reading, observing and browsing as it is about a kind of empowerment to *produce*. The Web site is a peculiar media form that allows the transformation of information into formats that resemble centrally produced and mass distributed traditional media. Without large institutional/corporate support, the personal Web page can look as good as an expensive glossy magazine on the newstands. Its combination of colour images and blocked and columned text has taken the empowerment formerly associated with 1980s desktop publishing and placed it on the Web. The fundamental difference with Web publishing is that distribution – the deathknell of the small desktop publisher – is a non-issue when it is circulated on the Internet. Reproduction and print runs – another cost of publishing – is eliminated as a cost of production. The Web provisions the user to eliminate the natural divisions between production, distribution, and exhibition as the network makes these divides meaningless.

Imbricated in this development of the user as producer is a shifted notion of media literacy. Cultural studies, in its development of the active audience through the writings of Morley (1986), Ang (1991), and Fiske (1989) among others, has identified a highly nuanced description of the process of making meaning from media texts. In a sense, the process of making meaning although it is derived from consuming/reception is a productive activity from this perspective. The activity of the audience reproduces the text into the negotiated space of the audience's lives. What cultural studies is underlining is that audiences are not passive but are in fact active. The general objective of this active audience research in cultural studies is to turn reception into production. Embedded into cultural studies is a temporary resignation that the disenfranchised have to 'make do': they have to work within a hegemonic structure of meaning creation of their cultural forms and make them fit into their pleasures and practices (Fiske 1989: 4). The text of cultural studies' approaches to media is the repressed will to produce meaning quite directly and unmediated by a dominant culture. The form of media literacy that is celebrated by traditional cultural studies' active audience approach is one of sophisticated reception. What the Web underlines is a form of literacy that is simultaneously about reception and production; the Web pushes analysis beyond the active audience thesis of past cultural studies to a focus on the ability to manipulate the cultural form for clearly new kinds of production. Conceptualizing the user of the Internet allows us to reorient the political dimension of how cultural studies has conceptualized media.

The desire to produce should not be seen as an exclusive domain of the Internet. The point here is that because of its architecture and its structure of access, the Internet allows us to witness and thereby conceptualize how the will/desire to produce is part of all media and part of a general cultural struggle. Enzensberger wrote in 1974 of a politics of production that in its position of taking control of production by communities and collectives would serve to make television a media form that is more democratic, accessible and, in his terms, valuable (Enzensberger 1974). Of course, by the time that Enzensberger had developed his theory of the media, television had already been constituted as a centrally controlled, nationally distributed media form whose costs often weighed against a form of production that operated at the community level. Nevertheless, there is a strong history of community television that emerged from cable access channels in North America put in place by federal regulators who looked to access channels as a way to give a 'community dividend' from the profits of cable television providers (Linder 1999). Similar scenarios of the politics of large- and small-scale production have been enacted in radio; but with radio, the lower entry costs of producing and broadcasting as a community station allowed for a flourishing of cultural production across many institutions in economically richer and poorer regions and countries.

It is also important to see that cultural production is never purely separated from the activity of reception. One of the more interesting phenomena of recent television is how it has attempted to appropriate the desire to produce into its new hybrid formats. Lifestyle programming, a clear international growth market through pay and cable television, is generally focused on reproducing the desire to produce. Cooking shows invite the audience to reproduce that which has been made; a spate of programmes from the franchised *Changing Rooms* to gardening programmes and home improvement shows all evoke a sense of desire to transform and change one's environment. Most of these programmes assume an audience that is in fact propertied and can therefore freely transform their homes and gardens (the programmes also work at another level of producing a desire in the non-home owner to buy a home in order to be able to transform, construct and produce). Another generation of documentary style programmes are celebrations of audiences as performers: several versions of a programme that begin as quasi-competitions but presented as 'fly-on-the-wall' documentaries of a popular music group being formed (*Pop Star*) or groups of contestants competing on a deserted island (*Survivor*) have circulated around the globe. Others involve the 'documenting' of a lifestyle by presenting a series on the trials of a fabricated shared house (*Big Brother*); and still others attempt to document a class as they go through the rigours of driving school, vet school or diving school.

All of these new formats are working in the interstices of production desires and representing them as television programmes for reception. Television as an industry has become more sophisticated at packaging the desire to produce in a hegemonic shift that may be a response to the shifted mediascape produced by the Internet towards more widespread production.

The Web has at the very least been successful at offering this promise of production to its users. Because of its relative newness, the Web puts in relief the politics of cultural production that have been buried in past struggles and contestations in previous media forms. In some ways, the Web's exponential proliferation of personal Web sites resembles the emergence of the portable 'Brownie' camera at the beginning of the twentieth century. As photography and reproduction had done throughout the nineteenth century, the personal camera further democratized the control of the image. Walter Benjamin (1968: 221–3) described this 'mechanical reproduction' as a means towards the destruction of the aura of the artwork; likewise the photographic image became the province of the middle classes and within reach of the working classes. Mantelpieces of personal images at the turn of the century bear a striking resemblance to the homepages of personal Web sites in their celebration of the personal for public display. The photograph, like the Web site, reconstructs the private, personal world through an appropriation of the media technology of representation. The distance and aura that a technology may have produced through its complex scientifically derived origins is broken down in this appropriation by the populace.

Part of the attraction of making a Web site is that it transforms the aura of production that has been the province of skilled graphics departments of major magazines and places it within the reach of a massive number of people. Add to this the aura of distribution and exhibition that the Web allows through its network, and one can see that personal Web site production is a play with past forms of media power (Cheung 2000: 43–5). The software to produce Web sites has been freely available as **shareware** or even in more commercial Web site production software. The tools are often made available for thirty-day trials which can be plenty of time to build the colourful, image and text-rich structure of a personal Web site. In fact, current versions of Netscape or Internet Explorer bundle a simple Web site producing software program as part of their free downloadable package. A Web site potentially becomes simultaneously a magazine, a picture gallery and an audio/video vignette. Its power remains potential despite its appearance of traditional media quality because the power of the traditional media is connected to their ability to attract a large audience. With the personal Web site, the cultural production is perpetually available to a vast audience of users, but few of them achieve the thousands of **hits** that would make the site equivalent to a traditional media outlet. Nonetheless, the personal Web site is a production of the self for public consumption and resembles the way the front garden of a house presents a public display of its occupants for passers-by.

The form of cultural production that the Web celebrates is not the discrete product such as a film or a novel. The Web site is heteroglossic, which not only refers to its fragments of **multimedia** formats that have already been described, but also the Web site's interconnection to other Web sites and other cultural productions. If the success of a Web site is related to its capacity to attract other users, one of the critical avenues for that success is how well the site is linked to other sites. This linkage, which we will elaborate upon later in this chapter, expands the cultural production outwards within the Web site's own architecture: it implies the presence of related universes and comfortably acknowledges that any user may jump via a presented **hypertext** link to another Web site.

There are two related insights to be drawn from this form of cultural production of Web sites. First, the interconnection of Web sites via the Internet has been one of the principal means of constructing or transforming the content of any individual Web site. The pattern of linkage has allowed for the exchange of graphics, **icons**, **avatars**, useful sites, Web editors and so on. The Internet's origins as an exchange of shareware continues in various forms, where individual Web sites freely allow their material to be transposed to other Web sites. This interchange has allowed for the incredible growth of cultural production which is at the centre of the Internet experience for most users. The expansion is related to both the will to produce and the relative ease at producing because of these linkages.

Second, the interconnection of Web sites produces what we could describe as a sensation of cultural production in the activity itself. The term interactivity has often been associated with this experience of the Web. Because of its overuse, it has become more and more difficult to use interactivity without imbuing the technology with some sort of supremacy over past media and cultural forms. Also, interactivity is seen as the golden fleece of technical perfectionism, where an artificial environment is compelling enough to be more interesting or sensorially complete than real-life. Although the Web can rarely make claims of virtuality and sensory immersion that some computer games with gloves and headgear promise, it has been seen as more engaging than film or television. Its interactive quality relates to the elaborate feedback structures that are part of Web design and its linkages, so that the user is included in the process of establishing what s/he actually sees, reads and hears. The Web is an *invocative* medium (Chesher 1996) where it invites you to make decisions and choices about what link you are going to take by pointing and clicking: film and television, in contrast *evoke* an emotional connection to the narrative. There is a feeling of constructing one's Web session through this process that aligns with an affective feeling of production and creativity.

Conceptualizing the Web in terms of cultural production also underlines how the Web's software has reduced the technicist quality of computer mediated communication to the point that its intrinsic ease of use allows for its very proliferation and expansion into greater parts of our everyday life. What we are referring to here are two dimensions of *access* (Marshall 2002). On one level, the Web is not difficult to learn to use and thereby presents itself as an inclusive technology like television but with the added quality that its use has an element of 'productivity'. This dimension of access has connected the Web to a massively democratic will to produce and an equally massive drive to connect people to the Web in developed nations and a strong desire to wire less developed nations. It must be remembered that actualizing that will to produce is only currently realisable by a limited demographic and a severely constrained part of the globe, despite all the rhetoric that has connected the Web with **globalization**. On a second level, the Web through its use begins to function in a McLuhanesque sense as an extension of ourselves outwards through the technology of interconnection and linkage. As we have indicated above, greater portions of our personal and professional selves are placed online for exchange and interchange in order to connect with contemporary information and communication flows. The Web's accessibility – its increasing affinity with the way we constitute our everyday interactions – moves the Web to the hub of production in whatever form in contemporary culture.

This proliferating productivity of the Web demands a closer inspection and a great deal more research from the perspective of cultural production. It is this cultural investment and engagement which is being actively harnessed by the so-called **new economy**. It is worth reminding ourselves that the Web has been routinely accessed through work by the information classes and therefore has always existed simultaneously as a technology associated with the productivity of work and the productivity generated from leisure pursuits. The Web's content reflects this hybridity and also reflects the increasingly less defined differences between work and non-work, entertainment and information in contemporary Western culture. There are attempts to service the forms of cultural production in commodity form by providing new versions of software, **Java**scripts, flash and multimedia capture technology; similarly computer hardware and telecommunications networking are servicing the Web's expansive reach and needs for data storage. There are also attempts to differentiate production so that certain sites are seen to be more professional, more validated, and ultimately of greater value. The forms of access to cultural production that the Web has embodied has produced an interesting struggle over the problem of *excess* content, communication and information: there are just too many sites for anyone to survey and evaluate and this excess produces an instability in determining the Web's economic and cultural value. Consequently, the Web as an incredible site of cultural production has also become the site for a struggle to establish new hierarchies of value that effectively work towards *exclusion* (Marshall 2002). Nonetheless, this cultural struggle is only identifiable in terms of cultural production and demands an approach to the study of the Web from the perspective of the cultural production thesis.

CONCLUSION: THE SHIFTING BOUNDARIES OF IDENTITY

In this chapter we have mapped several attempts to describe and reveal how identities are formed through the Web. We have underlined that the significance of the will to produce and the exponential growth in cultural production are connected to the heightened and engaged role of the 'user' as opposed to the role of viewer or consumer of the Web. In all these characterizations, from fluctuating identity (cyberculture theory) and social incoherence (negative social scientific studies) to consolidating social networks (positive social scientific studies), and the presentation of self in everyday life (Goffman's social construction approach), there is a general concurrence that the Web is an active site for the production and construction of identity. In a sense, the Web is a flourishing location for the negotiating of new boundaries and delineations around identity. The definitive 'effect' of the Web is somewhat elusive; but what we can conclude is that the Web highlights and challenges the boundaries around the following series of crucial identity tropes:

Anonymity

As we have seen, part of the allure of the Web is that one's identity may not be attached to one's physical body on the Web. One can transform via avatars and **handles** and Haraway's postgendering is possible in the anonymous Web. In some ways the pleasure of anonymity on the Web can be compared to the seductive qualities of the modern city, where one can enjoy what is on offer without being identified or at least without having one's identity being completely revealed. In contradistinction to this anonymous Web user is the reality that our Web activities leave remnants that can be traced, identified, and organized. So our anonymity or our reconstruction of our identity is elusive. Nonetheless, anonymity continues to operate as the boundary that one traverses as a Web user whether as a **lurker** in chatgroups or as a multiple 'personality' in usegroups and chatgroups.

Language

The question of language use is central to understanding the powerplays of identity around the Web. According to the World Lingo Web site roughly two-thirds of Web content is in English. However, in terms of users internationally, 43 per cent of users do not use English at all while online (World Lingo 2002; Global Reach 2001). In the early days of the Web the hegemony of English was felt as the United States articulated its cornering of the information economy and culture. That sense of English as the lingua franca of the Web and the Internet is now powerfully established. Because the Web is both an expression of work identity and leisure identity, this 'English' hold on the Web is increasingly tenuous. Moreover, the rapid expansion of the Internet in Asia and China in particular is shifting the language balance over the next decade.

Narcissism

As we have outlined, a large number of Web sites are personal Webpages. They are elaborate expressions of the self and are an example of how the Web blends the public and the private aspects of identity. Kitzmann (forthcoming) has shown that 24-hour **Webcams** focused on the everyday activities of an individual are part of this spectrum of the presentation of a public persona, where a desire to reach beyond and replicate media forms is part of the reason for the productions. Narcissism on the Web thus implies a kind of media voyeurism for completion. It demands an audience; however the Web does not privilege the simple audience in its celebration of the user. To produce an audience-effect, the personal Web site must reveal more and must transgress the public display into the private and intimate to achieve its sought-after audience. The Web more generally fits into a longer trajectory borne out of consumer culture where identities are in wider flux and are materialized through consumption choices. The user quality of the Web, where the individual personalizes its content in a variety of ways is an example of the apparent individualization of identity formation in contemporary culture.

Gender

Gender continues to be at the centre of identity construction. On the Web this remains a crucial marker of user difference if sometimes difficult to determine definitively on many sites. Because of the male-dominated history of computer-mediated communication, one might expect that the Web maintains the same gender bias. Early adoption of the Internet upheld this conception of Web identity; however, more recently and specifically in countries with high Internet usage the bias of use has virtually disappeared or even perhaps is slightly weighted to female users. What may be more interesting than the statistical divide is to think how gender has been implicated in the study of consumer culture and other media forms. Studies of consumer culture by Huyssens (1986) and Nava (1989) among others have pointed to consumer culture being linked to the feminization of the public sphere. Other studies (Shattuc 1997; Modleski 1982) identify particular genres such as soap operas and talk shows as demonstrative of feminized narratives in their non-linearity and multiple-story lines. From these perspectives, how should we interpret the Web? Does the ease of access and use that the Web expresses exemplify the feminization of the former masculine domain of computer mediated communication? Or does the emphasis on production challenge these now arcane binaries of production/consumption = male/female that have dominated the interpretation of media and is leading to a quite different 'transgendered' public sphere? There is growing literature that deals specifically with gender and computer mediated technology that work through some of these transformations of use that the Web has fostered and transformations that may define new differentiations in use along gender lines (see in particular: Green and Adam 1998, 2001; Green 1996; Youngs 2001; Graham 1999). The Web once again challenges us to think through these classical boundaries concerning the meaning of gendering contemporary culture in new ways.

Collective identities/collective networks

As some of the research has demonstrated, the Web is an elaborate hub for the formation of new collective identities. New political movements such as the antiglobalization movement have used the Internet and the Web to build a loosely configured and connected transnational organization that attempts to rival the transnational corporations and their supportive nation-states. On a more everyday level, the Web is populated by interest groups on every conceivable topic. It allows for these networks to flourish and develop into associations. In some instances, the Web produces another kind of collective – the audience – but as we shall see in Chapters 8 and 9, the traditional industries cannot assume that the same rules govern this kind of collective as those that have been formed by previous generations of television and radio. The Web produces a continuum of engagement from collective organization to audience. The user in his/her cultural reproduction of his/her Web space navigates between these collective identity poles.

Chapter 5

THE LOOK OF THE WEB

THIS CHAPTER TRIES to piece together the meanings generated by the design of the **World Wide Web**. In other words, we are deciphering and analysing the look of the Web. The Web's appearance has changed over time; but it has followed certain patterns that make at least some things generalizable. The techniques for analysing this structuring of content could be derived from past techniques of quantitative analysis of media forms; but this chapter will focus more on qualitative approaches to the study of content and design. The analysis works through the antecedents that have informed the look and architecture of the Web by recalling what graphic structures were developed for personal computers as well as what graphic structures were drawn from other screen industries (particularly television). Connected to this analysis is understanding **hypertext** both as a technology of connection and as a transformative aesthetic form of expression. From that historical contextualization of the Web's appearance, the chapter then moves towards a **semiotic** analysis of the Web, first through defining the generic patterning of Web content and then by a more focused reading of the Yahoo! Web site. Ultimately the chapter is a study of the new Web aesthetic, through identifying what it relies on from past media forms such as magazines and television and then how it is constructed to be clearly distinctive from any of its precursors. The new Web aesthetic emerges from these mediating layers where past media forms are embedded into its present. Web aesthetics is like an onion and composed of various past media layers that often confuse and complicate a Web aesthetic.

To begin this study, it is important to isolate on some of the features of the Web that have become so standardized we no longer think of them as new or different. Any Web page is composed of layers of scripts and commands that produce the graphic interface that we associate with the

Internet, but where does this graphic construction actually emerge? In our intense focus on the present, there is wide-scale amnesia about how this look of the Web developed. To break down that structure, we are going to look at some of those origins and map their place into the contemporary Internet. Once we have charted these origins, we can begin to dissect the construction of Web sites in order to determine how their meaning is defined by their architectural look and their relationship to these origins.

THE MOUSE AESTHETIC: APPLES, APPLETS, ICONS AND WINDOWS

In the mythology of the emergence of personal computers, there has developed a narrative that rivals the biblical tale of David and Goliath. On one side, there was the monolithic IBM, the largest corporation in the world, who had little interest in the development of individualized computers (or so the story goes). On the other side was the company that was not part of the manufacture of large super computers that IBM had developed, but was specifically a company that developed the individualized computer – Apple Computers. Although there were a host of other manufacturers including Altair, Commodore, and TRS-80 (Tandy), that were producing personal computers by 1977 when this divide developed, it was the Apple Corporation that provided some of the key developments that made the computer **user**-friendly and for over a decade incompatible with other operating systems. Apple Computers developed by 1984 what was called the **graphic user interface (GUI)** for its new computer called the Macintosh (Stranahan 1999). This interface made the recently developed mouse an integral element in how to use the computer. To make the mouse usable, its click was on **icons** rather than the user typing a series of commands. From this basis, operating a computer became an interlinked system of commands from images. The actual graphic look of the Mac was a series of lists with **applet**s that could be opened into their full screen version. This relationship of icons to larger applications is essentially the architecture of the Web and even the **menus** of the individual Web page. Its ease of use that we have referred to in other chapters led to the establishment of the Microsoft Windows system for IBM-compatible computers by the end of the 1980s and early 1990s. Application software, from spreadsheets to wordprocessing, from graphic programs to computer games, was modelled on this graphic interface between commands and their program. Over time the distinctiveness of Apple's intuitive and icon-driven screen had dissipated as other operating systems, particular Microsoft, transformed into graphically rich interlinked systems (Lessard 2002). In public access systems, the screen itself became modified to be touch sensitive and thereby emulate the mouse click for movement among menus of programs.

Further building blocks for the look of the Web were allied to the emergence of hypertextual dimensions of personal computers. Once again, Apple computers system developed something called the hypercard for its Macintosh models by 1987 which used a hypertextual language behind the icons presented on screen. The hypercard was not synonymous with hypertext as it is used on the Web. As a system, it provided greater graphic capability, faster movement between software and a more malleable interface for moving around the materials on the computer (Sanford 1996–2002). So, it should be understood that the emergence of the **hypertext markup language**, known generally as **HTML**, as we understand it now was heavily built on the layering of coding that was occurring in the development of personal computers.

To further map the integration of hypertext into its fundamental association with the Web, there are two histories that need to be outlined. First, the aesthetic development of hypertext that was not initially dependent on the Internet but connected to it originally in a form of science fiction imaginary. And second the development of the graphic display of the Internet via **browsers** that resembled the enhanced graphic quality of the home computer 'desktop'.

THE HYPERTEXT IMAGINARY

The conceptualization of a system of automatically interconnected texts is typically attributed to Vannevar Bush's 1945 *Atlantic Monthly* article on the memex system. Bush imagined a machine that on the basis of a particular command in an existing file could search and retrieve another file of **information**. In his conceptualization, there was still a relation to the actual physical file folder achieved; nonetheless, his writing has been identified accurately as the conceptual precursor to the linked nature of the Web.

By 1965, the term hypertext was coined by Nelson to describe this interrelationship between texts and files. Nelson explained hypertext in this way in 1974:

> Ordinary writing is sequential for two reasons. First, it grew out of speech and speech-making, which have to be sequential; and second, because books are not convenient to read except in a sequence. But the *structures of ideas* are not sequential. They tie together every which-way. And when we write, we are always trying to tie things together in non-sequential ways (see nearby). The *footnote* is a break from sequence; but it cannot readily be extended (though some, like Will Cuppy, have toyed with the technique) . . .
>
> (Nelson 1987: 29)

We can understand hypertext as a term that describes the extension of an existing text into other areas and other domains. Thus embedded in one text are a number of other related texts. On a very basic level, this hypertextual imaginary has to be linked to the ancient and scholarly use of footnotes that provides the way to find the connection from one text to another in traditional citations of academic and theological manuscripts. Hypertext also implies a superior form of text perhaps in the speed with which it makes this link or the automatized connection from one text to another. And finally on a theoretical level, it is an automatic acknowledgement of the intertextual nature of any writing: the origins of any piece of writing call forth its predecessors in a long chain of signifying connections. Conceptually, this intertextual quality of hypertext connects it to a strain of post-structuralist thought: instead of thinking of authorial origins of texts, it is more accurate to think of the various interconnections that are embedded in a text and acknowledge that the author operates simply as a way of grouping texts.

Wedded to the emerging concept of hypertext, was playing and implementing it in writing, communication and cultural forms. By the 1980s, this form of writing was growing in practice. By the early 1990s, hypertextual examples of writing had emerged in a number of genres and forms. In children's novels, the new genre of 'choose-your-own' stories plays with alternate story paths that resemble hypertext. An emerging group of writers including Michael Joyce (1987) began developing the hypertextual novel and experimented with how readers would engage with multiple platforms and different pathways and 'sites' to gain their mastery of the non-linear narrative. Strategy computer games such as Myst which was first released in 1993 by ID offered multi-levelled and structured paths to work out the story and satisfy the goals of the game. Particular parts of the screen became links to new passages and directions. Platform games produced for Nintendo such as Donkey Kong or Super Mario similarly had particular hotspots or hypertext links or applets that moved the player to the next level.

Some writers have thought of hypertext and **hypermedia** in clearly utopian terms that have dovetailed with the general euphoric relationship to the Internet and the World Wide Web as a liberating technology. Landow (1992) was one of the first to theorize about hypertext and revel in its non-linearity. Controversially invoking the philosopher Gilles Deleuze's and Felix Guattari's (1987: 6–7) conception of the 'rhizome', Landow described the movement in hypertext as non-hierarchical and ultimately liberating from the constraints of linearity. Although Deleuze's and Guattari's conception of the rhizome was much more aligned to a critical reading of contemporary capitalism, Landow appropriated the idea of the rhizome to underline a non-authoritarian structure in both reading and writing in hypertext and the idea was further expanded by Moulthrop (Moulthrop 1994). In nature, the rhizome is a form of propagation of a plant along runners and pathways that run along the surface of the ground. The organization of the rhizome is that there is no centre discernible in its structure: a network emerges of merely interconnected parts/plants. This metaphor of both connection and engagement becomes the way that hypertext can be understood to transform the aesthetics of reading or writing a text. Landow's early writing predated the proliferation of the World Wide Web and it is important to see the various extrapolations of the idea of hypertext have been taken in that context.

THE WORLD WIDE WEB AND HYPERTEXT

The integration of hypertext into the World Wide Web emerged from Tim Berners-Lee and the Swiss-based **CERN**. HTML as a mark-up language that encoded links between networked computers was put into operation in 1990 as the system of **http** and **universal resource locators** or **URLs** were put in place. At that time, the look of this interlinked network bore little resemblance to the graphically enhanced browsers that we are now used to. Hypertext onscreen was often a simple series of lists. Systems such as **gopher** that supported this hypertext Internet presented the links as a series of underlined units of text – the underlining and perhaps an asterisk border were the only graphic embellishments (Zakon 2002; Internet Society 2002).

Hand-in-hand with the development of hypertext and its coding of linkages was the advancement of a graphic user interface that would make the **navigation** of **cyberspace** simpler and intuitively obvious. Synergistically aligned with the graphic development around hypertext and hyperlinkages was the expansion of the use of the Web beyond a relatively small research culture and early **modem** adopters and users. From 1990 onwards, there was a rapid **convergence** of the aesthetics of desktop graphic user interfaces and the Internet. The key development of this convergence was the establishment of browsers that organized the production of links into a recognizable look. Before its commercial reincarnation, the first successful browser overlay for the World Wide Web was released in 1993 under the name MOSAIC and came from NCSA at the University of Illinois Urbana-Champagne. When it was redeveloped into a commercial entity with the financial backing of Sun Microsystems in December 1994, MOSAIC became the industry standard under the name Netscape (Zakon 2002). For the next two years, Netscape had a **virtual** monopoly of the graphically enhanced browser with its easy-to-use applets to link to other resources. That structure of the Web page browser became the template from which all Web pages are framed. By 1996, Netscape's preeminence was challenged in two directions. AOL, the largest Internet provider also bundled a browser in their software. More significantly, Microsoft developed Internet Explorer as its Web browser which was included in the software when computers were purchased. Internet Explorer now dominates the browser world and Netscape has been relegated to less than 10 per cent of users (Upsdell 2002).

In terms of the development of Web pages by individual users, browsers by the late 1990s provided software for aiding in the quick production of Web sites. The coding was once again hidden by a further graphic layer so that users would have what is often called **wysiwyg** – what you see is what you get – when they developed their pages. Similar programs were offered by services that provided free **e-mail** such as Geocities, Yahoo! or Hotmail. Commercialized wysiwyg software programs such as Dreamweaver provided a more sophisticated Web production software that also graphically overlaid the markup language through its applets.

THE DEVELOPMENT OF THE WEB IMAGE

The Web's graphic capability has permitted the interlacing of text and image on Web pages and it is important to realize that the ease with which photographs and other images can be put into a Web site has led to this general hybrid look of the Web that we can liken to magazines. Placing images into Web sites depended on the development of standard **digital** coding for these files. Two standards developed for images: j-peg or gif files. Software on personal computers allows for the ready importing of these images. The massive image bank on the Web now has become the raw material for personal Web sites.

This integration of the still image describes only the most basic Web site. Part of the drive to more sophisticated Web sites was to differentiate commercial Web sites or at least the commercial banners from the homegrown variety. New coding was developed that allowed for images to move – in effect to be animated – and these became another standard Web practice for Web designers. Javascript was the coding language to produce this moving image that we often see in **banner advertisements**. They shimmer or produce repetitive looped movements which are designed to draw the eye of the user and ultimately the mouseclick on the banner where an embedded hyperlink is located. The software Macromedia Flash provides the user with the tools to animate complete pages and allow images to transform and appear when the mouse is dragged over them. Along with Javascript, software such as Flash has shifted the Web out of its graphic antecedent of the magazine into something quite unique. Although these techniques of animating pages are gaudily flashy, they do identify that key function that envelopes the look of the Web and that is distraction. As much as hyperlinks, hypertexts excite the layout of the page being viewed, they also are constructed to offer a way out to the next site and onward to what is potentially more interesting. The Web continues to relate to one of its roots – of being a showcase for what it can do and not necessarily what it does. This potential of the Web is certainly part of a maturing media form, but it also is part of the relationship among Web sites and their interlinkages.

Beyond the Flash and Javascript forms of animating pages, there is also the integration of moving image and sound. **MPEG** files were the standard digital vehicle for the placement of moving images online. Any moving image also relies on the existence of the software. In the dual tradition of the Web, these software decoders were available in free versions and more complete paid versions. Nonetheless, Quicktime, Real Media, and Media-player have emerged as the most common platforms for the display of moving images. What is interesting about moving images online is their widely diverging quality. When video images are **streamed** they are often compressed in order that they can be displayed in real time. The **compression** of the image means it is presented with fewer **bits** of information, so that if you made a video and audio-streamed news report into a full screen it is almost unrecognizable what the image actually represents. Downloaded files however are not compressed and can produce DVD quality on the computer screen. The **downloading** of the image however pulls the user away from the Web experience in a way that the streamed audio or video maintains the user onsite.

TELEVISION AND GRAPHICS

Although the development of the computer graphic interface was foundational in leading to the interlinked structure of the Web, it is important to identify some other sources in the Web's emergence as a particular aesthetic construction and presentation of information. An often overlooked site and precursor is how television has transformed as a disseminator of information over the last fifty years. From its emergence purely as a live broadcast entity and to its disseminator of both current and recorded events and programmes, television as an industry has worked towards an equally particular architecture for the dissemination of information. Building from radio, television has developed a pattern of presentation of flow – that is, programmes follow on from another in succession and the networks and channels generally try to link viewing across often diverse content over time (Williams 1974). American network television, for instance, through their news programming at the beginning of prime time attempted to maintain viewers for the entire evening. The rest of the evening's programmes would be heavily advertised to ensure that there was a flow-on of viewers. This idea of flow can also explain how television moved from its programme content to commercials. Programmes were designed to encourage viewers to continue watching the programme by promising something even more interesting to follow a commercial break. The presentation of an entire newscast would be predicated on holding one of the most interesting reports for the end of the programme. We could label this style of programming flow to maintain

viewers as part of a general **promotional aesthetic** that enveloped television. The promotional aesthetic is one of perpetual anticipation, and this
structure of anticipation is part of the way that the Web presents its own
forms of information in hierarchies and further mouse clicks.

Structured into this television/promotional aesthetic flow were the promotional 'trailers', and the network and station identity 'stings'. Along with
the commercials, these bits of interstitial programming were heavily reliant
on graphics and animation. Images of the logos of national networks were
regularly inserted into the broadcast day to 'brand' the channel. The branding of television networks is part of the emerging aesthetic of television that
allowed more than one form of information to be presented simultaneously.
By the 1990s it was standard television practice to have the network brand
superimposed on the television screen no matter what programme was
being shown. The graphic overlay of content is one example of the way that
television's style of presentation became something of a model for the
Internet. Although the computer and television screen are far from identical, they are similar technologies of exhibition in terms of screens and
images. Television has developed patterns of placing information that were
eventually incorporated into the way Web pages organized their information. The crossover point in terms of screen use can be seen in the historical
development of television graphics.

In early television, graphics were physically placed in front of the image,
usually at the bottom of the screen. This style of graphic presentation grew
from the use of intertitles from the silent film era. Other use of graphics
resembled therefore the title sequences of films. On television a programme
would be introduced with the same graphic development that superimposed
the animated text over a stationary or moving film image – they would be
'cutout' of the background image. Because television is an electronic
medium, graphics were eventually generated as electronic inserts using blue
screen or chromakey techniques to generate more than one image in the
television display and put together through a switcher. In television news,
the blue screen was used to superimpose a related graphic or photograph to
accompany a new story. It was often located to the left of the newsreader's
head and compiled in the control room. This play with graphic overlays was
experimented with greatly in weather forecasts, where the weather presenter
was placed in front of a weather map that was not there and had to point to
weather systems through looking at a monitor of the weather system image
that was off-camera.

Graphics were particularly integrated into live sporting broadcasts from
the 1960s. Statistics on players would be presented as an overlay along with
running tallies of scores and results. The screen during sporting broadcasts
thus resembled the more diverse image of a computer screen. Information
during these telecasts was multilayered. Indeed, in many commercial broadcasts, even short advertisements were graphically overlaid on sports such as

ice hockey and soccer when the 'action' could not be interrupted long enough to insert a commercial. Gradually, through the 1980s, the development of television graphics was generated by computers through the technology of computer-generated imaging (CGI). Whether one looks at the development of promotional identities of stations or the graphics during sports and news broadcasts, television graphics have become versatile and more pervasive in the flow of television because of the relative ease in their generation through computer software.

Developing simultaneously with the emergence of greater amounts of television graphics was the technology of reception. For instance, the remote control device (which first emerged in 1955 but was generally in use by the 1970s and integrated low-level infrared emitted beams to communicate with the television by the 1980s) transformed television by easing the movement between programmes on different channels (Bellis 2002). One can liken channel surfing to Web surfing. Likewise, VCRs led users towards timeshifting their viewing of programmes or creating commercial-free collection copies of their favourite programmes and films. And with these two technologies emerged a graphic transformation of the screen. Graphics were superimposed on to the screen to indicate to the viewer the new range of controls that s/he possessed through the remote control. Volume, colour levels, language, channel number, and recording information were some of the basic commands that were displayed on the screen. In addition, the television receiver had expanded electronic capabilities including the development of having more than one channel on the screen at any one time. The development of teletext was also part of the division of the screen into different parts or areas.

What is evident in current television is that the screen is no longer a 'sacred' space dedicated to a single image. Television has diverged from film in this way – its screen is divided in its presentation of information. Some channels have gone further in the divided screen. For instance, all news channels such as CNN provide a continuous news message board with breaking stories, no matter what the presenters onscreen are talking about. Bloomberg television has taken this division of the television screen into Web hybrid territory. Stock quotes sidle up beside another frame of world weather information. The Bloomberg logo operates as a large branding masthead. A minor percentage of the screen is devoted to the newscast image that is entirely framed by these other panels of information.

Although rarely referenced the emerging display of the television screen has been instrumental in the development of the Web, particularly as the Web has moved to the integration of moving images into its content. With the late 1990s' efforts to establish **WebTV,** where the television became the location for surfing both the Web and television channels, one can see a further expansion of the aesthetic convergence of the two media. Along with the computer's graphic user interface development, the Web is a hybrid of 'screen appearances' that draws from and was inspired by televisual, magazine/prints graphics and on occasion, film. All of these screen looks have built on longer histories of art that rely on traditional aesthetics where classical notions of balance and composition are significant. The Web is a complex sign system that requires this kind of intricate background knowledge to interpret its animated screen.

ANALYSING THE LOOK OF THE WEB: SOME SCREEN EXAMPLES

To complete our analysis of the look of the Web, it is worthwhile studying the design of specific Web sites in order to establish some patterns. Our form of analysis will be built from a semiotic approach to the study of signs and these readings of Web sites will assume a familiarity with the basic terminology employed in semiotics and **semiology**. One caveat should be underlined as we delve into Web sites: Web pages and Web sites change regularly and so the analysis presented here is not so much designed to be the definitive reading but indexical for your own analysis of any number of Web sites. What is most significant in this analysis are the new categories of analysis of how content is grouped and ordered on Web sites. Some of this analysis will intersect with and reinforce particular themes presented in other chapters. To begin that investigation, we will make some larger textual divisions of the Web; in other words, we will identify some genres of Web sites.

WEB SITE GENRES

To make the claim that there are specific genres on the Web is to link our analysis to how television, music or film is divided up into certain expectations. Television is composed of situation comedies, dramas, telemovies, news, sports, and reality television programmes to name the most prominent genres. Similarly music can be divided into pop, rock, hip hop, techno, folk, soul, dance and so on. Film also has its categories that we can see in evidence when we peruse a video shop: action, comedy, thriller, arthouse and Western are some of the most prominently displayed and advertised. How these genres develop in other media is a complex interplay between production and consumption: the audience develops certain expectations for pleasure and entertainment value and the genre emerges from an industry that for its own profitability tries to read these patterns of expectations and produce accordingly. So genre is neither completely an audience conceptualization nor an industry conceptualization but a constantly developing though relatively stable constellation or pattern that links the audience to the industry. It hybridizes and develops into subgenres. It is constantly reinforced through advertising, and it demands referencing to precursors to emphasize that the current version is part of the same genre. Genres are a comfort zone of a patterned sign system that both an audience and an industry can read with relative ease.

Web sites can now be grouped under similar patterns. Because the Web is generally more production-oriented, how genres have developed and how they continue to develop have some distinctions from other media forms. The key distinction is that the Web is much more continuous than discontinuous from different domains of activity. Thus one moves relatively seamlessly from commercial to non-commercial sites; likewise information and entertainment are also connected and not made discontinuous. Nonetheless, the Web has produced some of these comfort zones where expectations of how they work are known by users and met by those making the sites. Here are some examples of Web genres that have emerged to have some constancy:

WEBPORTALS: FROM SEARCH ENGINES TO PORTALS

Because of the Web's abundance of information, one of the key genres to develop is either organizing its content for retrieval or providing a channel through which searches can be done. Partially emerging from **search engines** and their amorphousness has been the **Webportal** that organizes information for the user. The commercial Webportals such as Yahoo! work to customize the user's relationship to information with an organized homepage structure. In addition to categorizing searching, they have worked to organize new and entertainment content for their users. As a commercial entity, Yahoo! has been successful at providing an easily usable site that can be personalized. Because its goal is to ensure that it has subscribers it has also linked its service to providing e-mail and Web site space.

Other portals work to provide background and advice for further searching in a particular area. Sites that deal with education, health and film are often portals to other sites with lists of links. Axel Bruns (2002) in his study talks about the emergence of resource centre sites that serve as portals but also try to establish an allegiance to users who can contribute their own content to these sites. Bruns indicates that resource centre sites vary in their involvement of their users; but as a subgenre of portals they are an expanding and stabilizing feature of the Web and successful resource centre sites can have hundreds of thousands of **hits** per month. Portals attract interested Web surfers, not only drawn there by searches, but also drawn by the way portals concentrate interests. Portals then are organized access points that allow the user to move outward via **WebRings** of linkages on particular areas of interest. One can find portals that link the user to **Webcam** sites, travel information, guides to Web pornography, or the range of media sources on the Web to highlight a few of the hundreds of portals on a wide variety of topics. As diverse as their content may be, portals pattern the Web and are clearly a genre.

THE MEDIA SITE

Some of the most powerful Web sites are those connected to some other media form. Thus a local radio station will have developed a Web site that handles its promotions and provides background materials on its talent and shows. Television networks provide similar passages through their programmes. Greater details about stars, possible online chatrooms about particular issues or personalities are set up. Indeed, reality television programmes can be expanded through their Web site. For instance, *Big Brother* in its many international incarnations, had Webcam coverage of the house activities twenty-four hours a day – well beyond the weekly or biweekly programmes. Newspapers generally have online versions as do many magazines. Because media sites enter the Web world with high recognition and cross-promotional possibilities, they often become locations where many millions of users pass. As a group, they are about expanding the presence of the media company to ensure its centrality with its target audience. It is rare that Web sites will become financially more lucrative for a media company than its original media outlet. Media Web sites thus must be seen as primarily promotional and techniques to extend the brandname of the media company.

TELEVISION AND THE WEB: *24* AND *DAWSON'S CREEK* AND IMMERSIVE MEDIA

Web sites for television programmes operate within apparently limited parameters. The programme on television is the principal commodity and the Web site is therefore a support structure. In the tradition of music videos, the television programme Web site inhabits a promotional aesthetic; yet even within this straitjacket innovations occur and new potentials for aesthetic and cultural exploration develop. The Web sites for WB's *Dawson's Creek* and Fox's *24* express an emerging hybridity between television and the Web. Christopher Pike of Sony Pictures Digital developed something called 'Dawson's Desktop' to support the *Dawson's Creek* programme. While he acknowledged that the 'whole existence' for the Web site was for 'marketing the show', he saw his objective as keeping fans through the seven-day gap between instalments of the serial – in other words, making the Web site 'seem alive'. *Dawson's Desktop* is thus a simulated computer desktop of the lead character and in that space there are chatrooms that connect the characters, picture galleries, e-mail correspondences and a digitalized version of a handwritten diary. Moreover, there are spaces for the audience to engage in debate through their own bulletin board. The key innovation was that the desktop integrated into the programme by providing background information about the characters. Motivations and feelings were accentuated; relations were identified. As the week moved closer to the next episode, the content foreshadowed without revealing the direction of the next show. The programme has had a devoted teenage following and the Web site allowed for the exploration of issues and concerns that were spawned by the characters and the programme. The producers expanded its desktop idea to bridge the lack of new content over the summer between seasons by rotating the desktop amongst the lead characters. The Web site served to connect to fans and allowed for a channel of feedback: with over 200 fansites devoted to some aspect of the series, Sony Digital connected to the top twenty-five and established an Advisory Board that connected the fans to the programme. The Web is leading to a shifted development in the cultural economy, where the audience is integrated in new interactive ways into the flow of television and its construction of meaning.

Fox's series *24* used its Web site to provide further background to the programme as it hoped to immerse its audience in the various possible directions of the action/suspense series that each week presented sequentially an hour of a day that involves counter-terrorism, kidnapping, conspiracies, attempted political assassinations and misinformation. The Web site opens with a game to test the fan's knowledge of the minutae of each hour. Emulating *Dawson's Desktop*, it has a site that replicates one of the younger character's computer desktop, complete with e-mail and arrested chat. It provides extra detail about the characters to the point of creating an entire press kit for the presidential candidate Senator David Palmer through a series of Web news reports. Images from each hour of the programme are **hotlinks** to further information about the show's content. With a programme genre built on gradual acquisition of audience information to achieve a mastery of the text, the Web site embellishes the narrative game.

Sources: Christopher Pike, Sony Pictures Digital (2002); http://www.dawsonsdesktop.com/dawson/; www.fox.com/24/

There are also entirely Web-based media companies such as a **Web radio** station or a site devoted to downloading popular music. The greatest success in translating a media form to the Web has been through popular music and the proliferation of genre-specific music sites that operate without commercials has become a popular way to listen to 'radio' via one's personal computer.

THE COMMERCIAL SITE

As Chapter 6 will discuss the Web has moved towards a much greater commercial presence. The Web's power is connected to its ability to become a major location for trade and commercial transactions. As a result, one of the major genres of the Web is the commercial site. Because of its sheer size, the genre is best understood in terms of subgenres that we can list below.

The company/corporate Web site

With the Internet boom of the late 1990s, most companies felt enormous pressure, partially economic but primarily cultural, that a Web site was now a necessary part of doing business. Thus, there are millions of sites that are heralding a company's presence in much the same way that the Yellow Pages have worked. Many of these businesses have no means of selling anything online, but they continue to maintain Web sites as a way to ensure their presence in searches for their particular service or commodity. These Web sites can be elaborate if the corporation is large; more often these are Web sites that are somewhat dated and static in terms of new content.

The commercial trading site

Many companies actually trade and take orders via the Internet. Some of these sites have no real entity outside of the Web. Most have a bricks and mortar outlet that is supplemented by online commercial transactions. The embodiment of the stand-alone Web site is Amazon.com. Travel agencies such as Travelocity or Orbitz also work entirely online.

Institutional site

Although not perfectly commercial in function, institutional sites resemble other commercial sites through their various services and functions. Information provision becomes the core feature of institutional sites. Government departments and services are the best examples of institutional sites: reports, press releases and forms populate institutional sites' page architecture. Libraries, universities, schools, charities and non-profit organizations have similar institutional sites and thus belong to the same subgenre.

THE PERSONAL WEB SITE

The range of Web sites that represent the individual which can be called the genre of personal Web site is quite vast. Subgenres include fansites, Webcam sites, diary sites, **Weblogs** (as discussed in Chapter 4) and family album sites.

Some personal Web sites have objectives beyond heralding one's presence and attempt to operate as portals concerned with particular interests. The commercial drive sometimes envelopes personal Web sites: making a site a popular destination can ensure commercial sponsorship possibilities through display advertising. In general, however, personal Web sites are expositions and exhibitions of the self by presenting the public display of the domestic world. Their ubiquitousness is partially driven by both the ease with which a site can be developed and that most service providers facilitate their development through space provision on their **server** and tools for their construction.

BREAKING DOWN THE MEANING SYSTEMS OF WEB SITES

The generic differences in Web sites shape much of the look of the Web. As users of the Web, these genres help us decode how a Web site functions and what kinds of expectations around information and entertainment are privileged and therefore foregrounded. Nonetheless, Web sites share features across genres and in order to work out the meaning system that produces the look of the Web, we need to break down Web sites into smaller units of analysis. As we have already discussed, the Web has been built as a meaning system from its antecedents. The key antecedents that we have identified are the generations of computer graphics, television graphics and the organization of the screen in all its manifestations. Embedded in this development as we have underlined is the Web's incredible connection to the graphics of text, print and image. We have underlined the hypertextual dimension of the look of the Web; but we now need to consider further how these various screen dimensions of the Web are reconstructed into 'pages' of presentation. To undertake this analysis, we are going to look more closely at an individual Web site to develop the chains of signification that the Web has developed.

CASE STUDY: YAHOO.COM

Any Web site could serve as a starting point for our analysis; but it is useful to work through a textually rich site so that we can identify some of the key forms of signification that occur through presentation. Yahoo.com is a site that serves as a sophisticated commercial portal to the Internet and is integrated closely with search engines. What Yahoo! has accomplished is something that in its own structure embodies the **loose Web**.

To get to the production of meaning on the Web let us break down its sign system. In breaking it down, we have to be aware of the different ways of signifying that part of the Web. To accomplish this we need to generate a few extra forms of signification that can be conducted on any Web site. These new categories are:

Personalization

How does the site allow for its own reconstruction into something that is driven by the user to recreate?

Interactivity

How does the site engage the user with responses and transformations? Connected to this notion of **interactivity** is the basic integration/application of hypertext.

The interplay of media forms

The Web has the capacity to emulate other media forms and each Web site provides a particular ratio of media forms presented, organized and sometime hierarchically connected through hyperlinks. We can divide these media forms into magazine, video/TV, radio/audio and newspaper. This interplay of media forms is another way of understanding and interpreting the phenomenon of media convergence. Although differentiations between media are becoming less distinctive via the Web, in order to analyse Web sites it is useful to instantiate in archetypal form the essential features of each medium and how these are now interconnected and interspersed on Web pages.

STAGE ONE: THE BASIC SIGNS

Figure 5.1 on page 98 is a facsimile of the Yahoo! opening Web page. It is static as opposed to dynamic but it gives a rendition of how different signs are constructed by Yahoo!

Colour and textual dimensions

Although each computer can vary the colour of the default settings produced for any page, it is clear that Yahoo! contrasts its own logo from the rest of the text. While the rest of the text is dominated by hypertext, the Yahoo! logo is red. Moreover, while the rest of the text is displayed in a conservative Times New Roman font, Yahoo! is given personality through its irregularity. Even the choice of term Yahoo! which connotes an affective emotional outburst is in deep contrast with the plethora of categories that are listed below it. The brand Yahoo!'s signifying chain is layered in its appellation of irreverence and its emergence as an entity is connected to the sensation of freedom and independence of the Internet and the Web. It is connected to the *Wired* generation of the Internet where there is active blending of play and work in the emergence of the information economy.

As is commonly known, Yahoo! is usually connected to the acronym *yet another hierarchical officious oracle* and with its origins connected to two doctoral engineering students putting together categories of their favourite sites in 1994, the name acknowledges and celebrates the past and somewhat hides the corporate quality of its current form (Yahoo 2001).

From a larger perspective, the Yahoo!'s page is completely dominated by text; but it is a peculiar text that diverges from conceptualizing the content like a magazine. The text is a series of categories that reveal very little. The use of sentences is rare as these categories predominate its structure. Yahoo! is a Web site that is organized then by its categorization and as their name suggests, they have provided a hierarchical architecture for this categorization. The signs of the Yahoo! homepage then are connotatively invitations to explorations. The categories themselves are stabilized around genres of information and entertainment. The choices of news headlines is driven by a **cybernetic** sense of a national audience's desires that is designed to transform with each national and language version of Yahoo! graphically and hypertextually presented at the very base of the homepage. The text then is completely dominated by hypertext with the logo 'Yahoo!' being one of the few locations on the site that cannot be clicked upon to transform the content. As Yahoo! has commercialized, the categories have moved towards consumer cultural pursuits. Shopping is highly prominent and categories that are more serious appear further down the homepage. The connotation of Yahoo! is that it is driven by the characterization of the Web as a form of media entertainment while making appropriate genuflections to the Web's role as information source. The frame structure of the homepage works to rank these interests. The prominence of games, the position of the banner advertisement, the invocation of chat, interpersonal correspondence and e-mail, shopping and entertainment issues indexically point to Yahoo's open call to a middle class domestic use of the technology. Yahoo! as a Web site has moved to the epicentre of the consumer Web.

The overall colour scheme of background and text also connotes accessibility without threat of unwanted images and meanings. The grey colour background is in contradistinction to the prevalence of black and red backgrounds on pornographic sites where the photographic image is foregrounded and the illicitness is accentuated. The Yahoo! colour scheme also points to personal transformation that we will analyse below.

Icons: interestingly, Yahoo! does not produce a great number of images on its homepage. Its hierarchical structure of providing links has mandated the lack of particularity that a photograph connotes for the user. Moreover, photographs slow down the loading of the page and by their elimination, Yahoo!'s industrial strategy of quickly capturing its user base on its first page is achieved. Thus, we are left with the prominence of the banner ad and the relative banality of the icons arrayed at the top of the page. The icons at the top convey an interesting signifying structure: they resemble the

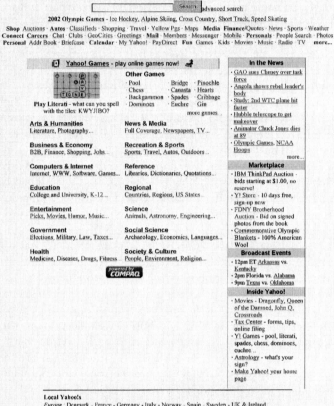

Figure 5.1 Yahoo! Web page

Source: Reproduced with permission of Yahoo! Inc © 2000 by Yahoo! Inc. YAHOO! and the YAHOO! logo are trademarks of Yahoo! Inc.

avatars and handles that populate the Internet. In their nostalgic style, they resemble the graphics of 1980s desktop newsletter publishing. Why would a sophisticated Web/media company allow itself to convey such an unsophisticated image? The answer lies in unpacking the signifying chains of these images: they evoke earlier generations of the Internet and their lack of sophistication again allows Yahoo! to maintain its cultural politics of openness that defined its rather simple origins. In a sense, Yahoo! is domesticating the Web and making it familial for easier use. The objective of Yahoo! is to produce a comfortable navigating environment that prompts returns after searches. To produce that effect, the homepage must provide signs of 'home' and reassuring icons of the personal desktop.

STAGE TWO: THE WEB SIGNS – ANALYSING SOME OF THE LINKS OF YAHOO!

Web homepages are the starting points of explorations. In commercial sites such as Yahoo! the architecture and design of the site is to work towards creative containment. We can understand what we mean by creative containment through analysing some of the links provided by Yahoo! as interlinked sign systems and as attempts to provide signifying chains: even though the connection between one page and another is weak and loose, it is the objective of Yahoo! to provide the central page where one returns after a Web exploration. This sophisticated structure of signifying chains is complicated by the reliance on content from other companies. Nonetheless, the interconnection – the six degrees of separation if you will – means that Yahoo!'s essential business is maintaining elaborated WebRings that provide a slightly organized parameter to your Web experience. They embody the idea of the super homepage with all the domestic and familial connotations that can be associated with such a site. We shall analyse these links through our new categories that are Web specific.

PERSONALIZATION

Web sites are often structured towards some possibility of personalizing content. Thus commercial portal sites such as Yahoo! offer ways to transform what appears to be generic into individual patterns. Not only do they provide potential chat sites and the means to meet others online, they encourage you to join and be part of Yahoo.com. Free e-mail, and personal Web sites lure the Websurfer into a more permanent relationship with Yahoo! As a subscriber who has provided personal information, one is also invited to reconstruct a homepage of news, information and content that is driven by individual interests. One can choose which sports teams to be updated, what weather reports from which cities need to be present and what corporate stocks and currency exchanges to display. Different categories of news can further customize the Web page generated by Yahoo! Thus local news and technological news along with entertainment sites can be organized and ranked by the user. The user of Yahoo! has the sensation of control that we have identified in Chapter 4. Although constrained by what Yahoo! categorizes, the surplus of categories available means that there is always the sensation of personalizing one's information sources. The connotations of possibility and freedom and mobility are maintained as Yahoo! connects to the spirit of the Web. Moreover, the page that is called 'my Yahoo!' can be transformed in terms of colour, sizing, and frames. Again this underlines the sensation of cultural production and self-actualization that the Web has historically offered its users.

INTERACTIVITY

Yahoo!'s homepage, as we have described, is simply a series of links to other locations. On that basis alone, the page is driven by a form of hypertextual interactivity. In the language of the Web, the user is 'pulled' to the next site and location and, unlike television, is not pushed with the content. Much like most Web sites there is the active click which defines how the user moves and transforms the content. The sense of interactivity is reinforced through the personalized homepage that we have described above. Interactivity is indexical of an investment and we see this most strongly in the Yahoo! site and more generally across the Web through the online game sites. On some of its commercialized versions, Yahoo! presents the opportunity to engage in a variety of games that connect one user to many users. What they offer is partners to play chess, pool, literati and a host of other card and parlour games. On sidebars, there are further opportunities to move into buying current versions of top computer games and downloading the trailers and software. Interactivity is best thought of in terms of a spectrum of investment that moves between the user and the site or the user and another user. The game sites provide this close connection between users because each player actively responds to the moves or play of someone else. Yahoo! creates such an environment of interaction that is a microcosm of larger online game sites. Network/online playing of games thus represents one of the most immersive forms of interactivity on the Web. In online versions of Doom or Quake, the screen is an explosion of virtual worlds that construct not only avatars or skins of other players but also the sensation of three-dimensional space. The experience is intensified precisely because of its online/Web status and that actual people are operating the other entities onscreen. This online world of gaming that is **hyperlinked** to Yahoo! deserves greater exploration as an interactive virtual world. What Yahoo! presents are the paths to this form of interactivity and engagement.

Other structures on the Yahoo! site permit the movement of content.

Clicking on a news story offers the possibility of e-mailing the story with a further click. Augmenting this form of interaction models itself after news sites such as CNN.com with a plenitude of message boards that are linked to specific news stories. Interactivity becomes an elaborate game of links and connections that move the content presented from common public spaces into interpersonal domains such as usegroups, e-mail, chatrooms and message boards. The more financially endowed the site, the more likely that these standard techniques of interaction are operating.

Augmenting these techniques of providing interconnection among users of Yahoo! are the accordion-like hyperlink extrapolations of stories from a single site. The accordion-effect is not so much driven by linearity, but a wider reach of potential interconnection. For example, an AP story entitled 'Grammy show no favorites for a Sweep' (26 February 2002, http://story.news.yahoo.com/news?tmpl=story&u=/ap/20020226/ap_e n_mu/grammy_preview_2&cid=529) sidebars the actual stories with a further eight direct links to other Grammy-related stories with a further link to all the nominations for 2002 (http://story.news.yahoo.com/ news?tmpl=story&u=/ap/20020226/ap_en_mu/grammy_preview_2&ci d=529). The accordion unfolding of any story on the Web is structured and hierarchized for the user by Yahoo! and thereby Yahoo! is providing a guide. Further supplementing the news stories and opinion pieces about the Grammy awards, Yahoo! provides a link to the official site grammy.com – this site is the eleventh link in the sidebar that accompanies the story. The list then goes on to magazine, audio and video files that take you further into the world of the Grammy awards. The actual article navigates you to a list of potential search sites of particular performers. In all, the Yahoo!-related article had thirty links that provided a WebRing around the Grammy awards that would accentuate the centrality of Yahoo! to the organization of that flow of information. Yahoo! thus is at the centre of user interactivity with its banner emblazoned across each link that the user alights.

THE INTERPLAY OF MEDIA FORMS

Web sites are **multimedia** forms and Yahoo! structures itself to produce a woven interplay. There is no doubt that the Web is still dominated by what can be called the **Graphic Internet Stage** (Marshall 1997). The Graphic Internet Stage refers to the dominance of text and/or text and photo-image in the organization of Web pages. Other media forms are available, but the Web architecture of the Yahoo! site, like many others, ensures that it is an extra click or link to get to moving images and sound. So the look of Yahoo! or the personalized categories that are linked to my Yahoo! resemble newspaper and magazine displays. Images are prominent, headlines traditionally employed, and advertisements are positioned strategically around the content much in the way that the front page of newspapers such as *USA Today* or the *Metro* structures its content mix. Connotatively, Yahoo!'s stories are 'news stories' derived from producing information in classic inverse pyramid fashion. Links are likewise hierarchized as the news genre prevails the formatting of Yahoo!'s interlinked sites. Indeed, although restructured and reformatted, the principal news agencies and presses predominate the presentation – from the *New York Times* to *Variety*, from AP to *Sports Illustrated*.

But the Web has expanded from its Graphic Internet Stage into an interesting flow of moving images and sound. Yahoo! provides these kinds of inserts into its content as the user moves to news stories and information. In a service called Yahoovision, Yahoo! divides its video clips into *Financevision* and *News*. The moving image can be played in through a number of devices and it remains a televisual style of presentation. To ensure rapid and continuous access of the moving, streamed image, the resolution is poor. Also, the image can be transformed as to its location on the screen – from a dominant position of occupying the entire screen to the more normal 1/5 screen size. What makes the image different from television is that it is surrounded by text and other still images that are in some way connected to the streamed image. It is classic intertextuality that has crossed over into the way some television stations present the news as we have discussed earlier in this chapter. On *Finance Vision*, the default screen allows one to view stock exchanges, text background on the specific story, and a host of links to related daily financial news. Sound clips can be similarly displayed; but sound can be streamed with much greater ease. Although Yahoo! is not positioned in this way, one of the most prevalent uses of Internetworked computers is as a source of Internet radio stations.

To overcome the limitations of streamed video, Yahoo! and many other sites have invested in a **hybrid media** structure which is called **slide shows**. A series of related images to a news event are sequentially linked into a 'show' that any user can click through. The richness and the array of images along with the expediency with which the user can find them makes them far more accessible and detailed than a newspaper or magazine could be. This range of images on the Web underlines the play of plenitude in its structure and its method of overwhelming more traditional media. Instead of the single chosen image about a particular major news event that is highlighted in newspaper coverage, thousands are quickly locatable. One only has to move through the archives of images of the terrorist attacks on the World Trade Center to realize the massive catalogue of images, both still and moving, that are now part of the networked Web. Each Web site like Yahoo! attempts to provide a loose containment or pathway through this plenitude and through this rationalization and organization of content hopes to encourage the floating user to return to the epicentre of the site.

WEBART – PLAYING WITH THE MEANINGS AND AESTHETICS OF THE WEB

One of the critical dimensions of the Web is that it has permitted new levels in the manipulation of images and text. From an artistic perspective, this is a new open season on fabricating artifice and practice. Like the Web itself, it is next to impossible to encompass all the artistic activities on the Web – they are too diverse. They move from the experimental to the reinstitutionalization of the art museum in a virtual space. Some work to play or subvert the Web image and hypertext; others to replicate its promotional structure or are concerned with formalistic dimensions of the technology.

The Web offered the possibility of breaking down the 'art commodity' and a movement loosely associated through the term netart attempted to undermine the institution of art and bring it back closer to the avant-garde push of linking artistic practice to everyday culture. In any case, netart presented an interesting discussion of the Web and its uses: at irrational.org one can stumble into sites that play with the surveillance possibilities of the Web and the fears around losing all your information with a networked computer. The famed *Grammatron* by Mark Amerika experimented with word, image, and flash/animated images to comment on the transformation of meaning and spirituality in the era of IT. Etoy.com is a site that replicates the many commercial sites but subverts their 'buying' premise in its own design and sloganistic message: 'etoy:twistingmarkets; capital, power, culture'. Etoy.com led to a whole struggle over the actual domain name with the commercial entity.

Even the aesthetic taste of the Web has been institutionalized – there are now the slightly irreverent but nevertheless coveted Webby Awards that celebrate the best practices in a very wide range of categories. Webart is impossible to summarize; suffice it to say that creative interventions populate the Web and push us to ponder the structures and signifying patterns of the dominant 'digital aesthetic' (Cubitt 1998).

Sources:

(http://www.irrational.org/tttp/watch/second.html) – created by Heath Bunting

http://grammatron.com/about.html – created by Mark Amerika

http://www.mowa.org/ – the Museum of Web Art

http://www.Webbyawards.com/main/ – the Webby Award homepage

Alison Hearn for her insights

CONCLUSION

To establish the aesthetics of the Web is a task that is categorically imposs-ible. The nature of the Web is that it engulfs content into its structure. Any image, any textual form, and any graffiti can be made or at least made to reappear in facsimile on the Web. This chapter has worked through the reasons why the presentation of the Web has followed certain patterns and certain alignments despite this continually expanding engulfment of pro-duced content. It has mapped out its lineage backwards to other screen sources such as television and has further underlined the relationship the Web has to the emergence of the interactive quality of the graphic user interface that developed for personal computers. The Web aesthetic has a trajectory that is evident in its variations of fashionable styles: like the per-sonal computer the screen image is designed for accessibility of use and some sort of intuitive relationship to the movement through its layers, pages and sites. As we have indicated, Web sites are often structured to produce a comfort zone of familiarity and recognition. With the exponential expansion of the content of the Web, the continuous effort to structure its use by major Web-based corporations is inevitable. The aesthetic developed on commercial sites often works with past aesthetics that have legitimacy (the newspaper or television screen) in order to validate and authenticate the content. Simultaneously Web sites cannot hold to these structures because of the ethos of the Web for at least providing channels and paths through hyperlinks to other sources. As an aesthetic it is open-ended and constantly invokes and evokes intertextuality. Any Web site that overly con-tains its users suffers the lurking potential to be circumvented by the user who looks for the aesthetic of the loose Web.

Chapter 6

THE WEB ECONOMY

CHRISTMAS 1999 – NEW YORK CITY

AT THE NADIR of the old millennium, the Web was operating as the elixir of something new. The lead-up to Christmas 1999 in the United States seemed fundamentally different from past Christmasses because the **Internet** was heralded as something that could now make money change hands. The fears of previous years, where people resisted making purchases over the Internet because of trepidation over the security of using their credit card, was waning if not completely ennervated. Christmas, with its usual power to make it not only the season of giving but also the season where retailers made their greatest revenues, was the agent of transformation and the channel to accept the Web completely. Estimates for the Web-related sales for the Christmas season in the United States alone were in the US$ 4 billion range.

THE NEW AGORA

What changed? Why 1999? Part of the feel of change was related to the way Web retailers were comfortable with doing massive advertising campaigns on television and radio. Quite dramatically the presence of Ebay, Amazon.com and other **virtual** department stores rubbed shoulders with the national advertising campaigns of the largest department store chains. Indeed, even the chains such as Toys'R'Us made concerted efforts to have a Web presence and compete directly with the e-retailers. Equally significant was the importance of the warehouses and inventory that were now part of these electronic retailers' **networks** which meant that often Web retailers were the only source for the most sought after toys and games. In five years, the Web had moved from being a location for the distribution of primarily technology and software to catering for the selling of every possible product manufactured and every available service. As much as the Internet has been identified as a new public sphere, it must be emphasized that new public space resembles the agora or market place as the free exchange of ideas and development of free speech are embedded into this superseding code of buying and selling.

The agora is noisy, crowded and its flow of speech and **information** resembles the stream of consciousness of the best Joycian prose. At the core of the agora is barter, where goods are exchanged for other goods; but an ineluctable part of that process is the conversational haggle. The potential customer may even look disinterested in the product in order to reduce the price ultimately to be paid. The vendor might engage in techniques that make the potential customer feel that their relationship is special and the price offered is part of that special bond. The give and take may seem endless and the style of communication in parts of the world where an agora and marketplace still thrive is an artform which moves seamlessly between delicacy and braggadacio.

The other reality of the agora is that it is never simply a place of exchange. In an anthropological sense, all sorts of other negotiations are going on. The agora is where the classes cross paths and the display of class may be part of the scene. If you want to promulgate an idea the agora is your first stop. So, not only are goods and services available but there is an attempt to create public debate in the agora. The agora is the place for the flow of commerce, the flow of culture and as all these other dimensions intersect, the flow of politics.

The Web is producing a similar virtual agora. It is a cacophony of presentation and representation that deliberately violates divisions that we have set up through our modern institutions to operate distinctively. For instance, democratic political systems generally eliminate any commercial discourse to cloud the process. Thus, you do not see banners in legislatures advertising Nokia. Likewise most countries place controls on political advertising in polling stations where people vote. The concept is that politics and citizenry are sacrosanct identities of the individual in contemporary society and that the process of consultation and representation is above the commercial and the economic. Although the reality of corporate lobbying of legislators makes this more of a simulation or an ideal of the democratic process, it nevertheless underlines the division between one part of our society and another.

On a similar dimension, there are all sorts of policing strategies which separate the public world from the private world. In contemporary media that line is routinely crossed when we are invited to read about the most intimate details of stars, celebrities or the infamous; but we rarely expect our own private worlds to move into public debate. The Web and the Internet have made those delineations less clear as private correspondences such as **e-mail** are often not that different from what we reveal in the more public realms of chatrooms. The online world, whose interface is through the *personal* computer permits this bending of the private and the public: if we think of **Webcams** and their depiction of the everyday lives of people we can see the intimate becomes the entire content of certain Web sites. Although television is a technology that is part of the private home world, it has not been designed as a two-way **interactive** form: the Web in contrast occupies similar private domestic spaces in its use *and* provides channels for the exchange of private revelation that television just cannot fulfil.

The Web's agora is both public and private as much as it is a site for vociferous political debate and pure commercial drives. What we want to explore in this chapter is the nature of this political/economic universe and how that has produced this borderless **Web culture** that transcends its public status by routinely revealing the intimacies of everyday life of its **users**. It is a **new agora** that may resemble past market places, but nevertheless it has been structured from its history and early utopian ideals into something unique.

THE GIFT AND THE COMMODITY

Typical political economic analysis of the media begins by detailing who owns what and finishes with identifying the implications of such ownership on the content of our media. This form of analysis generally moves towards the need for safeguards and regulatory frameworks to reign in the excesses of ownership. It is an important form of analysis and one that we will pursue once we establish the kinds of politics that have been part of the Web's emergence and how that has had some effect on the movement of information on the Web. The central distinction that has to be developed to understand the Web's economy is between the gift and the commodity.

The gift has been a central component of the Web's history and has led to particular economic developments on the Web. From its early usage and close connection to university research, the Internet has often been about the free exchange of ideas and projects. Indeed, part of the history of computer culture is the **shareware movement** where computer programs were passed between users for free and a relatively benign request for donations. This process of passing software for free has accelerated through the Internet and the Web (Wayner 2000). There are sites for **downloading** free and accessible images, other sites for 'cheats' about computer games, and still other sites that have made the entire user base of the Web a potential library for the collection of music from the Web. As we have described in Chapter 2, the Web is about the circulation of **digital** information and it facilitates a borderless accessibility to appropriate that information – that is, download – and reform its content for one's particular uses. This ease in movement and exchange of information actually has been one of the principal reasons for the retardation of the Web economy and we will revisit this 'problem' later in the chapter. What is central to realize is that the Web has been connected to traditions that are somewhat outside of the economic structure of value. Let us concentrate on some of those features.

The Web has features that resemble a library

Although not all libraries are open to the public, the concept of the library is that it is accessible and, once you are a member of the community you have *borrowing* rights. The contents of a library may have been acquired from commercial publishers, but once they are in the library those materials transform into quasi-public domain. Users can be quite direct in their searches for information or they can browse. The contents of the material are cross-linked within their pages through the use of footnotes and bibliographies which provide the connection of one book or source to another within the library. Further cross-referencing has been developed in the original card catalogues to make the library's resources of greater utility and easier to locate; now search catalogues of the library system extend these cross-linkages.

All of these features of the library have served as a model of the Web itself. Once information is placed on the Web it also becomes available and accessible as it enters into the quasi-public domain of **cyberspace**. The digital quality of any Web-based material makes it available for borrowing; the difference between the Web and the library system is that the material from the Web can be copied exactly as it was originally produced whereas library photocopying can only produce a close facsimile. The cross-linkage system of the Web, which hearkens back to Vannevar Bush's model of the memex (1945), is in many ways a **hypertext** version of a card catalogue and a series of endnotes and footnotes. Indeed, because of the close affinity with the Web and its development of searching techniques, libraries through their information-science trained staff have been one of the major institutions that have embraced the Web. The Web offers a massive extension of the library system and, like libraries, does not necessarily hierarchize the value of the information. That construction of the value of information is determined by the Web **browser** as much as by the library user. The Web proliferates the expanse of the modern library. Recent estimates of the Web size vary a great deal. At the time of writing, the conservative estimates put the Web's size at 100 billion documents. Brightplanet.com, a firm with an interest in providing techniques for searching the Web, claims that there are in fact over 550 billion documents that are in the uncatalogued by **search engines** 'deep-Web' (Bergman 2000). Whichever of these two figures is chosen, the reality is that the Web represents a resource that is larger than any other library or combination of libraries on the planet. And most of that

Web remains as accessible as a library for the acquisition of information and knowledge.

The Web has developed clear connections to the government, public service and education

We are well aware of the Web's Internet origins with the American Defence Department ARPA which has always wedded the Internet to government interests. But the proliferation of the Web since the early 1990s has led to quite different parts of the government and their interest in the Internet. Al Gore, when he was American Vice-president has claimed that he coined the term the **information superhighway** as he set up the National Information Infrastructure (NII). These efforts by national governments like the United States have not only been about fostering a commercial Web, but more directly about connecting the Web to education and educational needs. Thus a series of programs of getting schools connected to the Web has been a policy initiative of the most wealthy nations from the United States and Australia to Europe and Singapore. The Web has come to represent the future for many countries and **computer mediated communication (CMC)** is now seen as an essential form of learning for children. Governments are reacting to a new **digital divide** that is restructuring wealth; as societies they are trying to ensure that information technology is prominent in the educational curriculum and the Web represents the most accessible resource and tool for computer use. All of these efforts are government initiatives to ensure their particular societies are not left behind these massive transformations with economies that are not information oriented and workforces that do not have the skills to take control and develop these new methods for the construction and movement of information.

It is also important to signal that the Web has elements that link it to how other utilities have operated in countries. Telephone services have generally been run by PTT (Post, Telephone and Telegraph) in the past, which are and were government corporations or departments that ensured there was an information infrastructure in each country of the postal service and eventually the telephone service. In some countries such as Canada, this service was private but highly regulated to ensure universal access to the telephone and postal systems. Currently, many of these telephone utilities have been privatized to allow them to compete more effectively in a deregulated international telephone market. Nevertheless, the Web's emergence has placed it as a service that, like telephones, should be universally accessible and governments continue to foster public access points for Internet usage in libraries, schools and public buildings.

The Web, in its affinity to the production of knowledge, possesses an ethic as a cultural gift

Every culture has divisions between what is an object of trade and what transcends the normal economic and commercial system and becomes a gift. Cultural anthropologists have studied specific societies that have produced remarkable variations in their systems of exchange. For instance, the Pacific Northwest Amerindians, Kwakiutl, have been studied particularly for their potlatch. At certain times, there are potlatches where a given chief's prestige is determined by how much he can give away during a festival to another village. Quite often the desire to give under these conditions has ruined a village (Leiss *et al.* 1990). In contrast, Western consumer society seems to produce a continuous spectrum of exchange where it appears that any product can be reduced to a monetary value. Nonetheless in most cultures, some things are transformed from commodities into gifts which are freely given and received.

In general, the economic rules of exchange are most likely broken where the emotional bonds and familial investments are strongest. Gifts are thus most regularly exchanged among family and friends. Gifts seem to be also connected to donations to religious institutions and charities; again the motivation behind the gift is a transcendence of the everyday into something spiritual and therefore beyond self-interest. However, some of the most deeply embedded gift-givings in a culture are those that are rarely seen. Knowledge is passed on from generation to generation without any clear economic exchange. Children learn language and skills from their parents. Even the contemporary universal access of education is at least connected to this normal movement of information. Information and its conversion into knowledge through acquisition and then application is strongly associated with the gift. Although controls of information through the Church, through controls on literacy, through the commercialization of education and where **data** is stored, and through the selling of books and newspapers make it appear that knowledge is a commodity it is always an uncertain commodity and unstable in terms of ownership. Intellectual property is a feature of an information-based society; nevertheless knowledge and information have deep-seeded qualities of the gift that have to be overcome in their conversion into products and property (Frow 1996: 89–108). As knowledge becomes more accessible and more widely dispersed it loses its exclusivity and is *common* knowledge. As common knowledge, it can be freely given precisely because it is generally held and widely distributed and stored in the consciousness of so many people.

The diversity of material on the Web makes it harder to discern that the Web is centrally about the production and distribution of knowledge. Because of that central activity, the Web treads the line between the gift and the commodity. The ethic of the exchange of information for the betterment of a culture is strongly positioned in the emergence of the Web. The ease with which one can access information on the Web makes its structure of providing information and thereby knowledge resemble the gift. That ethic is part of what fuels the proliferation of Web sites where more and more pieces of knowledge are shared globally. According to one extraordinary report as many as 7.3 million Web sites are added daily to the literally millions of terabytes of information available (Cyveilance 2000). There is genuine sharing of knowledge on the Web that has to be seen as part of the expansion of common knowledge and comes close to Levy's (1997) thesis about improving a kind of collective consciousness for the betterment of humankind.

The gift quality of the Web has frustrated the emergence of the Web economy, but not enough to arrest the now massive commercial nature of the Web. The Web as gift has shifted how value is transformed to accommodate the concept of the Web as free, accessible and a source of common knowledge. The Web continues to be an unstable and volatile economy as companies learn to negotiate this ethos of the gift that still inhabits the Web's core.

MAKING THE WEB MAKE CENTS: THE INTRICACIES OF THE WEB ECONOMY

For years, companies have worked to crack the code of the Internet as a commercial entity. Like the holy grail, some have sought the **killer application** – that is, some content or software that every Internet user would pay to have loaded on their personal computers. This search was more or less modelled on the rise of the personal computer itself: operating systems, word processing, accounting and spreadsheet programs, design and presentation programs and assorted games became the essential software that allowed companies such as Microsoft to grow into very large and powerful corporations. With the Web, the search is far from complete and has migrated over time. A good way to get a sense of these migrations of what is the central commercial feature of the Web is to look at the corporations that have surfaced with the rise of the **World Wide Web** and their efforts at growth on the **NASDAQ** stock exchange.

RISK CAPITAL: PICKING A FUTURE

NASDAQ is known as the stock exchange for new technologies and the most likely place for the launch of new Internet companies into the heady world of venture capital. Physically based in New York, it has become the virtual hub of the new electronic economy partly because it is entirely an electronic stock market that was launched in 1971 as the needs for financing new electronic ventures began emerging. It is a volatile exchange and is generally perceived as the most active American stockmarket in terms of sheer volume – over 270 billion shares annually (1999) (NASDAQ 2001). There are 4,800 companies listed on the exchange for a total market value in 2000 of US$5.38 trillion (NASDAQ 2001). Not all of these companies are Internet companies – they may be manufacturers, software or games companies. Of those 4,800 companies, 432 are grouped as Internet-related companies. Most of the remarkable stockmarket moments since the early 1990s have been related to the **initial public offerings** (**IPO**) of these Internet-related companies. Millions of shares are offered to the public to buy a stake in these companies and their capacity to generate profits into the future. However, the stock market generally and, to a much higher degree, the NASDAQ do not work in the world of profits and losses. Stock-markets are estimations of the current value and future value of any company listed. Investing in Internet companies has accentuated both the speculative nature of stockmarkets and the virtual quality of any company's value that is determined in terms of stocks. When a company is listed on a particular exchange they pay a fee and to maintain their status an annual fee and this is how the actual exchange makes its money. With both the number of companies that now look to be listed on NASDAQ as well as the names of the companies that have made a successful start there, NASDAQ as a stock exchange has not only cornered the American market for new technologies and the Internet, but has been the stockmarket of choice for many non-US-based corporations. It has become the place for capitaliza-tion, where a good idea attempts to expand outwards to market dominance.

Some major Web corporations, IPOs on NASDAQ, the number of shares offered, at what value, and their value in 2000 are presented in Table 6.1.

Table 6.1 Web corporation IPOs

Company name	IPO date	Offered shares (in millions)	Offer price	Close 7/21/00
AOL	3/19/92	2.000	11.50	57.500
Amazon.com	5/15/97	3.000	18.00	41.125
Ask Jeeves	7/01/99	3.000	14.00	17.000
Cnet	7/01/96	2.000	16.00	30.812
Ebay Inc	9/24/98	3.490	18.00	58.750
Netscape	5/9/95		28.00	
Inktomi Corp	6/10/98	2.254	18.00	129.750
Lycos Inc	4/2/96	3.000	16.00	58.812
MP3com Inc	2/5/99	12.300	28.00	12.125
RealNetwork	11/21/97	3.000	12.50	49.875
Saloncom	6/22/99	2.500	10.50	1.375
Yahoo Inc	4/12/96	2.600	13.00	138.312

Source: Wall Street Research Net – accessed 23 July 2000

There have been massive successes through these Initial Public Offerings. For instance, both Yahoo! and Netscape's debuts on the stockmarket established records for capitalization and transformation in value. From Table 6.1, one can see that Yahoo! has increased in value over 100 times from 1996. Amazon.com similarly has had an impressive stock release, although was severely affected by the downturn in Internet stock in 2000. It should also be clear that there have been less successful capitalization processes. Salon.com, which has been an interesting site for original articles on the Web by recognized writers a year after its IPO was trading at half its original value.

These stock price movements may be intrinsically interesting for those of us trying to determine the next wave of market frenzy; but our purposes here are to indicate how the Web has moved to centre stage for contemporary capitalism. As is clear, an entire stock exchange has emerged that rivals the traditional giants of New York (NYSE), London (FTSE), Tokyo (NIKKEI), Hong Kong (Hang Seng), Paris (La Bourse) and Germany (Deutsch Borse) in terms of activity and general interest. Its concentration on technology and Internet stocks means it has a clear definition and provides a clarion of where this **new economy** is headed. Many exchanges have a technology list that provides similar avenues for investment; but none is as tightly connected to the informational economy as NASDAQ.

However, it is equally important to realize that very few of these Internet companies have generated profits. They may have generated enormous revenues; but they are still operating at a loss. For instance, the giant Internet product distribution company that launched itself through bookselling, Amazon.com, turned a profit for the first time in the last quarter of 2001. Many individuals have made massive fortunes from having investments in these companies; but it must be said that capital's interest in the Web is still based on potential and the future. More often than not, Web-related companies have been overvalued as the hype around the 'affirmative future' takes hold over the collective investor consciousness. These are moments of what is called 'market correction': in April 2000 the Internet-related stockmarket went through a massive 'correction' where the **Internet investment bubble** burst and a re-evaluation of the enthusiasm for particular companies and the general stock values of all Internet companies dropped.

In what was called the dotcom crash of Black Friday, 21 April 2000 NASDAQ lost 25 per cent of its value. In the aftermath, thousands of technology based companies went into bankruptcy and a subsequent wave of mergers and takeovers took place. Nevertheless, there remains a foundational understanding that the Internet and the Web will expand their commercial presence in the coming years as greater aspects of retailing, services, information resourcing and entertainment become mediated through the Web.

THE KILLER APPLICATION – WEB PORNOGRAPHY

Although many forms of electronic commerce suffered downward spirals since April 2000, pornography on the Web has grown. Indeed, since the expansion of the Web from the early 1990s, pornography has consistently been the leader in transforming the Web into a marketplace where users suddenly are comfortable with revealing their credit card details online. Some of the statistics are revealing of this development. One study indicated that in 1998 e-commerce was a 9 billion consumer industry with 11 per cent of that generated by the porn industry. One year later, the e-commerce had doubled to 18 billion and the porn industry still generated 8 per cent of this larger pie (Rosoff 1999). Dennis MacAlpine, an investment analyst who specializes in the entertainment industry concurred with many others that the size of the online industry and the entire pornography industry was difficult to discern but he ventured the following guestimation for the United States in 2002: 'The Internet is probably, rough guess, two, three, four times larger [than the 1 billion dollar **pay per view** television industry for pornography]' (Frontline 2002). With the worldwide pornography industry estimated at 56 billion (Cronin and Davenport 2001), and 200,000 commercial pornography sites (Frontline 2002) the actual international economic dimension of online pornography is enormous. One study in 2000 revealed that from a survey of 1,031 American adults, 20 per cent or the equivalent of 40 million had visited a 'sexually-oriented' Web site (Family Research Council 2000). Nielsen's surveys also reveal a high frequency of porn-related sites: in January 2002, there were 27.5 million visitors to porn sites in the United States with 72 per cent male and 28 per cent female users (Nielsen Netratings 2000). Moreover, although the most popular search items terms have varied somewhat, it is a truism that the word 'sex' has been at or near the top of searches for many years and according to Alexa Research, 1 in every 300 searches was for 'sex' and other terms such as 'porn', 'nude', 'xxx', 'erotic' were all among the highest twenty (Business Wire 2001).

Apart from capturing new subscribers through search engines the shape of this economy is revealing in terms of how people are passed from one site to another. Danni Ashe, CEO and performer of the 8 million dollar a year Web site Danni's Hard Drive, explains the idea of driving 'traffic' from one porn site to another: '... Essentially what happens is an adult Web site will buy a thousand visitors, for instance. Of those thousand, maybe two or three will subscribe, so the 998 people who don't subscribe, they'll say, "Hey, I'm going to sell 'em to the next guy." The next guy will buy the 998 visitors, and then maybe one or two will subscribe. And so people just keep getting moved around. And, you know, the initial philosophy was, "Hey, you know, maybe this guy doesn't like my Web site, but he might like this other person's Web site, so let's give them more choices." But it's gotten to the point now where people are getting moved around and bought and sold too much ...' (Frontline 2002).

Although the pornography business has been a saviour for many technology workers after other dotcom businesses collapsed, it also is an industry that treads the line of legality in many countries. In order to generate customers it must reveal some of its wares for free in the hope of grabbing subscribers. This has resulted in the Web reality that it is difficult not to stumble upon sexually explicit material when surfing the Web. Pornography sites advertise heavily and regularly send massive e-mail-outs to unsuspecting free e-mail users whose addresses have been sold. The industry is under constant surveillance by government regula-tors and even in self-regulating terms by the major **Internet Service Providers**. Nonetheless, pornography has been the killer software appli-cation of the first decade of the Web.

SIZE DOES MATTER

Peeling the waves of hype around the Internet is difficult partly because the assets of the Web economy are not very tangible: the product itself is often virtual; the activity is only in the realm of electronic transactions and the actual bricks and mortar of property may be miniscule. Even the various efforts to chart the economic activity may be generated by companies that have vested interests in maintaining the illusory but seductively exhilarating exponential growth statistics of the Web. Getting a sense of the amount of economic activity is an important form of analysis – even if it needs updat-ing regularly so that the facts and figures that are contained in this book will need to be both challenged and amended each time it is read.

Jobs

One way of gauging the impact of the Web is to determine the amount of jobs that are related to its activity. In an anecdotal way, one can sense that there has been a shift in the job responsibilities in almost every kind of industry. Whatever the commercial activity, e-mail correspondence and newletters may be now a routine way of servicing the needs of customers. Someone is clearly responsible for presenting and updating commercial Web sites. And still others are responsible for retraining and educating workers in the skills of Web design over and above the growing number of software coders who are producing the tools that are employed to make Web pages. Also, as the software improves in its accessibility, a greater number of people are actually available for a number of other Web-related tasks because the skill-level necessary declines. The results of these transformations and integrations of Web-related software means that the employment structure of the Web economy is in continual flux.

Perhaps the greatest amount of statistical evidence about the Web and employment has been generated by the University of Texas at Austin's Center for Research in Electronic Commerce. Their information refers specifically to American labour, but they indicate that nearly 2.5 million workers are supported by the Internet economy in 1999. In relative terms, this makes the Internet economy larger than the American communications industry or insurance industry and twice as large as the airline industry or the property industry. The rate of growth in Internet-related work in one year according to the same report is just over 30 per cent. (Internet Indicators 2000). The four divisions/layers of work and activity outlined are equally interesting and need further exploration.

1   Internet Infrastructure layer: Internet service providers and those provisioning equipment and service for providing access to the Internet represent almost a third of the Web economy labour force. Large telecommunications firms such as AT&T in the United States, Telstra in Australia, major service providers such as AOL.com and Internet security firms are included in this layer of activity.
2   Internet Applications Infrastructure layer: this work is involved with producing software and services that 'facilitate(s) Web transactions and transaction intermediaries'. The applications infrastructure layer also includes designers of Web sites and portals, consultants and those who maintain the Web sites for continuous use for **electronic commerce** transactions. Twenty-six per cent of Web employment is primarily connected to these applications. Firms such as Microsoft, Oracle, Adobe – who produce software for designing Webspaces – would be the higher profile companies that employ in this layer.
3   Internet Intermediary layer: This layer of work is not so much involved in the moving of goods and services and therefore cannot be labelled electronic commerce. Rather, these are workers and activities that help *mediate* the movement of goods and services. This layer is composed of the content providers, the advertising agencies who produce the **banner advertisements**, the search engines who provide access to content and advertisements. Also included here are the online brokerages, the online travel agent work, internet advertising brokers and the many portals that open specific content and knowledge about specific products. In terms of workers, these 'intermediary' workers are about 13 per cent of the entire Web economy.

4   Internet Commerce layer: workers in this layer of the Web economy are
     involved in companies that are actually selling products and services
     online directly. The quintessential firm would be Amazon.com in its
     selling of all sorts of entertainment related products. Direct sales by air-
     lines are included here as various companies circumvent the agents that
     have traditionally sold their products or services. Thirty per cent of Web
     employees work in this layer. Although many may be employees of
     traditional firms, their jobs are related to increasing and servicing trans-
     actions online (Internet Indicators 2000).

The new economy work in Europe

Similarly, in Europe there has been a transformation in work that is related
to the new economy. The results of a recent European Union (EU) study
(2001) on the exploitation and development of the job potential in the cultural sector in the age of digitalization identifies these current and future
shifts. Continued employment growth in the creative occupations of the
cultural sector is to be expected in the future since the demand for cultural
products and services is strongly increasing, both from private households
and from companies. Employment growth in the area of distribution will
also increase, but not at the same rate as in the development of cultural
'products'. 'Content producers' seem to be in greater demand than marketing and sales persons.

   Generally speaking, the rapidly increasing digitalization of cultural products will result in 'traditional' cultural media, such as books and printed
matter, losing significance, while new media, such as Internet Web sites, will
come to the fore, also in terms of employment. The 'digital culture' is the
result of an interaction between 'traditional' culture (content), the **TIMES**
sector (technology) and services/distribution. The increasingly used term
TIMES sector (Telecommunication, Internet, Multimedia, E-commerce,
Software and Security) is used to cover the whole audio-visual sector, i.e.
the entire **multimedia** sector, including culture industry areas such as television, publishing and the music industry. The TIMES sector in the EU is
characterized by very small companies. Only 13.2 per cent of the companies
have more than 50 employees. There is a very high share of freelancers, with
1.3 freelancers for every regular employee. In contrast, at 30 per cent, the
share of women is very low. The percentage of women employed in creative
occupations is even lower, and when it comes to company start-ups, only 20
per cent of new TIMES companies are set up by women. Digital culture
demonstrates enormous employment dynamics, particularly in the areas of
multimedia and software. These two sub-sectors are those with the greatest
demand for content and creativity and therefore represent the best employment opportunities for creative workers. There are currently approximately
1.5 million companies in the EU active in the areas of multimedia and

software, representing a total of 12.4 million workers. Assuming a declining annual growth rate over the next 10 years from 10 per cent in 2001 to just 3 per cent in 2011, we can estimate 22 million jobs in the year 2011. Thus, approximately 9.6 million new jobs will be created in multimedia and software in the next decade.

However, the TIMES sector is currently already experiencing great bottlenecks of personnel on an EU-wide level. This shortage of qualified personnel represents the number one hindrance to growth in the TIMES sector. In digital culture, completely new job profiles and qualification content are presently emerging which are extremely interesting for cultural workers. The rule of thumb which can be applied to this sector is that the entire technical segment, including technology, infrastructure, hardware and printing, will undergo a period of relative stagnation or even decline (with regard to both jobs and contribution to the value adding process), whereas all content-oriented work, that is, creative areas of employment, will continue to show high growth rates (Web design, advertising, publishing, media, education, entertainment, etc.). Digital culture has acted as an employment motor in the past, and will continue to do so in the future, primarily based upon the strong demand within the TIMES sector for creativity and content.

Revenues

Another way of determining the relative importance of the Web's economy is in terms of revenues and incomes. Here the figures vary wildly and widely which once again underlines the enthusiasm and hyperbole that has surrounded the emergence of this economy. One Internet research company claims that electronic commerce generated 132 billion dollars worldwide in 2000 (ActivMedia Research 2000). This American report indicated that only 1.7 per cent of retail sales are done through e-commerce. Yet another source with a running tally of 'global Internet commerce revenue since 1998' puts the figure at 161.4 billion dollars by the middle of 2000 (NUA Internet Surveys Europe 2000). In a European survey, an estimate that more than US$50 billion of purchases would have been made during the year 2000, while approximately 22 billion was spent in 1999 online (NUA Internet Surveys 2000).

Interestingly the Scandinavians were clearly the largest consumers in the 12 EU countries surveyed. Whatever the statistic on Web-related revenues of this new online economy, the basic point is that it has been growing and continues to expand rapidly. Although there have been moments of decline, these are generally where there is a rationalization of a particular sector of the Web economy down to fewer companies and fewer players. What attracts so many investors and business people to the Web economy is that it appears to be free from the constraints that operate in other industries.

This can be translated to the sensation of capitalist frontier for the Internet. It is important to realize that floating with electronic commerce is the fear and anxiety of illegitimate, frequently illegal and phantom company activities. Indeed, the Web as capitalist frontier has been an inhibiting factor in Web businesses expanding as users through fear of the cross between crime and capital are held back from traversing that delicate psychological threshold of releasing their credit numbers online.

The divides that are developing in this Web economy are related to two types of commercial activities. On one level, there is the business-to-business transactions (**B2B Internet**) which is dependent on even higher levels of access security for it to operate smoothly. This level has been expanding rapidly as the supply of equipment and parts is serviced by the Web and the Internet from one company to another. The second level, business to consumer (**B2C**) transactions, is the one that has exploded from 1999 to the point that over 200 million online consumer transactions occurred in Europe that year. (NUA Internet Surveys 2000). Both forms of commerce are leading to major transformations in the way that business operates. The size of the Web economy may be less important than the perception of the Web's significance as a channel for business activity. This perception is fuelling a rapid proliferation of Web presences by small businesses. A survey report by Prodigy Communications indicates that 37 per cent of American small businesses (1–90 employees) now have a Web site and of those surveyed 90 per cent believe that the Internet would benefit their businesses in one of three ways: to promote their products or services, to actually sell online and/or to improve their customer service (Prodigy 2000). In a similar vein, NUA estimated that 56 per cent of American companies would sell their products online in 2000 (NUA Internet 2000).

As the revenues and the believed potential revenues from the online economy go up, the impact of the Web on the overall economy works in a multiplier-effect way. If actual producers and providers of services begin to sell their wares directly online, there is a breakdown of the divisions of retailing and distribution that have organized consumer production and consumption for the last century. Although department store chains can begin to produce a Web presence that replicates their presence in the cityscapes of the world, there is no reason why the online economy would not work towards direct sales from manufacturers. At the present time, these patterns of business–consumer structures are not clearly in place on the Web. As a result, the Web represents a possible location for a transformation of our consumer society and a moment where new 'department' store equivalents such as Amazon.com emerge from the wired world to surpass their twentieth-century giants such as Walmart. Moreover, the process of Web retailing works without national borders which also allows for rapid expansion of particular electronic retailers in transnational ways that would take years to develop in traditional distribution and retail structures.

THE IMPORTANCE OF COUNTING ON THE WEB: THE MAKING OF THE 'AUDIENCE' COMMODITY

There is no question that electronic commerce makes us think of the Web as an entity that goes well beyond a media form. The Web produces an economy that intersects with all industries; television in contrast tends to intersect with many parts of the industrial culture through advertising and its direct sales through home shopping channels provide a stunted relationship to retailing. Yet to comprehend the operation of the Web's economy demands a general understanding of how commercial media make their income because at least 20 per cent of the Web economy is similarly constructed.

Whether one considers television radio or magazines the economic engine of these industries is related to constructing audiences. Audiences are the product – the commodity – that is manufactured by media industries that rely on advertising revenue. Television stations and networks for instance sell their audiences to advertisers who buy the audience's time. The placement of a commercial within a programme relies on the programme to generate an audience. The serial form of entertainment that we are used to in television is at least partly related to producing consistency in audiences that advertisers of certain products can rely upon to return to each week or each day.

With the production of this peculiar product – the **audience-commodity** – an even more peculiar media economy develops. Instead of the audience paying for its entertainment as they might be asked to do if watching a film at a cineplex, the television audience is given the programs for 'free'. But as Dallas Smythe (1981) and others have emphasized this free lunch structure of commercial television for the audience actually is dependent on a clear economy of watching. The audience's presence and viewing of the commercials generates the economic value in the system. Smythe has called this audience-labour, that we as audience members are actually working while we watch and are an essential component of the contemporary economy and its structure of value. This form of adding value as an audience-commodity is the reason why newspapers are relatively cheap to purchase; the advertising revenue covers as much as 80 per cent of the revenues of newspapers and magazines. In its most extreme form, television advertising rates for the annual football Superbowl are the most expensive on American network television.

To construct this value, there has to be some system in place that enumerates the size of the audience. In the development of each media industry, techniques have been developed to calibrate and then classify the audience. For instance, television has ratings that are now determined by a select number of households which have 'peoplemeters' that monitors each household's viewing practices. Magazines have a service that not only determines subscribers but also the larger readership of any particular issue. The music industry at one time determined its ratings or charts in terms of surveys of record store managers; it now gets virtually instantaneous ratings through the electronic information generated from the barcode on the sale of each CD. As Ang (1991) has conceptualized these various forms of counting audiences and then classifying them into demographic and psychographic categories has generated a 'mythic' audience that is used in each industry to organize their advertising rates.

A parallel history of counting has emerged with the Web and much of that counting is trying to determine the value of any particular site. Certain types of counting economies have developed on the Web to organize this value. The most readily generated of these economies simply is counting the number of **hits** that any Web site achieves. On the basis of these hits and reloads the number of visitors are determined. Because each hit leaves a residue or **cookie** of what **server** and user has connected to any site, there is a large industry that has developed that tries to organize and sell this information. Interestingly, the largest and most successful audience research company Nielsen's has become one of the major players in this world of counting. Their system of measurement is sold to particular clients who are given greater demographic and projective details about the movements of visitors on particular Web sites. Other smaller Web counters are also being used throughout the Web and are free to download their meter reading systems and have basic information of where in the world your particular site is successful at attracting visitors.

This first type of counting economy is designed to convert the Web into a media form modelled on the broadcasting free lunch system. Paid subscription systems on the Web, where the user pays to visit a particular site have only been consistently successful with pornographic locations. To a lesser degree business to business subscriptions of information have been moderately successful at achieving paying members and some business publications such as the *Wall Street Journal* have also had relative success by marketing the exclusivity, ease, and reliability of their business information. The overwhelming pattern on the Web is free access by all users to sites and the generation of money through the 'selling' of the aggregate of users to others who would like similar levels of visitors to either their sites or to know of their activities. The description here sounds more complicated than it really is. What has developed is an elaborate system of advertising on the Web. Companies pay for the regularity of hits on particular sites by putting banner advertisements on the sites. The host site to sustain this revenue source from advertisers must maintain a regular flow of visitors so that the rates it can charge to advertisers are consistent or improving. The function of the counting companies such as Nielsen's is to authenticate the basic advertising transaction: they guarantee to both the site and the advertiser that the 'audience' for that site is in fact a certain size. Counting companies are essential for brokering the selling of advertising on the Web. They help the industry develop what are called **click-through rates** which calibrate the advertising rate for a site by the number of times the advertiser's banner is clicked upon by users.

The kinds of statistics generated in this counting economy reveal a great deal about the uses made of the Web and how that is being filtered into a system of commercial value where an audience-commodity can be determined. On the first order, it is essential to establish the 'universe' of the Web. So companies such as Mediametrix or Nielsen's netsizer attempt to establish the definitive number of users of the Web. The global total of active users at the end of 2001 was 254 million worldwide (Nielsen Netratings.com 2000). Since advertising is divided into regional and national markets there are further statistics about the size of the universe within particular countries. According to the same counting company, Table 6.2 reveals the statistics of users for some critically significant Web-nations:

Table 6.2 Internet usage

Country	Number of active users per month (in millions)	Hours of use per month	Number of sessions per month	Number of unique sites visited per month
Global	254	9:20	17	43
United States	104.8	11:27	21	47
Canada	10.4	9:40	21	23
Japan	21.6	10:18	19	55
Australia	6.1	7:58	13	38
Sweden	3.6	6.55	14	36
United Kingdom	17	6:45	14	42
Singapore	0.83	8:46	16	43
France	7.2	7:25	16	48
Germany	17.9	8:15	17	58
Finland	1.3	5:12	12	32
The Netherlands	5.5	7:15	15	52
Ireland	0.64	4:05	9	30

Source: Nielsen/Netratings – Data from December 2001 and January 2002
Note: Information is presented from home Internet usage. Global samples size from twenty-nine countries: 164,648

THE POP-UP ECONOMY

As one moves from Web sites to commercial Web sites, a curious phenomenon begins to develop: Web sites pop up on top of the original site. Once the user crosses the divide from user to consumer by clicking on some product or service, the chainlink structure of the Web economy begins to emerge. Porn sites advertise on other porn sites establishing a **WebRing**. Because of the automatic nature of the pop-up window series it is difficult for the user to escape from the onslaught of connected porn sites. Travel services pop up on airline booking sites which may be similarly linked to hotel services. Deals, prizes and offers of money frequent these pop-up rings. Metaphorically, the commercial Web is becoming more Las Vegas-like as it works to target the potential consumer with gaudy door prizes and games of chance. The promotional promise of the Web is forever foregrounded for the user and the sense of nineteenth-century hucksterism and outright fraud haunt the development of electronic commerce.

The universe establishes the potential reach of any particular Web site, the same way as statistics about television are determined by their virtual saturation of every household in many countries. On a basic comparison, Web advertising is working with a much smaller universe and a much more dispersed universe and on this basis is less attractive to advertisers. However, the statistics are more nuanced. The universe becomes much more focused when the statistic divides the users into the 'active' Internet and the wider user statistic. For instance, Nielsen assesses that in a week in January 2002 there was an active Internet user base of 104.8 million in the United States and a further 41 million at work. It then goes on to assess three other significant statistics: the time per month that a user is on the Web, the average length of time spent on any page and the gender of the user. The average length of use varies considerably from country to country and is primarily determined by local phone rates and secondarily determined by the relative average wealth of each country's populace as we can see from Table 6.2.

The detail of information for the American market isolates on a number of other elements of Web users. For instance, in mid-2000, an average of twenty Web sites are visited per week in the United States and 200 Web pages per week of content are perused by each user. What these statistics indicate is that there is a high concentration on particular sites and a related high return factor to any of these sites by a particular user (Netratings 2000).

Other details of use have been developed. Gender divide is regularly

surveyed by the media survey companies providing another way to comprehend the particular success of Web sites. Countries such as Singapore and
the UK have a male to female user ratio of 60:40, while the American
market is generally perceived to be 50:50. Increasingly, the age range of
users is incorporated into these compiled statistics: universally nearly 30 per
cent of each country that Nielsen surveyed is composed of users in the
35–49 year old age demographic (Netratings 2000).

An added dimension of the counting economy is built from these basic
statistics that establish the groundwork of thinking that an 'audience-commodity' however different and interactive it might be from other media
forms is produced by the Web. Many Web sites demand some extra
information from the user where a questionnaire that establishes the user's
basic demographic statistics is demanded before access to the site is granted.
In other words, this counting economy not only generates a massive **database** on users, it also provides the groundwork for connecting interests,
economic background and consumer choices in a manner that is far more
accurate and sophisticated than anything other media industries such as
television have been able to generate. Moreover, once a particular user is
identified as a subscriber, his/her Web identity can be tracked by the
cookies or identity markers that are left upon visiting a Web site on their
machine. As we have discussed in Chapter 2, the Web permits the surveillance of the user's activities that makes the 'audience-commodity' generated
very valuable. Peter White has developed this understanding of the new
economy where a great deal of effort and capital exchange comes from what
he calls the 'transactional economy', a space where information can be
generated once a connection is made between one element and another
(White 1996: 4–11). The Web has allowed for the transactional economy to
accelerate and intensify as valuable information is generated about users that
can be packaged and sold to companies interested in targeting certain
demographic groups.

HACKING AS COUNTER-ECONOMY

Coursing through the veins of the new Web economy are some elements
that work to counter its overriding hegemony of what the future should be.
The Web economy's fragility is that because of the very network of networks upon which it is built, there are possibilities that the security and
'firewalls' designed to protect the citadels of the Web economy can be
compromised and challenged. Emerging from the freeware and shareware
movement, the hacker culture has a loose political strategy that attacks corporations such as Microsoft who try to commodify if not monopolize the
Internet. This is not a completely organized counter movement; rather it is
as Best has indicated a new politics that is not connected to 'public democracy' but a re-reading of 'more individualized and identity-based politics'

using computer networks as a 'tool of protest and dissent' (Best 2002). Hackers are certainly not unified under one banner of activity; but they are demonized if not mythologized by the popular press as incredibly adept 'criminals' that make the Internet unsafe and its commercial patrons insecure. It is more accurate to characterize some but not all hackers as a vanguard class of the Web and the Internet that are trying to protect a relatively free flow of information exchange via the Internet. Although individual hackers are testing their abilities to break codes to enter into inner sanctums such as the Pentagon or a particular Web site, through their mischief they do destabilize the commercial Web. The **viruses** that are generated by hackers are similarly destructive of the corporatization of the Web even when it appears to attack the most innocent of users in their efforts to undermine the corporate entities that have been transforming the Web into yet another domain that is capitalist-driven.

SUMMARY

As much as the economic size of the Web economy is considerably smaller than prior to the April 2000 devaluation, it is important to realize that even with this contraction of commercial activity, there continues to be expansion in using the Web as a source for the exchange of goods and the commodification of information. What is developing is the routinization of the uses made of the Web via networked computers. More is bought online; more information is first sought out through online sources; greater numbers of business feel obligated to have a Web presence. And concurrently, the 'audience' of users is becoming increasingly comfortable with paying for products and services by the Web. Airline travel, books and video purchases, software and hardware, are examples of the way that young adults in particular are shifting how they buy and sell. The Web's various auction sites are equally successful because of the wealth of objects and the wealth of ready buyers. The Web economy has not achieved this development as if the market were free, uninhibited and unregulated. It is also significant that the strength of the Web economy has been dependent on government and regulatory support as we shall see in the next chapter.

Chapter 7

THE WEB OF POLICY, REGULATION AND COPYRIGHT

Our industry will be changing the way people do business, the way they learn and even the way they entertain themselves, far more than I think people outside our industry expect.

(Bill Gates, 1996)

I N THIS CHAPTER we want to address the transnational discourse surrounding the **Internet**. We will argue that what we are witnessing in public fora, government documents and industry advertisements is nothing less than a political myth based upon an **ideology of information technology**. This growing ideology is a **convergence** of **technological determinism**, new liberal politics, and free market economics, and has direct implications for framing issues of policy and regulation.

In the 1990s the **information** highway, the Internet and the **World Wide Web** became household words. Terms such as information technology (IT), global information infrastucture (GII) and national information infrastructure (NII) have not only become popular in public discourse but governments internationally have developed active responses. Policies are being developed, funding is being allocated, and investments are being made. A question that arises from this situation is how these terms can be seemingly so uncritically accepted by governments as a basis for policy action.

THE SIGNIFICANCE OF METAPHORS

Technologies more often than not end up being used in ways that their inventors did not foresee. Sociologists of technology, Bijker, Pinch and Hughes (1987), have pointed out that the social function of a technology is not uniquely determined by its material construction but is rather subject to 'interpretive flexibility'. In this perspective, different social groups character-istically see different possibilities in the usage of a given technology and thus develop divergent social meanings and expectations for it, thus leaving the direction of its subsequent development somewhat contingent. A critical look at the history of information and communication technologies reveals just how unexpected their fate can often be.

One can argue that the metaphors or conceptual frameworks which we use to make sense of new technologies can be either emancipatory or limit-ing. But because explanatory metaphors for new technologies are often drawn from our understanding and experience of previous technologies, the new technologies are often cast in the image of the old. For example metaphors based on the railway industry were the basis of understanding and regulating the telegraph system. In turn, metaphors rooted in the form and function of the telegraph industry guided conceptualization and regula-tion of the telephone system (Sawhney 1996: 295).

Parallel trends can be seen in early discussions of radio where two com-peting metaphors were circulating. One was a metaphor based on news-paper publishing. This entailed notions of editorial control, advertising support and circulation. Not surprisingly AT&T applied the model of the telephone to radio. Its model assumed that potential broadcasters would purchase and use broadcast time in much the same way as the telephone **user** would use a public pay-phone. Ultimately the difference between the two models was based on conceptions of the mechanisms which would make broadcasting an economically viable enterprise (Sawhney 1996: 295).

Similar observations have been made about early conceptions of electric light. Marvin (1988: 175) has shown how electric light was conceived as a public spectacle and entertainment medium well before it was considered as a useful illumination device in private homes. And when the telephone was being promoted for domestic use, one European entrepeneur ignored its one-to-one communications possibilities and used it for the 'broadcasting' of music and news to subscribers (Briggs 1981: 51). In the US the tele-phone was promoted as a substitute for the telegraph which would enable the transmission of commands and orders so that goods could be ordered and traders summoned to the home. It took some years before telephone companies promoted the telephone as an instrument for maintaining social links (Fischer 1992: 75). While hindsight is often amusing, these examples should warn us about uncritically adapting the metaphors of the current developments in media and communications.

Raymond Williams (1989: 178) has discussed the importance of how we use metaphors as a ground for political consciousness: 'representations are part of history, contribute to the history, are active elements in the way that history continues; in the way forces are distributed; in the way people per-ceive situations, both from inside their own pressing realities and from outside them'. Williams suggests that that history is far more complicated than its images, for just as representations help us to understand the past, they must also be understood as part of the material culture of the past. Clearly, we are faced with a complex problem of trying to determine the nature of the Web within the current situation of flux and convergence.

IDEOLOGY OF INFORMATION TECHNOLOGY

Terms such as 'information highway' must be seen as metaphors and as such, they do not have a precise meaning, least of all in political terms. While recognizing this, it cannot be denied that many governments have been prodded into action to respond to the challenge of information technology.

It must be recognized that specific events underpinning the information highway concept often have antecedents. Much of the action taken by governments in the communication technology area to date has occurred in a context of the rapid rise in popularity of the Internet and the transformation of monopolized national telephone and media **networks** to more liberalized market structures.

The current ideology of information technology first emerged in the United States when federal government policy favoured scientific and technical research with development in the private and public sectors that would contribute to economic growth. Industry and successive federal governments actively pursued a strategy that promoted the virtues of the free market, the need to give priority to competitive innovation and greater productivity over social welfare issues, the demand for greater efficiency in all areas of public and private enterprise, and the glorification of science and technology as a means of achieving these ends. This strategy supported high-tech developments, including information technology, by the private sector, university researchers, and the military.

The push to equate productivity growth and information technology, found support in the social analysis provided by scholars, management gurus, and populist futurists who asserted that we are moving away from an industrial society into a high-tech postindustrial **information society**. It was often asserted that this change was occurring in major historical waves or megatrends, driven by the inevitable forces of technological change alone. Daniel Bell (1973), Peter Drucker (1994), George Gilder (1994), John Naisbitt (1982), Nicholas Negroponte (1995), Alvin Toffler (1970), and many more reinforced the view that we are witnessing the emergence of a postindustrial economy whose primary resource was information and whose workforce would consist of an elite class of knowledge workers. Thus, the demand for information, for more sophisticated technologies for production and distribution, and for more privatization were part of the drive to increase productivity in a global information economy.

In the **new economy** dedicated to an ever expanding supply of goods and services, information, produced and sold by the private sector, was considered a necessity for a prosperous economy. As inflation, unemployment, and economic constraints intensified and manufacturing moved to Asian nations, increasing emphasis was placed on creating a high-tech information society as a strategy to meet the challenge of a highly competitive international market. The wedding of free market values and information technology became even more prevalent when boosted by the success of US President Ronald Reagan and UK Prime Minister Margaret Thatcher in advancing a political agenda that advocated less government through the privatization of traditional public services.

The US is widely acknowledged as being a leader in promoting the information highway idea. During the 1992 presidential election, Al Gore captured the support of many US academics and the information industries by promoting the idea of '**information superhighways**'. The idea was further articulated with the publication of the Agenda for Action on the National Information Infrastructure (NII). The document developed a plan for America to build 'a seamless web of communications networks, computers, **databases**, and consumer electronics that will put vast amounts of information at users fingertips' (US Government 1993: 5). In the agenda there was a heavy emphasis on deregulation in telecommunications and it stressed that industry would have to pay for the information infrastructure. The government's role would be to help pave the way.

The response from other leading countries was rapid and to the point. An Organization for Economic Cooperation and Development (OECD) report notes the significance of the American NII initiative:

> Many other countries have followed the United States in giving priority to the examination of convergence. This emphasis has included not only reviewing market structures and regulatory requirements which a merging of broadcasting and communications would entail, but the need to stimulate service development and diffusion of new technologies.
>
> (OECD 1992: 15)

The bonding of information technology with market needs was by no means confined to the United States. Reports in Australia, Canada, Denmark, France, Japan, Singapore and Sweden, to name a few, advocated that a shift from an industrial manufacturing economy to a technologically driven information processing economy was indeed a global phenomenon. In various government commissions and reports it was widely asserted that this technological imperative would revitalize capitalism in the developed countries, while developing nations were encouraged to embrace information technology within a free market economy in order to climb to a new era of worldwide prosperity.

GOVERNMENTS WEIGH IN TO THE FUTURE OF THE NEW ECONOMY

For example, Japan's *Reforms Towards the Intellectually Creative Society of the 21st Century* (1994) recommends to support the construction of an optical fibre network based on **multimedia** applications and needs. The European Commission (EC) Bangemann Task Force Report, *Europe and the Global Information Society* (1994) recommended matching the US and building an European Information Infrastructure which emphasized the importance of market mechanisms. Australia produced similar plans in the *Networking Australia's Future* (1994) report. Sweden's IT Commission produced a report entitled *Information Technology: Wings to Human Ability* (1994), while Denmark's Minister of Research and Information Technology published *From Vision to Action. Info-Society 2000* (1995). Singapore's *IT 2000: Vision of an Intelligent Island* (1996) and Canada's *Connection, Community, Content: The Challenge of the Information Highway* and *Building the Information Society: Moving Canada into the 21st Century* (1996) are equally optimistic in spirit and vision.

Consisting of over 3,000 pages, the different reports attempt to answer the questions formulated by governments in search of information technology policies. Common to all investigations, were three main objectives:

- to create jobs through innovation and investment,
- to reinforce Nation X sovereignty and cultural identity, and
- to ensure universal access at a reasonable cost.

One can also delineate five orienting principles:

- an interconnected and interoperable network of networks,
- collaborative public and private sector development,
- competition in facilities, products and services,
- privacy protection and network security,
- lifelong learning a key element of the Information Highway.

This discourse was concisely delineated in an Organization for Economic Cooperation and Development (OECD) report on information technology:

> IT developments, originally driven by defence and space needs, are increasingly geared to meet commercial and industrial demand. IT is now recognised as indispensible to many

economic activities, and industry experts consider broader IT
production and use as a basis for further economic and social
development. IT has become a strategic tool in the contemporary economic and political environment, as well as for the
opening up of new markets and patterns of demand.

(OECD 1992: 23)

The rhetoric on the virtues of information technology reached new heights
with the incessant references to the global 'information highway' and the
'Internet society'. In the United States the development of a National
Information Infrastructure (NII) became a priority of the Clinton adminis-
tration. Across a wide political spectrum politicians were able to endorse the
spread of information technology through their untested belief that it
would provide a new means of expanding a more democratic society, promoting economic opportunities while fostering electronic modes of
community.

The arguments supporting the NII initiative reflect the heavy burden
placed upon information technology as a means of revitalizing the
economy. A US Government document claims that, 'America's destiny is
linked to our information infrastructure'. It states:

> The potential benefits for the nation are immense. The NII will
> enable US firms to compete and win in the global economy,
> generating good jobs for the American people and economic
> growth for the nation. As importantly, the NII promises to
> transform the lives of the American people. It can ameliorate the
> constraints of geography and economic status, and give all
> Americans a fair opportunity to go as far as their talents and
> ambitions will take them.
>
> (US Government 1993: 16)

The rhetoric does not belong to America alone. We find the same intensity
in reports from governments around the world. A steady stream of government and consultant reports asserts, without providing any substantive evidence, that Nation X has shifted from a resource based economy to an
information economy where increased productivity is driven by information
technology. A Canadian report (which echoes that of most nations) on the
information highway claims that it will:

> stimulate research and development (R+D) in leading-edge
> technologies; it will facilitate the diffusion of innovative tech-
> nologies and information-based services; it will strengthen the
> competitiveness of large and small Canadian businesses; and it
> will provide cost-effective access to high-quality health care,

educational and social services. The information highway is essential for Canada's success in a new global economy in which value, jobs and wealth are based on the creation, movement and applications of information.

(Industry Canada 1994: 12)

The Canadian Information Highway Advisory Council (IHAC) reflects the faith in information technology. The low-cost, high-quality network 'will give all Canadians access to the employment, educational, investment, entertainment, health care and wealth-creating opportunities of the Information Age'. The information highway 'is a personalized village square where people eliminate the barriers of time and distance, and interact in a kaleidoscope of different ways'. The council goes on to claim that the information highway 'really is the next step on route to the **global village** that Marshall McLuhan described so forcefully and eloquently' (IHAC 1994: 3).

However, this conjunction of political rhetoric, free market economics and information technology does not represent any historical turning point, as many would have us believe. Rather, it can be viewed as a recurring manifestation of the dynamics of capitalism. Heilbroner (1992: 25) makes the observation that 'Certainly capitalism's most striking historical characteristic is its extraordinary propensity for self-generated change'. Throughout history this dynamism of capitalism stimulated recurring bursts of technological innovation: the steam engine, the railway system, electrification, the internal combustion engine, nuclear energy. These technological developments had of course major impacts on social and cultural life. Nevertheless, it is not technological innovation that is the fundamental force driving change; it is the inherent drive to generate and accumulate capital, the force of the free market.

From this viewpoint, the free market, demands technological innovation to perpetuate a vital economy. Information technology is only the latest in a long history of cyclical technological developments required of such an economy, rather than being a totally unique force for fundamental change. The building of the technological infrastructure, the demand for sophisticated software, and the potential consumer markets for information services and technology represent vast opportunities for investment and profit, but they are not the monumental break from the past as is so often claimed.

While we need not quarrel with capitalism's need for technological innovation for economic rejuvenation, we should be concerned about the tendency to impart to all spheres of social and cultural life the values of the market place, in other words, their commodification. The ideology of information technology holds that the adoption of information technology must be accompanied by the adoption of free market values and the commodification of information.

Many examples of this linkage can be found. Distinctions between information, **data**, and knowledge are collapsed into a vague all-encompassing concept of 'information', a commodity that can be packaged into **digital bit**s and marketed directly to consumers through the Internet. Institutions previously mandated and tax supported to make available information and knowledge as a public good for the promotion of culture, educational and political development of an informed citizenry are under extreme pressure to require users to assume more of the direct cost of access to the resources they seek. Private vendors of computer **databases** of information strive to bypass institutions fostering the widespread availability of information by offering their wares directly to end users or consumers for a fee. In other words, all needs for information should be fulfilled through an open market place transaction. Examples of this include public library fees for service, increased charges for government publications and data, copyright legislation favouring content owners over users, and the battle over who will build, own and provide access to the Internet.

Some observations on pattern can be made from the above. First, it would appear that the US has led the way in forging the information highway concept and other countries have been quick to respond.

Second, the initiatives taken by governments are not strictly identical but there are numerous common themes. Some of these themes emphasize the importance of information and information technology in economic development, the need not to fall behind competitors, the notion of vision with respect to the emerging information society, the notion of discontinuity in that the digital future will be both technologically and socially different from the past, and an essentially optimistic future based on new services and opportunities provided by information and communication technologies.

Third, the historical context suggests that the information highway idea is not too dissimilar in rhetoric from other technology developments in the recent past. Of importance here are the space race of the 1960s to put a person on the moon, laser technology and the Star Wars Defence project of the 1980s and biotechnology and the Human Genome project of the 1990s. This suggests as noted in Chapter 1 that there is a distinct link between governments and industry interests in gathering symbolic and instrumental forces behind technological concepts at particular points in time. Notions of prediction and futuristic visions involving technology are common in this regard.

A question that begs to be asked is if we are seeing the rise of a new 'political myth'? Political myth is a widely believed set of unquestioned political beliefs that give events and actions a particular meaning. It commonly takes the form of a story, a narrative which simplifies complex problems, and at the same time, overcomes contradictions. A political myth can provide; a guide to action; a way of making sense of the world; and a framework that can overcome the contradictions that can bring about political consensus. A political myth can include themes on how a certain society came into being, its present predicament and its likely direction in the future. A key feature of political myth is that it does not really matter whether it is objectively true or false. If it is widely believed, 'reality' is essentially created through myth. Examples of political myths abound and more specifically political myths about technology are prevalent. For example, the postindustrial society and information society concepts can be construed as political myths. They tell a story of discontinuous change from an industrial society to a postindustrial society based on the driving force of new technology.

PRIVATE SECTOR SUPPLY AND STATE-STIMULATED DEMAND

The role of the state in the hoped for new competitive setting should, it is argued, be limited to establishing simple, clear and stable regulations. But things are not as simple as they appear at first glance. While it is limited to a minimal supply function, leaving the entire field to private initiatives, the state is strongly urged to play an active, indeed primordial, role in the generation of demand. It must first of all become a model user, quick to introduce IT in its own services. It must also incite citizen-consumers to enter the game as quickly as possible. The education system is seen as the preferred means of achieving this end. From the creation of information systems, the emergence of an information society is quickly deduced, in which, to be sure, education is conceived as a *key conceptual component*. The logic here is impeccable. Qualified workers and sensitized consumers are required in order to respond to industry's new needs. And the state is relied upon to fulfil both requirements.

On the supply side of matters, the state is not limited to creating a regulatory framework. With respect to research and development, for example, the state is called upon to provide active support by way of income tax credits or other facilitating measures. It is also proposed that the state provide financial support for the creation of national products and applications. In fact, the private sector is not really asking for the complete withdrawal of the state. It is simply asking that state action be better attuned to private sector interests.

It is thus somewhat imprecise to claim, as does the Canadian Council report, that 'in the new information economy, success will be determined by the marketplace, not by the government'. In our view, it would be more accurate to say that the creation of the information highway will be the result of a close collaboration between the public and private sectors. But would an overly explicit acknowledgement of the state's role not carry the threat of legitimating possible demands that private sector beneficiaries pay back the public financial support they received in the development of these new markets? Is it not time to take a more serious look at the kind of social and political regulation needed to keep in step with the changes occurring in our societies?

POLITICAL MYTH AND THE IDEOLOGY OF INFORMATION TECHNOLOGY

The question of the relation between innovations in information technology and economic productivity is interesting. In recent years there has been a lively debate as to whether investment in information technology leads to productivity growth. Studies comparing the investment in or the use of information technology by country, industry, firm, and using various economic indicators, have failed to establish a strong correlation between such technological investment and growth in productivity (Landauer 1995). This does not mean that the mythical quality of high technology and information technology in particular has been dispelled. An OECD report recognizes that:

> That will not happen as long as high technology is regarded as an automatic and instant panacea for all manner of economic ills. The essence of a myth is that it can have value in the absence of analytical assessment, and high technology has great value as political myth.
>
> (OECD 1989: 36)

The ideology of information technology promotes the idea of less government. Yet the development of a national information structure relies as much on government participation and support as did the development of the nineteenth-century industrial infrastructure. As noted above the military was an important early financial contributor to the research and development of information technology. The development of information technology infrastructures and their widespread use requires the investments of billions of dollars, some of which will be sought from government by the private sector through research grants and subsidies. This is also an area that is presenting complex challenges to government regulatory agencies as major companies in the computing, communications and cable industries jostle to dominate the information highway.

Clearly, goverment cannot be excluded from the dynamics and politics of information technology. Consequently, it is critical that the ideology of information technology be challenged by a political will that transcends any particular media used for the transcription and transmission of information and knowledge. There is nothing inherent to information technology that it must be wedded to one ideology over another. Information technology can be used to make information widely accessible, as is the case now with those who have access to the Internet, or it may not. Information technology will continue to affect many spheres of our cultural and economic life, but it is not the sole force for change. The more profound cause is the ideology of information technology, and ideology that derives from capitalism's inherent need for change, growth and new markets. The issues arising out of the challenge of the ideology of information technology must rightly be resolved by the entire body politic.

REGULATION AND COPYRIGHT

In most countries around the world there is great uncertainty on behalf of the state as to how best to regulate the Internet in the interests of the citizen body.

The United States Government's National Research Council, recently released a report on what they describe as the 'digital dilemma' in which they eloquently point out some of the contradictions of the Internet.

> The information infrastructure – by which we mean information in digital form, computer networks, and the World Wide Web-has arrived accompanied by contradictory powers and promises. For intellectual property in particular it promises more-more quantity, quality, and access – while imperiling one means of rewarding those who create and publish. It is at once a remarkably powerful medium for publishing and distributing information, and the world's largest reproduction facility. It is a technology that can enormously improve access to information, yet can inhibit access in ways that were never before practical. It has the potential to be a vast leveler, bringing access to the world's information resources to millions who had little or no prior access, and the potential to be a stratifier, deepening the division between the information 'haves' and 'have-nots'.
>
> (NRC 2000: 1)

The new digital technologies represent both a promise and a threat to many of our traditional institutions. The rapid growth of the Internet has seen many stakeholders in these institutions attempting to protect the advantages they enjoyed under traditional mass media conditions. These attempts are often met with resistance from those who view the Internet as a new form of media with radical implications for communication, business and public life.

The threats to the future of the Internet have been clearly identified in the public's mind; censorship, accessibility, privacy, and pornography, that is to say the agenda set by the mass media. Away from the public eye, in national and international legislative fora the real battle over the future of the Internet is taking place and it is a tremendously complex one; the battle over intellectual copyright in **cyberspace**.

At stake here are the powers to determine content, to assign legal liability, to regulate the development of new technologies, to create new categories of copyrightable material, and to redraw the public/private realm distinction. The results of these decisions will fundamentally influence the development of the Internet, making it almost unrecognizable from the Internet we have known thus far. Indeed many argue that the greatest danger is from overzealous intellectual copyright protection. Moreover, when we take into account the borderless nature of networked information, we realize that in this era of increasingly globalized trade in information-based products, the stage is being set for upheaval on a global level.

The battle over copyright compels us to revisit such fundamental – and generally uncontested – pre-digital copyright assumptions such as creation, author, distribution, copy and public and private realms. John Perry Barlow, in a provocative 1993 article in *Wired* entitled 'Putting old wine into new bottles: the economy of ideas', summarizes the quandary of digitized intellectual property thus:

> If our property can be infinitely reproduced and instantaneously distributed all over the planet without cost, without our knowledge, without its even leaving our possession, how can we protect it? How are we going to get paid for the work we do with our minds? And, if we can't get paid, what will assure the continued creation and distribution of such work?

At first glance, the attempt of copyright holders to protect their wares on the Internet sounds fair. After all when one thinks copyright holder, one thinks creator, with the invariably romantic notion of a gifted individual struggling to bring to life an inspired idea. And indeed this is an image the copyright holders would encourage. But it is vital to bear in mind that most copyrights are held not by authors, but by corporations who have bought the rights. Although creators are recompensed for their effort, the lion's share of the money made from their works goes to the holder of the work's copyright. Copyright-based corporations are of course big business and include such household names as Microsoft, Sony, News Corporation and Time Warner.

Nor should we underestimate the financial benefits accruing to copyright holders, especially in an increasingly information-dependent world. Intellectual property is big business, and nowhere more so than in the United States, the world's biggest exporter of intellectual property, much of it in the form of entertainment products. According to a pro-copyright American trade group, the Creative Incentive Coalition (1996), 'The copyright industries are one of the largest and fastest growing segments of the US economy, contributing over a quarter trillion dollars to the Gross Domestic Product and providing jobs for more than 3 million Americans.' Given these figures it should come as no surprise that the United States is spearheading copyright reform to respond to the unprecedented challenges of the digital age.

The debate then, should be framed not as creators versus the public, but as copyright holders versus the public. In the words of copyright lawyer, Pamela Samuelson (1997: 9): 'The (copyright) battle shaping up in the digital era pits media conglomerates against users as never before.' Lining up opposite the copyright protectionists are a variety of groups, with different stakes in the issue. Some represent the general public, including 'netizens', others academic institutions, while the third major group are software and hardware manufacturers and **Internet Service Providers**. All, for various reasons find the moves of the copyright holders to carve a niche for themselves in cyberspace unacceptable.

What follows is a further examination of some ways in which basic principles of pre-digital, pre-network copyright are radically challenged by the new technological properties embodied in the Internet. As well it will look at the main legal and technological manoeuvres being undertaken to protect, and even extend, traditional copyright in cyberspace. Finally, it will address the implications of this copyright debate for the future of a digitally distributed media society.

BASIC CONCEPTS OF COPYRIGHT

Intellectual copy laws are a relatively recent development in the history of the law. They were born in the wake of the invention of the printing press – the world's first mass medium. Although they evolved with the introduction of each new media technology, the essential concepts remain intact.

The first copyright legislation was the Statute of Anne (the 1709 Copyright Act) of Britain. It sought to prevent printers and booksellers from selling books which had been published without the author's permission. Implicit in this law is the treatment of intellectual work as property, one of the key concepts of copyright. Thus copyright was 'invented' to help authors earn a decent living from their writings.

The copyright holder, then, is the owner of the work, and as such exercises different rights over it, for copyright is really a bundle of rights. The exclusive rights of a copyright owner include the right to reproduce, publish, perform, broadcast, transmit and make adaptations of a work, and these rights can be sold or transferred to another person, though in practice the main rights are to authorize reproduction (i.e. the making of copies), and to authorize the distribution of those copies. Also, it is an economic right, meaning the owner may or may not be the author, and can sell the rights to someone else.

However, intellectual property is a problematic concept. Although one person may have articulated an idea, or created a piece of art, nothing is born *ex nihilo*. All ideas and creations are informed by their antecedents and in turn they provide inspiration for future ideas and creations. So the argument has been made that intellectual creations belong to society, not to the individual who came up with them.

Laws and intellectual property practice differ from country to country and will most likely remain different despite vigorous attempts at harmonization. Cultural attitudes towards intellectual property and the premises on which law is founded may also differ. Many 'civil law' countries (e.g. much of Europe) have in their intellectual property law a notion that the creator of an artistic work has an inalienable right, called a *moral right, droit morale* or *droits d'auteur*. This moral right protects both the artistic integrity of the work and the artist's interests against the unauthorized modification of the work, which would damage the artist's reputation. The concept arose in the aftermath of the French Revolution. Moral rights are intended to protect an author's name, reputation and work, which are seen as integral to the act of creation, and is why they are regarded as perpetual and irrevocable as long as the work exists (NIC 2000).

Article 6 of the Berne Convention states: 'Independently of the author's economic rights, and even after the transfer of the said rights, the author shall have the right to claim authorship of the work and to object to any distortion, mutilation or other modification of, or other derogatory action in relation to, the said work, which would be prejudicial to his honour or reputation.' Thus the moral right survives any sale of the work.

The US, British and Canadian tradition sees works of authorship differently, instead seeing them as commodities to be bought and sold, under the control of whatever person or corporation holds current title to it. This allows authors a broad freedom of the right to contract, including the right of an author to divest themselves of what would otherwise constitute moral rights. This is most frequently seen in the entertainment industry where the 'all rights' contract in routine use grants the purchaser of the rights to a work the right to adapt, change, modify or otherwise alter the creative work in any manner the purchaser may choose (NIC 2000).

In China and most Asian cultures there is no accepted concept of intellectual property in creative expression. Acts of individual expression are seen as rooted in the contributions of ancestors, and are regarded as one person playing the role of scribe for ancestors and other contemporaries. Thus, one who expresses an idea has no private right to it, as it is a social expression, not an individual one, and part of the process of passing on a society's cultural legacy (Alford 1995). Most countries, however, have some provision for what is usually known as 'fair dealing' (in Canada), or 'fair use' (in the US). These provisions allow private citizens, including those involved in academic pursuits, to make a small number of copies of a copyrighted material for personal use.

THE PROBLEM WITH COPYRIGHT LAW

Stanford law professor Lawrence Lessig in his book about computers, the Internet and how the legal system deals with them, *Code and Other Laws of Cyberspace* (1999) explains the problems with existing copyright law. For years now, Lessig and other critics have maintained that inflexible copyright rules as they exist often just protect entrenched – and usually uncreative – interests at the expense of virtually everyone else, including many of those the copyright rules were originally supposed to protect.

Lessig points out, for example, that when Congress first enacted copyright law in 1790, the protection extended for a term of fourteen years, which could be renewed for another fourteen years if the author was still alive. Congress has since increased that term to the life of the author plus 70 years. Given current life expectancies, that means a corporation can now bank on preventing a piece of intellectual property produced by a thirty-year-old today from falling into the public domain for more than a century.

Lessig maintains such practices run contrary to one of the main reasons copyright law was conceived in the first place. Originally, he says, copyright and patent laws sought to balance two competing interests: protecting and rewarding innovators for their work, but also making sure innovations were available for reuse or repurposing by others after a reasonable length of time.

The rationale for that policy is that the first person who figures out a new invention deserves to be fairly compensated. But that person should not have a right to prevent others from using his or her invention for so long that future progress is hampered. What is often missed by the private-property stalwarts and big-company lawyers is that the intended goal of the copyright system was to provide incentives for creativity not only for the originators of new ideas but also for others who want to use and build on those ideas in other ways (Lessig).

Unfortunately, over the years concentrated financial interests have convinced Congress to steadily shift that balance. Privatized rights have won favour over the public interests that were once a far more essential aspect of copyright protections. That trend has only accelerated recently, as Congress has agreed to one demand after another from Microsoft and other big media firms, to 'strengthen' copyright protections for a variety of high-tech digital goods.

THE INTERNET AND TRADITIONAL COPYRIGHT

The Internet poses a challenge to traditional copyright conceptualization by virtue of its technological configuration, and the social attitudes and practices that have developed alongside it. A number of examples can be summarized as follows.

Information on the Internet is digital

Although digital content was available before the advent of the Internet, it was mainly available on physical media, such as diskettes or CD-ROMS, and distributed, priced and sold as physical goods.

Information on the Internet is malleable

Because information on the Internet is not in fixed form it is malleable. It can be changed inadvertently or intentionally. Yet, inasmuch as, the exercise of property rights includes purchase and sale, both the buyer and seller have an interest in the property being what it is said to be, that is, in authenticating the property or text.

The Internet transforms systems of reproduction

Information on the Internet is easily and cheaply reproducible, with no limit to the number of copies, and no appreciable cost difference in the making of each copy. Moreover, for the first time it is possible to make copies without any degradation of quality from the original.

The Internet transforms systems of distribution

The Internet provides a virtually free distribution system by cutting out the costly distribution channel, where all participants along the way take their respective cuts of the revenue. Also, a digitized network environment creates havoc with the traditional 'first sale' rights of copyright holders which allowed subsequent sales of the material. In other words, a person was free to sell a book he had bought and read, since the publisher had already been paid for the initial sale. But on the Internet, where information can be perfectly copied endlessly, first sale rights have no meaning.

Another fallout to traditional distribution of intellectual property that the Internet produces flows from the fact that on the Internet distribution is ongoing, that is to say a document is theoretically always available in cyberspace to be accessed rather than there being a one-time acquisition of it; information is also vulnerable to being withdrawn. Online information providers can at any time shut down their site, thereby cutting off users.

Use of the Internet is transparent

Unlike with mass media information services and products which we consume, generally, anonymously, the use of digitized networked information is not private. It can be monitored by parties which have the technology, and the will-for whatever reason – to do so.

This means that private use of distributed information is not really so, as use can be monitored. This has radical implications for privacy and legal liability. For example, if Internet Service Providers host subscribers who infringe on copyright materials, who is to be held responsible? If these providers wish to avoid a lawsuit by a copyright holder, they might have to resort to spying on users.

A further consequence of this transparency is its effect on pricing structure. Whereas a book costs the same no matter how many times the buyer reads it, it is conceivable that each time a person views material on the Internet there will be a charge, in other words **pay-per-view**. This is possible through the application of a pre-digital concept of copy, in which viewing gets regarded as transmission and, since each transmission makes a 'copy', therefore each viewing creates a 'copy'.

Internet use fosters new attitudes and practices

In addition to the unique technical properties of the Internet that make it a challenge to traditional copyright, there also exists a set of attitudes and practices specific to the medium which bolster its destabilizing effect. The Internet is the result of historical circumstances. It had no central planning body; it evolved in response to the tastes, values, and needs of its community of users. As a result, the users of the early days have shaped a certain netizen ethos unlike that which exists about any other media technology. The attitude towards information that has evolved on the Internet is that it should be free ('Information wants to be free') and easily accessible, obviously not attitudes the copyright holders are happy about.

LEGISLATIVE REFORM OF COPYRIGHT LAW

There have been two major legislative processes on intellectual copyright. They are represented by the United States' National Information Infrastructure (NII)'s Working Group on Intellectual Property, and the World Intellectual Property Organization's (WIPO) Bern Convention. The work of the NII has become the international touchstone for debate on copyright in the digital age. It formed the basis for the WIPO discussions, and as such provides us with a convenient starting point.

The NII Working Group's White Paper, called 'Intellectual Property and the National Information Infrastructure', was released in 1995. This document addressed the question of how copyright law might apply to the Internet. From the beginning, the private-interest bias of the Working Group was evident, as they chose to view the issue of intellectual property as solely a legal issue, and thus setting the tone for future debate. The result was that no one representing the public interest testified, save a few librarians and academics. Most people making representations were lawyers of copyright-rich corporations, usually entertainment conglomerates. The Working Group concluded, ostensibly, that old copyright legislation was still viable in the era of digitized, networked information. It recommended some statutory changes, 'which it characterized as minor updates and clarifications of copyright law', but which in fact were anything but.

Among its proposals were the running of a public education campaign (including in schools) to change the general perception of the Internet as a medium in which information is free for the taking. Such a campaign would presumably alleviate the worry of this corporate CEO: 'We're concerned about the use of metaphors for the NII such as information highway, digital library or universal service, that imply that all of the information available might be free.' The same would apply to the corporate lawyer who said: 'We're training generations of (people) to love getting music and content over the Internet and training to think of it as a public utility, like water: free or virtually free.'

Another controversial proposal was the call for a 'ban on devices, "the primary purpose or effect", of which is infringement of copyright'. At first this seems unproblematic, but, such a measure demonstrates a lack of understanding of how technology develops, assuming as it does, that the 'primary' purpose of a technology can be ascertained. Indeed the evolution of the Internet from a secret military project to the public's network of networks itself vividly belies such a notion. Knopf (1996: 62) observes that, 'if such a ban had been in place in its proposed form in 1950, we would probably never have seen the development of tape recorders, VCRs, satellites, or indeed, computers themselves'.

Another key recommendation of the White Paper was to hold legally liable Internet Service Providers for any copyright infringement activity that takes place on their system, whether or not they were aware of it. In effect, this would force ISPs to spy on their subscribers, something not difficult to do with digital technology.

By far, the most controversial 'minor' adjustment to existing copyright law advanced by the White Paper was the addition of a short phrase to define the making of a copy as equivalent to the transmission of a copy:

> To 'transmit' a reproduction is to distribute it by any device or process whereby a copy or phonorecord of the work is fixed beyond the place from which it was sent.
>
> (NII Copyright Protection Act of 1995–S. 1284)

Such a measure highlights the key question about digitized work, a question arising from its nature as an electronic transmission: is it a reproduction, or a distribution, or both? The upshot of this clause is to effectively render illegal common practices such as browsing. The rationale is that each time a computer accesses a Web site, the RAM automatically makes a copy. The transmission proposal highlighted how the copyright stakeholders seized the new possibilities to extend their reach that digitized networked information offers. It was also the major issue that launched public interest in the proceedings.

The United States Congress ultimately rejected the White Paper and instigated a more public forum for the debate at large. In 1998 the US Congress passed the Digital Millennium Copyright Act, ending many months of turbulent negotiations regarding its provisions. Two weeks later, on 28 October, President Clinton signed the Act into law.

The Act is designed to implement the treaties signed in December 1996 at the World Intellectual Property Organization (WIPO) Geneva conference, but also contains additional provisions addressing related matters. As was the case with the 'No Electronic Theft' Act (1997), the bill was originally supported by the software and entertainment industries, and opposed by scientists, librarians and academics.

It would not be hyperbolic to characterize the two opposing sides of the Digital Millenium Act as David and Goliath. Supporters of the Act's proposals included the Creative Incentive Coalition, a powerful trade group consisting of the world's media and software leaders, for example Time Warner, Viacom and News Corporation. As mentioned earlier, the financial stakes they have in seeing copyright protected on the Internet are staggering and this fact is well known to Washington, which helps explain the ironic situation the *Economist* magazine (1996) pointed out:

> ... in Jefferson's day, legal copyright protection was young (the first statute was passed in Britain in 1709); and Americans, as Britain's authors endlessly complained, were notorious for pirating other countries' publications. Now that the United States is the world's biggest exporter of intellectual property, its politicians think differently.

By contrast, those contesting the act were a variety of groups, none as longstanding, well-financed, or well-connected to politicians as their opponents. Samuelson (1997: 61) explained the mismatch of foes, pointing out that:

As long as copyright largely regulated industry-to-industry relationships, identifying who owned which set of rights that would need to be cleared before some new commercial exploitation of the work could be undertaken – it made sense for policymaking about copyright to be done by highly trained technicians.

In other words, previous copyright legislation largely ignored individual users, and thus they have never had to come together to represent their interests. However, at this time it is too early to judge how regulations in

---

The general highlights of the Digital Millennium Copyright Act are as follows:

1 Makes it a crime to circumvent anti-piracy measures built into most commercial software.
2 Outlaws the manufacture, sale or distribution of code-cracking devices used to illegally copy software.
3 Does permit the cracking of copyright protection devices, however, to conduct **encryption** research, assess product interoperability and test computer security systems.
4 Provides exemptions from anti-circumvention provisions for non-profit libraries, archives and educational institutions under certain circumstances.
5 In general, limits Internet Service Providers from copyright infringement liability for simply transmitting information over the Internet.
6 Service providers, however, are expected to remove material from users' Web sites that appears to constitute copyright infringement.
7 Limits liability of non-profit institutions of higher education – when they serve as Internet Service Providers and under certain circumstances – for copyright infringement by faculty members or graduate students.
8 Requires that **Webcasters** pay licensing fees to record companies.
9 Requires that the Register of Copyrights, after consultation with relevant parties, submit to Congress recommendations regarding how to promote distance education through digital technologies while 'maintaining an appropriate balance between the rights of copyright owners and the needs of users'.
10 States explicitly that '[n]othing in this section shall affect rights, remedies, limitations, or defenses to copyright infringement, including fair use . . .'

the Act will affect the private, non-commercial activities of users, and to what extent it will redraw the public/private distinction in copyright law.

Opponents of the Act include the Internet community at large, as represented by, for example the Digital Future Coalition. The DFC is a twenty-seven-member group founded in 1995. Members include 'netizen' groups such as the Electronic Frontier Foundation and the Electronic Privacy Information Centre; educational groups, such as the National Education Association; various library associations; as well as the Computer and Communications Industry Association, 'representing a broad cross-section of the industry, including equipment manufacturers, software developers, telecommunications and online service providers, resellers, systems integrators, third-party vendors and other related business ventures'.

THE WORLD INTELLECTUAL PROPERTY ORGANIZATION

The White Paper and Digital Millenium Copyright Act recommendations have been the basis of negotiations at WIPO's conferences to consider possible treaties to bring copyright into the digital age. The two relevant to this discussion are the Digital Treaty, which aimed to adopt an international treaty to address copyright on the Internet, and the Database Treaty, which was forwarded by the European Union and supported by the United States. Although both the Digital and the Database Treaties generated much debate, the latter was by far the most controversial and holds the most import for framing the discourse on the Internet.

The treaty sought nothing less than to create a whole new category of intellectual property, just for the protection of databases, and without any clearly defined fair use exemptions. Moreover, as the DFC argues, whereas databases must have required at least a minimal amount of creativity to be produced under copyright, no originality or creativity would be required to receive the new *sui generis* form of protection. In other words a collection of addresses, or a listing of credit ratings could conceivably be eligible for this protection.

In their open letter to the WIPO Delegates, a coalition of treaty-detractors, including Ralph Nader's Consumer Project on Technology, pointed out that the Database Treaty would give sporting leagues the right to licence box scores, give stock exchanges permanent 'ownership' of financial data and define the practice of creating abstracts of scientific journals or Web pages (as **search engines** do), as infringements of database extraction rights.

The most noteworthy may well have been that the importance of fair use and other balancing principles was recognized. The preamble to the WIPO Copyright Treaty talks about, 'the need to maintain a balance between the rights of authors and the larger public interests, particularly education, research, and access to information'. In the next step of the WIPO process, the focus shifts to national legislatures. Thirty countries must ratify each WIPO treaty before it comes into effect. Upon ratification at WIPO, countries will then have to bring their national copyright laws in accordance with the international treaties.

COPYRIGHT PROTECTION TECHNOLOGY

Concurrent with legislative attempts to protect copyright, are the determined attempts to solve what the law may not be able to. Enormous sums of research money are being poured into the development of technological means of protecting digital works against unauthorized use. Such technological means include: digital envelopes, encrypted signal streams, software metering schemes, digital watermarks and copyright management information affixed to digital copies of work.

The current favourite is digital-rights management technology. Digital-rights management systems can embed code that provides proof of ownership and copy protection. The systems can detect when alterations are made, track the movement of content through serial numbers, and metre content so the appropriate royalties can be paid to the information provider.

In an illustration of how technological solutions to copyright holders' concerns may actually extend their advantages, is the natural synergy of digital rights management systems and micropayment systems. Micropayment systems are designed for high-volume, low-value transactions, with charges ranging from several cents per transaction to several dollars. Beyond the new technological solutions to combat copyright infringement on the Internet, is existing technology, which could be pressed into service. For example the indexing and abstracting tools, such as search engines, can be used to identify unauthorized use of works.

As the reach of the Internet increases, along with the volume of its information, and the role it plays in people's daily lives, the efforts to control it are intensified. Copyright holders have an ambivalent relationship to this phenomenon. On the one hand the prospect of a giant network of information in which their investments reap no reward is terrifying. Yet some among them also realize that the technology of the Internet may present them with an opportunity to extend their reach and take on new rights.

Opponents to legislation argue for a different approach. They advocate resisting the urge to jump in and regulate when conditions are changing so quickly, holding it is better to wait and see how the Internet develops, rather than straightjacketing it so that it fits into a copyright mould. Indeed, this would be in keeping with the organic nature of the Internet's development, which was not constrained by bureaucratic imperatives of centralization and control.

Barlow even goes so far as to say we should declare, 'a moratorium on

litigation, legislation, and international treaties in this area', arguing persua-
sively that, 'Ideally, laws ratify already developed social consensus', and that
cyberspace has not existed long enough for there to have evolved 'a social
contract which conforms to the strange new conditions of that world.' He
adamantly asserts that, 'Intellectual property law cannot be patched, retro-
fitted, or expanded to contain digitized expression . . . We need to develop
an entirely new set of methods as befits this entirely new set of circumstances' (Barlow 1993). However, the underlying principle of all legal
changes to copyright must address the vital question of how to balance the
interests of copyright holders with those of the public, especially given how
the technology of the Internet does not fit into traditional copyright concepts of private and public.

The debate over the future of copyright on the Internet is intensified
when we keep in mind the boundary-indifferent nature of information. Not
only is there the problem of digital technology rendering irrelevant the legal
jurisdictions of the physical world, there is also the monumental problem of
how to harmonize different nations' copyright traditions given their cultural, political, social and economic differences.

For those of us interested in the evolution of the discourse about the
Web, some important observations about the copyright battle can be
drawn. Underlying the 'copyright maximalists' position are some fundamental moves to discourage the Web from performing according to the full
range of its technical abilities, more specifically by realizing its truly innovative nature as a multidistributed public medium. They want to desensitize
people to the properties of the Web that position people as producers of
information, and not just consumers of it. It is just as technically easy to
create a message as to consume one in digital networked environments. Of
course for those who have a vested interest in us continuing our roles as
consumers this ability to communicate our understanding of the world to
the world is terribly disconcerting.

One simple way to keep people positioned as audience, and to enhance
the perception of value of copyrighted material is to disparage the existing
material on the Web. The NII attempted to characterize the Web as an
empty medium awaiting worthwhile content. The mass media, for example,
frequently runs stories about pornography on the Web. To the contrary,
there is a great deal of valuable content on the Web, and, it can be argued,
its value is due to its non-commercial nature. The danger of a Web with
more commercialized content is that this content will 'drown out' the
voices who inhabit it now, and it is these voices – real live people unaffili-
ated with any corporation, as well as non-profit organizations, public institutions and interest groups – who have made the Web a viable alternative to
the conventional, institutionally-derived world-view found in the mass
media outside it. In short, the Internet represents the public, at a time when
the public desperately needs to be represented. Under seige by a conservat-

ive ethos pervading governments and markets, the public has seen its interests squashed by private, that is to say commercial entities, or their representatives (i.e. governments).

As Godwin (1997a: 12) reminds us:

> The greatest interest at stake ... is the interest a free and open society has in ensuring that everyone can learn the facts, regardless of their economic background. We should regard our nation's investment in the knowledge of its citizens, and in their ability to participate knowledgeably in an open society, as the highest and most precious intellectual property we can ever protect.

The debate over copyright on the Internet represents an historical window of opportunity for the public to assert itself. With the great institutional fallout over this question, while everything is in flux, the time is ripe for old notions and institutions to be re-examined and re-evaluated, and then to be retooled to better serve people. As the 'givens' of copyright are being questioned during this debate of its role in cyberspace, what seemed rigid and intractable will hopefully prove to be responsive to the public after all. Technology will not in itself create a new world, but the upheavals that attend its introduction and evolution can give us a chance to remake parts of our current world.

In his most recent book, *The Future of Ideas* (2001), Lessig makes a convincing case that the health of the Internet and the tech sector in general is being choked off by increasingly successful efforts to erect proprietary bottlenecks that prevent competition. The most obvious example is Microsoft's Windows operating system, which remains the subject of federal antitrust litigation. But there are many other similar, although less well-publicized, cases that could prove equally worrisome over time.

Lessig says the solution can be found in the age-old idea of the commons – that is, the notion that society and the economy are better off when certain resources are protected and made freely available. Public streets, for example, provide accessible places where businesses can set up shop and where goods can be transported. Likewise, laws that prevented phone companies from discriminating between voice and data traffic allowed free use of those lines for other purposes, which in turn helped create the Internet.

CONTENT REGULATION

The entertainment industry is often blamed for the erosion of decency in society because of its insistence on providing programming and advertising messages filled with sexual messages and 'immoral' themes. Changing moral values and the rise of the Web combined to make obscenity more pervasive and easier for children to access. From a legal perspective, defining obscene material is problematic and often inconsistent. Moral issues quickly turn into 'moral panics' framed by politicians, religious leaders and community spokespersons. Disagreements about the extent of obscenity and pornography on the Web and certainly about what to do about it gains much media attention and often polarizes public opinion.

One can argue that when pornographers discovered the Web, politicians were forced to react. In the US, V-chip legislation was passed as part of the 1996 Telecommunications Act. The V-chip, a programmable circuit built into new televisions was designed to help parents control the amount of violence, sex and language that their children could watch. That the technology did not work well and was plagued by problems did not go unnoticed. The US government's attempt to regulate obscenity and pornography on the Web was important as it marked a turning point of sorts in the regulation of electronic media in the United States (Samoriski 2002: 265). Arguments were heard and choices were made, and with the passing of the Communications Decency Act (CDA) and its successor, the Child Online Protection Act (COPA), the US Congress envisioned a less liberal vision of the future.

FREE SPEECH VS CHILD PROTECTION

Key points in the conflict:

1996   US Congress passes the Telecommunications Act, which includes a clause on V-chip technology

1996   US Congress passes the Communications Decency Act, which makes it a crime to send obscene or indecent messages over the Internet to anyone under 18.

1997   US Supreme Court strikes down the Act, calling it too vague and broad.

1998   US Congress passes the Child Online Protection Act. The law targets 'material that is harmful to minors' and applies only to World Wide Web sites, not **e-mail** or chat rooms. It also covers only communications used for 'commercial purposes' and lowers the age of the children protected to under 17. The American Civil Liberties Union and online publishers challenge the law, saying it violates free speech rights.

2000   US appeals court strikes down the act, objecting to its reliance on 'community standards'.

2001   US Supreme Court rules that using community standards to identify 'material that is harmful to minors' does not, by itself, make the statute too broad for First Amendment purposes.

Source: Biskupic 2002

The US courts subsequently rejected government efforts to impose content regulation on the entire Internet, a decision that will have long-term effects on freedom of expression well into the future. They argued that the law would have also restricted freedom of expression on the Internet by limiting what everyone could and could not send and receive. The issue became a rallying point for free speech on the Internet supported by an alliance of the media industry, library interest groups and civil liberty groups. While the last word on the issue has not been said it is important to see how the Internet will finally be conceptualized by law – as a print medium, broadcast outlet or common carrier (Samoriski 2002: 280) and what that will mean for the future of cyberspace.

SUMMARY

It can be noted that the issues surrounding the Internet and copyright tend to focus on digital intellectual property and derive much of their complexity from the varied nature of the stakeholders and their wide range of concerns. The broad classification of interest groups can be delineated as, the creators of intellectual property, distributors, schools and libraries, the research community and the general public. The needs and desires of the different stakeholders sometimes coincide but often are in conflict.

There is no question that there has been a dramatic change in the way governments regulate in the era of the Web. As we have detailed earlier in our overview of policy documents, regulation of the Internet was about government as a stimulator of the new information economy, and not so much as a guarantor of a public ethos.

Contrary to past forms of regulation in media and telecommunications, the Web has been less about controlling corporations and more about facilitating their expansion. Thus we have seen that many countries aggressively pursued policies designed to ensure their place in the new information economy. Public access, while very much part of the rhetoric of all of the policy documents, was in fact a hoped for secondary byproduct of economic stimulation.

The form of regulation generally promoted internationally has fostered the notion of the **loose Web**: regulation has not been able to totally determine the Web's constitution. What regulation has promoted is an Internet that can be thought of as both open and closed. From the standpoint of the economy and business, the Web remains a territory for consolidation of economic interests; from the standpoint of the user it is still a contested space where commercial ends often chafe against the desires of a less-defined public. We will see how this difference of Web perceptions plays out in the field of entertainment where unregulatibility is a major issue for the music industry. The loose Web is both these competing perceptions of its future and the reality that its digital nature makes it slip through the nets of past forms of regulation.

Chapter 8

THE WEB OF INFORMATIONAL NEWS

The archdeacon contemplated the gigantic cathedral for a time in silence, then he sighed and stretched out his right hand towards the printed book lying open on his table and his left hand towards Notre-Dame, and he looked sadly from the book to the church. 'Alas, this will kill that'.

(Victor Hugo, Notre Dame de Paris)

IN THIS FAMOUS passage, the French writer Victor Hugo observed that the printed book rose to replace the cathedral and the church as the conveyor of important ideas in the fifteenth century. Will the **Internet** and new forms of **digital** news delivery and the related myriad of online discussion forums develop to replace the current news media? There is no doubt that the answer to this question is visible in some of the current changes in how people get their news and information. The Web is clearly already a major source for how people become informed and all the major news entities have established a presence on the Web. How people use the Web, however, fundamentally challenges some of the basic premises around the generation, distribution and reception of news. In this chapter, we argue that the Web has led to a shift in how we recontextualize news around a much larger search for information. It is important to comprehend the effect of this shift via the Web and the Internet on the organization of contemporary society.

NEWS AND THE WEB

Most people read the newspaper, watch television news, and listen to radio newscasts to gain public knowledge necessary to participate within their local, national and global communities (Schudson 1995). However while the quantity of news has increased, the time available to use this news has not. As such, news seeking behaviour satisfies different task requirements at different times.

We can define news traditionally as information about recent events of general interest, especially as reported by newspapers, magazines, radio or television. Digital news is the integration of such news into a **multimedia** presentation delivered over the Internet. Digital news is different in three fundamental ways: its relative short lifespan, its immediacy, and the capacity to link to other sources. The amount of raw or source **data** from which stories are selected is enormous and much of it is later archived. Although the **bandwidth** to deliver digital news to large numbers of people is an issue today it is predicted that soon the problem will be selecting the right news stories from an enormous flood of information in order to deliver personalized news. The archiving of several terabytes of news daily and retrieval from those archives present considerable challenges both for producer and **user**.

The development of digital news represents a major shift in the infrastructure, logistics and ethos of the traditional news (newspaper, television, radio) delivery services. In contrast to the current model of broadcasting news by the delivery of a discrete product (a paper or news broadcast), digital news can be characterized by the narrowcast delivery of **interactive** digital items of various media integrated into a single multimedia presentation. In discussing digital news systems, we must understand what people expect to gain from getting the news and how they accept new forms of news.

In the field of the media, the **convergence** of different equipment and **network** technologies and of different industries has, among others, given rise to various new media forms such as interactive television, video on demand and interactive teletext. In recent years, some of these forms have been made available to the public. The question which arises with respect to this technology push, is to what extent the consumer is going to use such new forms. The success of new forms of news delivery – and thus of organizations which bring these new forms – depends on the answer to that question.

The Web emphasizes some new forms of delivery: new forms in the field of news. These forms are referred to as 'interactive news programmes' and can be described as those forms of digital news delivery by which an individual consumer is given the ability to influence certain news programmes to such an extent that reception on an individual basis becomes possible, i.e. at the chosen time, with the chosen content and/or in the form chosen by the consumer.

THE USE OF NEWS

To be able to understand and determine to what extent people will use interactive news in the future, it is useful to study the question why and how the public makes use of the news. With regard to the motivations people have to use the news, Wenner (1985) provides important clues. He refers to Cutler and Danowski who distinguish content gratifications and process gratifications. This distinction indicates that there are gratifications that stem from the use of media messages for their direct, intrinsic value to the receiver and gratifications that originate from the use of messages for extrinsic values that are not related to content characteristics (Cutler and Danowski 1985). Rubin (1983, 1984) mentions another, but somewhat similar difference: instrumental versus ritualized media use. Instrumental use is intentional and reflects a selective exposure to specific media content. Ritualized use is more related to the medium, instead of media content, and is associated with habit, pastime and companionship reasons and a greater exposure to and affinity with the medium. Rubin and Perse (1987) relate audience activity to motives and attitudes towards news viewing. They find that instrumental motives are related to audience intentionality, selectivity and involvement with news. Ritualized motives are related to nonselective exposure and coviewing distractions. Instrumental and ritualized motives are sometimes linked to parasocial interaction: the interpersonal involvement of the media user with what he or she consumes, for example with television newscasters (Williams, Rice and Rogers 1988).

When these concepts are regarded in the light of the Web, it becomes obvious that the relation between needs or motives for media use on the one hand and actual media use on the other hand is essential. Especially in the case of an interactive medium, which requires a certain activity and selectivity from the user, motives for media use and news consumption seem very important.

The basis of the media selection process is formed by needs, goals and/or motivations which lead to the selection and use of media. After that, the choice is evaluated and possible feedback is obtained. This process takes place within a certain context. Demographic and psychological variables, attitudes towards news and habits and experience with respect to the use of media all exert an influence upon this process.

If people choose and therefore use interactive, digital news sites, it can be assumed that they find that such forms of new media offer added value in comparison with existing media. Such interactive news sites must offer certain advantages which correspond to peoples' (conscious or unconscious) motives, needs or goals. These needs or goals must be important enough to motivate people to fulfil them.

APPROACHES TO THE DELIVERY OF DIGITAL NEWS

There are several approaches to the delivery of news digitally. These include online access to newspaper **databases**, browsing the **World Wide Web**, newsgroups, and digital news systems which deliver news to the reader.

News databases

A distinction must be made between the task the user is performing when accessing newspaper databases and when viewing digital news. To access a newspaper database, a user attempts to satisfy an explicit information need and must be able to express this need in terms of a question or a profile description. Newspaper databases with online access are essentially document retrieval systems in which individual news items are treated as discrete units, i.e. news items are treated as documents (Berman 1993). Such systems typically provide retrieval in response to a user query and/or personalized clipping services (selective dissemination of information) based on user profiles. Many newspaper databases have associated **search engines** that range from rudimentary, providing simple string searches, to much more sophisticated systems.

Newspaper databases can perhaps best be explained by a uses and gratification theory of news reading that implies that optimal content and form can be determined once the particular goal is known. So one could strive to predict and select items for individual readers based on their information goals.

Web browsers

Early implementation of digital news systems on the Web provided the user a Netscape-like metaphor, i.e. a single scrolling window with one news item displayed at a time. However, research on news systems has been reflected in more recent Web-based systems, providing the user with a more newspaper-like metaphor. The newspaper metaphor is a newspaper layout of text and photographs, supplemented with television video, integrated into a coherent presentation.

There are several reasons for the newspaper metaphor being preferred by the readers. Newspapers follow a well-recognized format and functionality that is well known to large numbers of users. Readers understand the sectional organization, i.e. national news, sports, entertainment and so on, and have expectations with respect to the contents of such sections. The newspaper format provides excellent scan and browse spaces containing both headings and partial stories so that linking to more data is often not necessary. The juxtaposition of items, particularly with the integration of photos and video clips, makes an interesting and varied information space for the reader. Furthermore, advertisements are an accepted part of the metaphor rather than an added on feature.

One can appreciate that Web **browsers** are an important step towards the development of news delivery facilitators and that the improvements on the current presentation capabilities of Web browsers could be made that would better accommodate news delivery, particularly with the recent availability of such environments as **Java** and Flash. For example, item selection could be done by negotiations amongst the reader, software agents, and editors, and the physical layout of presentation of the news items could be determined by client software. In fact, there has been a marked movement away from a single story per screen presentation towards a newspaper-like metaphor recently.

A special case of Web sites as news **servers** are newspapers that provide single site current and archival news data, such as *San José Mercury*, and others. The data in these sites are by-products of the production of the newspaper and provide an alternative to the paper version. The CNN.COM site while currently 'state of the art' is also best understood as a complement to the TV channel. Online services, such as America OnLine, provide a broad based news service to multiple news sources with some selection and editing activities provided but the onus remains on the reader to assemble appropriate and adequate news coverage.

NEWSGROUPS

In general, the content and structure of data in **Usenet newsgroups** differ substantially from the content and structure of current event news. Newsgroups offer a narrow subject focus rather than broad coverage of events and are usually defined by an area of interest, such as operating systems, graphics, cultural groups, journalism or activity. The items available in a newsgroup are posted by the readers (i.e. subscribers) of that newsgroup. Authorship and readership are related activities and the role of editor, if present at all, is reduced to that of a moderator. In a newspaper, on the other hand, there is a clear separation of roles: authors create news items, editors select a set of those items, and readers read the news.

The design of newsgroups present some features that need to be considered for inclusion in the design of digital news delivery systems. In particular, newsgroups allow multiple threaded 'conversations' to occur simultaneously. The postings to individual newsgroups are threaded (i.e. arranged in a hierarchical fashion) for each open conversation. Responses, and responses to responses, are kept together and kept in the correct sequence. This concept of threaded topics is relevant to reading the news, as readers often follow events from day to day. Even within a single day's edition of the news, threads occur from article to article, and from article to editorial or letter to the editor.

Personalized news

In 1996 **push technology** made a breakthrough and became the latest of buzzwords in an ever accelerating digital lexicon. These digital news systems are designed to work over the Internet, thus making it possible to deliver personalized 'editions' of the news. Systems like *Pointcast* use retrieved data from a single site as the basis of a dynamic screen saver in which the text, photographs, and graphics are presented in a simple broadsheet format. Push based technology is based on blunt user profiles. The creation of fine-grained personalized editions is very difficult and the object of much research. Allen (1990) attempted to develop user models for reading news and found that the task involved makes it very difficult to do. He found that it was virtually impossible to predict what items a reader will read in today's news, based on a history of the items a reader has read over the previous few days.

Personalized filters remove data from a data stream that satisfy the criterion of a personal profile (Foltz and Dumais 1992). There is always a fear that a very narrowly defined user profile will defeat the function of news by filtering out all news except that identified by the profile, i.e. the reader will be exposed to no new items of potential interest, and the reader may not receive the necessary information to participate fully in the local, national and international community. This is a problem indeed when information technology is touted as a tool for increased information, knowledge and democracy.

In Table 8.1, the features of the various approaches to the digital delivery of news are summarized.

The differences between traditional news delivery and digital delivery have been summarized by Watters *et al.* (1998: 140) in the following issues; first, the content will be an integrated collection of multimedia multi-source news items; second, the provider will have less control in the packaging and delivery of electronic information; third, the reader will have more control in the packaging and delivery of the information; fourth, the selection, classification, and prioritization functions of the editing activity may be supplemented by third parties who have familiarity with a variety of content sources for a subscriber fee or advertising revenue; fifth, the layout will be dependent on the display facilities (software and hardware) provided by the reader site; sixth, delivery will be through a third party (the telephone and/or cable company).

If the newspaper publishers, radio and television news broadcasters hope to capitalize on their current areas of expertise as news packagers in an effort to become competitive in this rapidly evolving environment they will have

Table 8.1 Features of approaches to digital news delivery

Feature	News database	WWW browser	Newsgroup	Personalized news
Editor	no	yes	no	yes
Topic breadth	query-based	wide	narrow	wide
Browse/task	task	browse	task	browse
Presentation categories	no	by section	by thread	by section
Entire/partial document	entire	entire	entire	choice
Columns	single	single	single	choice
Media types	multimedia	multimedia	text	multimedia
Two-way communication	none	none	lots	some
Personal filtering	no	no	no	yes
Advertisements	no	some	no	choice

Source: Adapted from Watters *et al.* 1998

to expand their functional territory by providing a value-added layer in the editorial and layout activities. To secure these objectives, the news packager must have access to a wide variety of news sources, databases, **authoring** tools, editing facilities and subsystems that will generate interactive customized news packages for digital delivery.

Lieb (1998) explains that 'layering' is a structure in which a top layer provides the traditional who, what, when, where and why. The next layer offers a historical context. Additional layers provide analysis, expert commentary, and reader discussion and feedback. These tools will need to include advanced facilities that support the types of links and cross-references currently seen in experimental cutting edge digital multimedia news involving an integration of archival data, current data and often dynamic or real-time data. That is, news should include references to previous items, now archived, to other related items residing in digital libraries, to other current news items, and when relevant, to live feeds of current events. In addition to semantic or content linkages, news items have temporal linkages that are very important and that change dynamically. For example, reports are often given before events occur, during events and after events.

DIGITAL NEWS SYSTEMS SCENARIO

Anticipating the capabilities of tomorrow's **broadband** delivery technology, numerous efforts are being made at building digital news delivery platforms that exploit the technology and serve the news related information needs of readers, journalists and advertisers. These advanced functionalities according to Watters *et al.* (1998: 144) include: the generation of personal editions with customized news content; the integration of news media, such as video clips, live television and radio newscasts, photographs, news text, full support documents; hyperlinks based on media versions, timelines, structure and content; interactive advertisements and advertisements targeted to specific market groups; two-way interaction, such as letters to the editor, requests for supplemental documentation; and dynamic access to rapidly changing data, such as that now available at specific Web sites for sports, financial data and the weather. Dynamic assembly and presentation allows readers to specify the 'look and feel' of the news display format. The broadsheet or newspaper format seems to support activities of browsing or skimming while the single document display may be more suitable to satisfying an articulated information task.

THE ROLE OF INFORMATIONAL NEWS

News has generally been seen as an essential element in democracies for its role in informing the citizenry. As the fourth estate, news and journalism are ways of checking the power of ruling elites with a conveyance to the populace of important and necessary information in order to lead to effective decision-making. Over the last two hundred years, as much as news has been a part of the democratic process, it has also developed into an industry wedded to capitalism. Newspapers, television networks, and radio are all primary sources for the production of news; they are also very large media corporations behind entities such as the New York Times, CNN (AOL-Time Warner), Fox News (News Corporation). As media corporations, their goal is to maximize their profits and this has been primarily done through securing their audience of readers, listeners or viewers for advertisements. Thus these various media/news entities were instrumental in the development of consumer culture as they advertised and helped foster markets for the mass-produced goods and services of consumer capitalism. Although, public corporations generated television news in many countries, the overall production of news has operated primarily within this kind of negotiated terrain between producing audiences and informing the public.

Within this system of production, news has become patterned to the point where we can identify it as a genre. It looks for the sensational or as Walter Lippman expressed it, 'news is not a mirror of social conditions, but a report of an aspect that has *obtruded* itself' (Lippman 1922: 216). Stuart Hall indicated that news in its study of the obtrusion actually reinforced the normal and the 'consensus' of what was the real world (Hall 1973). Although there may be subgenres of news such as television news, broadsheet and tabloid newspapers, current affairs programmes and tabloid television, the concept of news is very similar in traditional media: journalists collect information and build stories that are hierarchized into an overall determination of news value that is connected to the core audience's perceived interests. It is a paternalistic system of journalist and editorial decision-making that makes news relatively digestible and comprehensible for the public.

Media critics like Christopher Lasch have established a theoretical foundation which makes it possible to critique the news media and challenge the current practice of this media. Lasch (1995: 81) argues that; 'what democracy requires is public debate, and not information. Of course, it needs information, too, but the kind of information it needs can be generated only by vigorous popular debate'.

Applying his critique to the press, Lasch writes; 'From these considerations it follows the job of the press is to encourage debate, not to supply the public with information. But as things now stand the press generates information in abundance, and nobody pays any attention' (Ibid: 81).

The genre of news that has developed from this system no longer encompasses the kinds of news that have emerged and are emerging on the Web. In order to isolate on this change, it is useful to differentiate news from what is best described as **informational news**. Informational news identifies the different modalities of information retrieval and search on the Web. Informational news also identifies the kinds of information exchange that occur through a variety of dimensions from news sites to newsgroups, from **e-mail** to chatrooms, from institutional sites to alternative media sites, from search engines to resource centre sites and portals. The informational component of our term underlines the shift that the Web has produced towards much more raw and less edited versions of phenomena and events rubbing shoulders with much more 'journalistically' constructed stories of phenomena and events. As we developed in Chapter 2, one useful definition of information is the raw material for knowledge. What the Web provides is a larger informational news dimension of information that is much more loosely connected to the journalistic and media corporatized constitution of 'news' that had developed primarily over the previous two centuries. The informational component also underlines that this style of news is aligned with and services what Castells called the 'informational society'. Informational news intersects with the emergence of new networks of connection and community as much as it aligns with the needs of information movement transnationally and instantaneously. There are several dimensions to informational news that we need to investigate in order to understand the flows of information and news on the Web and how it differs from the exigencies of traditional news. What follows is an exploration of each of these dimensions.

The transformation of the reader/viewer/listener into the researcher

When it comes to news, the Web somewhat challenges our traditional model of communication composed of source-medium-audience. The Web offers increased choices of sources such as the technology itself, individuals, and other users, and interactivity, which can be seen as a form of source. Technology as a source can be so powerful that human perceptions of content alter depending on the medium of delivery (Kaye and Medoff 1999). In a media world that traditionally separates content and source, features of the Web blur that distinction. Thus it is often argued that 'the media technology is the source' (Sundar and Nass 1996). It is with this in mind that James Fallows (1997: 11), executive editor, *US News and World Report* states that, 'by definition, getting involved in the Internet requires some active volition on the part of the user. You cannot be a passive Internet user the same way as you can be a passive receiver of TV news'.

Despite the many efforts to provide channels for viewing current events and reading articles by the major **Internet Service Providers** and traditional news organizations, users are typically drawn to reconstructing their news from available sources. The Web presents itself as a repository of information that can be retrieved. It is up to the user to find the information via the many search engines that are available. News and information thus blend somewhat for the user as his/her activities can be likened to the traditional role of the researcher. Search engines, such as Google which indexes over 2 billion Web pages, have become regular inhabitants as the most popular sites used by Web users. According to Jupiter Media Metrix Google had 33 million users for the month of March 2002 and was the sixth most popular site on the entire Web (Graham 2002: 4D). This level of use implies that information retrieval is central to the Web experience and has shifted the user's relationship to news delivery. An actual article in an online version of a major newspaper represents one source among many on a particular issue and the user as researcher is moving among many possible sources as they research a given topic. Because the Web not only has currency in the provision of information but also the capacity for archives and storage, the search for information by a user can also move more freely backwards in time. The Web makes searching for information similar to searching through a large interconnected and temporally open database of material.

A new comfortability with a range of sources

Users as researchers can circumvent the former patterns of gatekeeping and editing that have been part of the generation of traditional news. Informational news implies that the user is more aware of a wider range of sources for their information and successful news-based Web sites work to integrate this wider range into their own sites. For instance, the Web allows for the exploration of corporate and institutional press releases directly from corporate or government Web sites directly, an accessibility to a different style of news for the user than its recasting in television news and newspapers. On a more visceral and everyday level, there are portals and resource centre sites that cater specifically to present alternatives to mainstream press. Instead of an edited collection of alternative press material as the magazine *Utne Reader* has done for decades, alternative media sites such as mediachannel.org provide an avenue for a panoply of national and international online sources as well as a steady diet of counter-interpretation from their own staff. Znet similarly tries to present a differing perspective on the news and interpretation (www.zmag.org). A host of other channels of information are available online.

THE ALTERNATIVES ONLINE: MEDIACHANNEL

Mediachannel.org is a site that resembles the old alternative media sources that presented the social left perspective. As it states in its own mission statement: 'MediaChannel is designed to engage citizens with their media and to attract a broad, general audience'. The difference from the older generation and the Web version of counter-media politics is that this site is constructed in bold colours and interesting graphics and it instantaneously connects you to a directory of over 940 affiliates that provide differentiated news coverage from the mainstream to the periphery of known media outlets. One can engage in FCC debates via the mediageek.org or move around the debates of media ownership via the completed report of the Productivity Commission in Australia. Working as a 'supersite' or portal for other media outlets, the site itself goes beyond the directory by providing commentary on pressing news issues. It critiques the headlines of the daily news from powerful news outlets. Danny Schecter, the founder, weighs in with a Weblog of his interpretation of his own news diet. Debates are regularly featured on such issues as **globalization**, women and the media and public relations. From those vantage points one can be drawn into discussions or pose a question through M-C Net where a search for information is extended through the users of Mediachannel such as one that was visible in May 2002 whose subject line read: 'Looking to contact journalists in Benin, West Africa re the environment'. Mediachannel is a major intervention in the flow of news and is designed to draw active journalists and concerned people into its orbit of connection. To underline its well-connectedness it has had the famous CBS former news anchor Walter Cronkite act as both its endorser and advisor.

Source: www.mediachannel.org

It is important to understand that news and media sites operate as one platform of this new dissemination of information. Newsgroups on specific issues and interests focus information for their users and provide a method for response and debate. **Weblogs** by individuals provide a further path to understand how daily events may be interpreted and become particularly significant and important Web sites in times of crisis and catastrophic events such as the 11 September 2001 attacks on New York and Washington. Photojournals and video images by individuals, not news organizations, have provided tremendous insights for users to understand how major events have affected people close to the event, unmediated by the **gatekeeping** structures of contemporary television networks and newsmagazines.

Users have become adept at reading and interpreting these different registers of news and information. Many go beyond the reception of this information and join discussions and commentaries that are connected to these various Web sites. Informational news allows for these quite different registers of news and information sources, from the personal to the alternative, from the corporate press release to major network outlet, from self-made analyst to the academic article to become the wider resource base

11 SEPTEMBER

Journalists recognize that more of the information in which the public is interested, is starting to come from people other than professional journalists. In an article about the 1995 Oklahoma Federal building explosion, Sandberg writes (1995: 6) that; 'in times of crisis, the Internet has become the medium of choice for users to learn more about breaking news, often faster than many news organizations can deliver it'. This was even more apparent during the terrorist attacks of 11 September 2001 on the World Trade Center and the Pentagon. People curious and concerned about relatives and others present on the scene turned to the Web to find out timely information about survivors and to discuss the questions raised by the event. Soon after the explosions, it was reported and discussed live on **IRC** and in newsgroups on Usenet such as alt.current-events, sept11firstperson and elsewhere on-line. Resources on the Web included photographs of the damage, official White House statements, eyewitness accounts and updated reports from local news providers. Several **ISP**s and other news services provided links to news agency reports and graphics. The Web helped facilitate a range and a depth of comment and information that no single news provider or medium could match. A pattern that can be noted is that many logged onto the Internet to get news from first-hand observers as a complement to turning on the TV to CNN or comparable news sources.

from which the user invested in an issue can reconstruct the debate and potentially provide a further contribution for others to build their own opinions.

Journalists have written about public criticism of the news media. Volovic (1995: 115) in discussing online encounters, recognizes some of the advantages inherent in the new online form of criticism. Unlike old criticism, the new type 'fosters dialogue between reporters and readers'. He observes how this dialogue 'can subject reporters to interrogations by experts that undermine journalists' claim to speak with authority'. Changes are taking place in the field of journalism, and these changes will have a profound effect on how we view the world and form opinions.

The will to hierarchize

The wide range of news sources does not necessarily mean that all users are drawn to the variety. Like reading the same morning newspaper, users enjoy the familiarity of how their news is presented precisely because the time-consuming process of searching is eliminated. Users begin to evaluate their Web sources and hierarchize their connection to these sources by establishing links to their homepages or even establishing a news portal as their home page for browsing. In a similar manner, media corporations attempt to differentiate their content from the myriad of pretenders to online delivery of news by establishing features, graphics, and software that cannot be easily replicated by non-commercial Web sites. Their news sites are professionally designed and their content is written by professional journalists. Moreover their branding of their content is foregrounded: we are very aware that we are on the *New York Times* site because the distinctive masthead is replicated for the online version. The recognizable news branding is the method that media companies that have established their credibility through newspapers and television attempt to ensure their status online. These efforts towards legitimacy of sources become even stronger markers in the online world where evaluating the verity of information is difficult and clear hierarchies become important for users. In addition, Web sites such as CNN offer themselves as transforming appendices to their televisual flagship and work to strengthen the currency and depth of their information provision (CNN.com). Despite the plenitude of news and information sources, one can see this will to hierarchize by both established media institutions and users looking for solid legitimacy in the sea of informational news.

The fluidity of media forms

What is fascinating about the Web's informational news is that it is often no longer attached to one medium of delivery. Web news is not divided among radio, television and print. On the Web, they are integrated into an interesting mixture of media forms and the most commercially powerful sites are often the location for the most elaborate interplay of cultural forms. Text and photo-images form the backbone of news sites because they require the least download times. Nevertheless, MSNBC.com, for example, provides videostreaming that connects to their televised content alongside an association with the online magazine version of *Newsweek*. This converged quality of commercial news sites puts sites that are media-specific at a distinct disadvantage. Web sites for news organizations imbricate a form of cross-media enterprise that in many countries could be seen as contravening regulations and laws. On the Web, the cross of media forms has become the norm and has transformed into an interplay among text, image, sound and hyperlinks to a host of other mulitmedia sites and pages.

THE *NEW YORK TIMES* ADAPTS

The *New York Times* has established various levels of service with its Web resources. Subscribers of the hard copy newspaper have access to a complete facsimile of the paper. For the rest of Web users, The *New York Times* is heavily linked into portals such as Yahoo! where individual top stories are listed for possible links to a selected listing of stories. In a manner similar to other elite papers such as the *Wall Street Journal*, the *New York Times* allows for greater interconnection for its subscribers. Paid users thus can 'track' news subject areas and have them posted to their e-mail address. Moreover they can download the stories with greater ease for up to a week after a story has appeared online or in printed form. There is the possibility to customize your mobile phone for delivery of key news and weather. What one finds as a user is that there is decidedly more interactivity and possible ways of using the content of the paper with its Web home. Indeed, subscribers have a way to contact online to complain about their hardcopy delivery! Progressively newspapers are standardizing their online delivery as part of the package of informational news that they provide to subscribers. Users likewise move between the portability of the hardcopy and the accessibility for storage and manipulation of the online version as well as its complete integration into the informational flow of the work environment of many professionals. Although online only subscriptions failed for *USA Today*, but have succeeded marginally for the *Wall Street Journal*, the *New York Times* hybrid-but-fundamentally-integrated strategy has become the standard for newspapers.

Source: http://www.nytimes.com/

Electronically delivered news has the advantage of instant delivery, reporting current events as they happen. In today's evercrowded media-scape, radio and television channels often interrupt regularly scheduled programmes with important news bulletins. The development of twenty-four hour radio and television news networks has improved access to the most up-to-date news, but audiences still must wait for a particular story of interest to air. The Web has been responsible for facilitating a new type of news distribution. It has enabled twenty-four hour a day news that can be delivered directly to computers, anywhere, and at anytime. The active user can download the news that is of particular interest, and access an archive of related stories that are readily available as links.

An extension of this cross-media structure is the development of a closer relationship of the media source via the Web to its subscriber/audience. Most news sites offer the possibility of updates and selected headlines sent directly to user's e-mail addresses. Although these efforts at connection are broadcast, because they arrive via e-mail they personalize the production of news in a manner that only business elites have been able to afford in the past through clipping services.

The global/community of interest

Informational news implies fewer boundaries and borders for the dissemination of information. Thus, fans of a particular television programme such as the *X-Files* can find out plots and storylines via informal news and e-mail groups and lists long before the final episodes would have aired in a particular country. In fact, the rapid movement of entertainment information has been a major factor in the coordinated release of films and the **compression** of time in the release of television series internationally.

What this implies is that informational news can produce new kinds of interconnected communities via their Web and Internet connection. The effect on coordinated promotional campaigns is only one transformation that is spawned by the Web's informational news patterns. It has also led to the concerted development of politicized groups that use both the Internet and the Web to inform, connect and coordinate interests beyond geographical boundaries. The anti-**globalization** movement has been particularly successful at linking disparate groups into unified moments of resistance. This technique of using informational news patterns was borne out with surprising effectiveness in Seattle in December 1999 and then repeated in Washington and Melbourne in 2000 and Quebec, Gothenburg, and Genoa in 2001. Much like the Internet is a network of networks, the anti-globalization movement is a community of communities that is a **loose Web** connected through the Internet in its various forms. The surprising politicization and street activism/protest against abstract economic organizations such as the WTO and the World Bank and the capacity to understand the connected and concrete social implications of contemporary capitalism and the **new economy** appeared to traditional news organizations as if it had emerged from nowhere; however, the new flows of informational news sources via the Web explain how new forms of oppositions can develop and prosper through wider rings of interconnection. The very concept of community is being redefined through the use made of informational news possibilities and potentials.

THE CONSTRAINTS OF INFORMATIONAL NEWS

Although these dimensions of informational news indicate a shifted boundary of what constitutes news and thereby imply a new plenitude of news, information and sources, it is important to realize that there are some limitations and problems that informational news generates in contemporary culture. In other words, informational news results in some constraints and its value has to be seen as a mixed blessing. The central problem with informational news is that it often produces exactly the opposite of its apparent potential for plenitude: as a form, it can actually *reduce* the content of what is read and viewed. This reduction in information is generated by some clear Web-based developments about how information is produced for the Web and how people tend to read the news via the Web.

Many users of the Web personalize their homepages with a variety of information sources. As we have seen in our analysis of the Yahoo! Web site in Chapter 5, users can focus on their particular interests and design their homepage to generate headlines that pertain only to those interests. Neither newspapers nor broadcast media news can categorically eliminate stories and thus these older media provide a potentially wider range of news materials from which to draw. As a Web site is personalized, the content can be progressively more and more narrow and so the news elements of the Web no longer serve the objectives of providing a generally informed citizenry and an active public sphere across the diverse domains of a culture if the Web becomes the primary source.

It is a truism of the Web that the lead stories of newspapers when they are converted to the Web are generally shorter in textual content. This brevity is not a necessity of the Web – after all, one of the Web's strengths is its capacity to store materials; rather, it is a result of the perceived and known reality that people will read less text from a computer screen than from a printed page because of the sense of eyestrain that the computer screen produces. Thus, contemporary news sites are organized with less text and a great deal more pictures and links than most newspaper copy. Users tend to surf through the links rather than dwell on detailed textual material on the Web. As Samoriski explains 'online reporters become "linkalists" (McNamara 2000: 31) rather than journalists' (Samoriski 2002: 351).

Similarly, with the effort to produce greater numbers of services that can be accessed through subscribers' mobile phones, content that is designed for both the Web and mobile use is often further reduced to pure headlines, sports scores and little else for ease of access.

Many news organizations today are worried about the possible impact of new interactive forms of news delivery. Some, for example, fear that once people are able to select the news themselves, there will no longer be a need for journalists to select the news for them. It is with this background that it is interesting to note that Steve Case, CEO of America Online (AOL), the worlds largest subscriber-based Internet Service Provider (ISP), claims that AOL does not hire journalists because AOL views itself as a 'news packaging' instead of a 'news gathering' company.

The newspaper business is rapidly changing as newspapers merge and often simplify stories without any local perspective. Reporters are equipped with cameras to take their own pictures, just in time to edit them on their personal computer and send them to the news room – all in an effort to collect news faster and faster, and with as few employees as possible. The increasingly fragmented 24-hours a day news journalism is taking over at the cost of depth and perspective of analysis. Users have to navigate this

FUTURE OF THE PRINTED PRESS

In a report on the future of the printed press commissioned for the European Journalist Centre in Maastricht, the situation is explained as follows:

> Newspapers are created by journalists, who now have to master a new set of tools to be able to make use of the online medium in the most relevant way. On the one hand, the Internet offers new ways of collecting and reporting information, and the integration of Internet access into the newsroom and economisation of the news gathering process will dominate future news production. On the other hand, making use of the medium to publish newspapers also requires a completely new set of skills, one that at this point few journalists have. They have to learn how to organise stories into structures conducive to interactive reading online. They might need to learn about using audio, video, animations, interactive maps, and databases. These narrative techniques and the critical thinking that goes into them appear to be among the most important skills for online journalists to possess.
>
> *Source:* van Dusseldorp, Scullion and Bierhoff 1999: 13

overflow of information production and the capacity to work one's way through the content is often determined by one's education, skill and economic resources. Thus, the increased speed of news journalism can lead to questions about how well it is serving democracy.

The Web's informational news is fostering a breakdown in a public sphere of knowledge and interest that has been generated by the mass media forms of newspapers, radio and television. This mass-mediated public sphere relied on commonality of discourse on a specific cluster of issues to maintain an 'informed' citizenry. The Web's production of personalized informational news cannot operate as a guarantor that the material users access is common. The dispersion of sources can lead to a breakdown in national political understanding among the populace. Moreover, if Web users no longer are connected to local news sources their connection to community political issues can be equally threatened. As much as the Web may have been instrumental in building transnational political movements such as the anti-globalization movement, it has weakened the fibre of many local political movements. It is at least questionable whether informational news patterns serve the local community well.

For a variety of reasons, informational news can lead us to debate its quality of journalism. Because the Web remains more of a promotional structure for most major news organizations and rarely generates income from subscription, news suffers from being subsumed to the exigencies of advertising and promotion to a greater degree than traditional media. Even the efforts by such organizations such as the quality online commentary magazine Salon (salon.com) to pay market rates for stories has not produced a profitable entity. In 2002, Salon shares had dropped from a one-time high of $15 to twelve cents (Gardner 2002) and dissolution rumours of its parent Automatic Media Company have been circulating since 1999. Thus, the content of informational news from the more commercial news Web sites is an overwhelming abundance of advertisements, entertainment information, and links that surround the news. The division between editorial content and promotion is much less clearly defined or refined on the Web.

Receiving news on the Web is often not as convenient or as pleasurable as using traditional media. Old media habits are hard to break. Live television is exciting, radio is current, and a newspaper does have a special feel and mobility about it. Certainly the worst Web news sites offer content that is first written for the traditional version of the medium supporting the Web site, and then repurposed or copied into a Web version. In contrast, on better sites where a news Web site is being continually updated with breaking stories, the Web version is the starting point with the print version rewritten at a later time. The distinction between print and Web-based editorial decisions then becomes increasingly more difficult to discern.

In the best examples the Web is adding new dimensions to the news delivery experience made possible through **hypertext** and its immediacy

METRO

Informational news has established clear formats for the delivery of simpler textual content on the Web; it has also led to a tranformation of the media industries themselves. Television has become more Web-like in its delivery of content. Likewise newspapers have taken on the look of the Web in their content. This organization of content is no more graph-ically represented than by the free transit newspaper *Metro*. *Metro* is the next generation of highly formatted newspapers that has taken the development that *USA Today* began 22 years ago as a satellite deliv-ered national newspaper in the United States to new heights of now international convergence. Although its content is language specific in 15 countries and 23 editions, its new stories are categorically Web-length articles. As its own publicity indicates, the newspaper is not long or difficult to read: '[It] can be read in a 16.7 minute commute'. In its relative short history launching in Stockholm in 1995, it is now the fourth largest newspaper in the world with 10.1 million readers daily. Targeting the reader that is now less attached to the usual daily news-paper, Metro has produced a publication that is comfortable for a new generation weaned on the Web's informational news. It provides a light mix of the international, local, national and entertainment in a paper that actually is stapled together for the convenience of the commuter and to maintain its presence when discarded for others to read. Distrib-uted exclusively at mass transit locations for free in cities with major commuter traffic, the paper has successfully targeted a younger reader-ship than other newspapers and an unusual 50 per cent per cent female readership. Metro represents the best example of the migration of the Web's structure of informational news outside of the online world.

Source: Boston Metro and the Metro International Web site
http://www.metro.lu/

through continuous distribution. The Web has allowed television and radio stations, newspapers and magazines, to go beyond the technical confines of time, space and mode of presentation by creating sites filled with colour graphics, audio and video and hypertext versions of stories complete with extensive links to satisfy the needs of their audience.

CONCLUSION: A QUESTION OF QUALITY

The model of online publishing brings some of the forces of commercial television to all content publishers: the direct drive to attract audiences, the short attention span of readers and the need to produce captivating material. Quality newspapers, with their established tradition of fair and objective reporting, are at the moment forming a necessary counterweight to the more superficial news reporting often brought to us by radio and television. This same quality could be brought to the Internet, from which more and more people will gather their main news intake of the day. Once online, however, newspapers with their trusted brand names can play much more innovative roles than has hitherto been the case. They can be the focus for public debate. They can guide their readers through the overwhelming mass of information that the Web offers, and they can try to regain their importance among a younger audience. For this option to become effective, newspapers need to treat their online versions not merely as an experiment but as a serious part of their publication's business.

Many research questions remain open with respect to the production, presentation, distribution and consumption of news in a digital context. McQuail (1992) identifies several dimensions for evaluating the quality of media contents including, factualness, accuracy, completeness, and readability. Because of the current separation of structure, content, and audience, we adjust our personal requirements on these dimensions by choosing different packagers (newspapers, television or radio channels), each of which presents a set of new items for our consumption. How then can we control these dimensions in our new Web environment where editors and editorial boards may be replaced with personalized search agents? The delivery of personalized news introduces questions that have to be asked with respect to breadth and coverage, bias, similarity and sameness of individual items from different sources and of possibly different media types, and reliability of news coverage.

How can we satisfy the required breadth and depth of news coverage without human editors composing editions? When both structure and content are determined by personalized news agents driven by individual profiles, then we remove the diversity provided by competing deliverers of news: different newspapers, television and radio channels, etc. The selection of items can now be driven by individual queries and personal profiles rather than third party editors. Automatic feedback and adaptive user models may result in more and more tightly constrained user profiles that accurately reflect the immediate interests and interest levels of a given user but no longer provide adequate coverage of real world events. Such news coverage may be self-fulfilling and become more narrow rather than maintaining the breadth required to satisfy news coverage criteria of density, breadth and depth.

How can we recognize levels of bias and accuracy in the news delivered in this new mode? Individual newspapers, television and radio sources gain a reputation for bias and reliability. For example, we have a perception that a report in certain newspapers may be more or less credible. Newspapers and television and radio stations often generate an impression of political balance or imbalance that the consumer uses to weigh or filter information coming from that source.

Certainly, one can hope that digital news will achieve the vision of Burnstein and Kline (1995: 241) to be 'a consumer-oriented service that recreates not the newspaper's content but its historic role online – a town square, citizen resource, community forum and civic glue'. Whether this becomes the case remains to be seen. One prediction that can be made with a fair amount of certainty is that a small number of large conglomerates will dominate the market for mass information. All will be involved in television, newspapers and Web publishing. As media mogul Rupert Murdoch (1999) noted in a speech to NewsCorp shareholders 'News and entertainment is changing its delivery system totally. We have to stay on our toes to make sure Bill Gates doesn't erect a tollgate in every house'. While matters of ownership are important, Edward Herman (1996: 201) reminds us that the Internet and news is no easy mix:

> Some argue that the Internet and the new communication technologies are breaking the corporate stranglehold on journalism and opening an unprecedented era of interactive democratic media. There is no evidence to support this view as regards journalism and mass communication. In fact, one could argue that the new technologies are exacerbating the problem. They permit media firms to shrink staff while achieving greater outputs and they make possible global distribution systems, thus reducing the number of media entities.

McChesney (2000) cuts to the fundamental issue of the nature of online journalism when he states that, 'if the Web fails to produce a higher caliber of journalism and stimulate public understanding and activity, the claim that it is a boon for democracy is severely weakened'.

The Web has been involved in a general shift in the quality of news. We can think of that idea of quality in two basic ways. On one level, the quality of news as it is now reorganized as informational news has questionable value in terms of validity and legitimacy. Although news organizations have tried to reassert clear hierarchies in what constitutes a legitimate news source, users are not totally defined and limited to their output. This new relationship to constructing one's own content through many sources of information on the Web is symptomatic of how the Web has engendered a much more loose structure. Although networks and clear patterns of readership have attached to major commercial news sites, it is equally true that users move beyond these sources. The most authoritative news sites must therefore acknowledge this new tendency and link to wider and wider rings of connection.

On a second level, the quality of news has shifted in terms of modality.

Our term of informational news is very much attached to a DIY (Do It Yourself) relationship to the news. The user then becomes in essence their own editor and selector of news stories as they work within the linked world of Web news. Moreover, informational news makes the user's activities closer to a form of cultural production, particularly if they integrate the other elements of the Internet – from chatgroups and newsgroups and e-mail lists – into their use of the Web.

Finally, news is becoming detached from particular media and the Web has been instrumental in this virtual migration of the content of news. It can now be part of a variety of electronic sources from personal computers, and mobile phones to personal organizers. This reconfiguration of news has challenged the conventions of its locations on broadcast media or in newspapers. Within that challenge is a differing connection to commerce, to promotion, to advertising and to opinion. The Web's development of informational news is producing a dramatic transformation in the way that we conceptualize what actually constitutes news and information in contemporary culture.

Chapter 9

WEB OF ENTERTAINMENT

Music is prophecy. Its styles and economic organization are ahead of the rest of society because it explores, much faster than material reality can, the entire range of possibilities in a given code. It makes audible the new world that will gradually become visible, that will impose itself and regulate the order of things; it is not only the image of things, but the transcending of the everyday, the herald of the future.

(Jacques Attali 1984: 11)

IN THIS CHAPTER we would like to focus attention towards how **digital** technology and the **Internet** are influencing the entertainment industry and more specifically the music industry. The entertainment industry is discovering that the information ecology is a reality in which centralized control is impossible to impose, and as file sharing of sound and moving image becomes a familiar daily activity this decentralized quality of the Web migrates to the whole mediascape.

The future of digital media in many ways coincides with developments in the entertainment industry. It has been well documented by McChesney (1999) that today's media environment is characterized by **globalization**, conglomeration, concentration and hypercommercialism. We are also seeing an important transition period in the media industry. Historically intellectual property produced has been defined by physical boundaries like the movie, video cassette, CD, the book. Now, because of advances in information technology, this physical boundary has been broken. The best example of this transformation is the music industry, where the music, which is the purest digital format, has left the CD, left the physical product and spread rapidly across new technologies and **networks** and in different ways found its way back to consumers. Specific digital technologies such as MP3 and Napster have facilitated this process.

Due to these developments media companies will need to embrace new technologies much faster and much more aggressively than they have in the past. For every new technology out there, there should be, in a short span of time, a business model coming along to enhance and take advantage of developments. Today we see new technologies and high consumer demand and use of these new technologies. The problem is that currently there are not proper business models in place, where the value of the intellectual property being produced is maintained.

McChesney (2000: 26) argues that the traditional media giants enjoy several distinct advantages over new media firms when it comes to developing new business models. First, they can plug existing digital programming directly onto the Web at little extra cost. Second, they can generate an audience based upon their existing 'brand name' by promoting their Web sites incessantly through their traditional media outlets. Third, the media giants are better positioned to acquire the major portion of Web based advertising. Fourth, using their 'brands' they can negotiate prime location from software makers and **Webportals**. Fifth, the media giants have the resources to buy out innovative, emerging new media firms. A Bertelsmann executive is to the point, 'Our goal is, quite simply, to eventually offer online all books, from all publishers, in all languages' (Nix 1998: 7). That ambition will indeed crave deep corporate pockets.

The media industry is going to have to be much more flexible about the new rules associated with new technologies. Industry cannot in these times of change, maintain a fundamental position, and expect that by keeping that position, the rest of the world will not change. History shows that industry cannot expect that the consumer is going to wait for industry solutions. The consumer always finds a way to get access to desirable media content. Artists have a natural desire to connect to audiences.

The search for profitable business models for the Internet is echoed by the following top level media executive (Schmidt 2000):

> The business we are running here works from one fundamental vision: Bertelsmann, as one of the largest content companies in the world, needs to be able to supply and drive this content over the three major platforms we see out there – the Internet, mobile and **broadband**. Our job here at the E-commerce group is to figure out which business models you can apply over these platforms to make the intellectual property and the contents available to consumers. That can be in either traditional physical formats or in new digital formats, including file-sharing and new mobile formats. Now, at the core of our business

> strategy is the consumer; for us, the consumer is the subscriber. Subscriber-based businesses are what we're going for. Because you can monetize that kind of consumer relationship. You can build and extend on it, and it's much more valuable.

Physical e-tailers such as Amazon.com and Cdnow.com may well evolve into an addition to the subscriber based business models of the future. There will always be physical products. People will continue to buy books, CDs, videos and DVDs because people like to own, collect and keep things. But in the future, that collecting may well be an addition and no longer the core business model.

These developments will not happen simultaneously around our digital globe. There are already fundamental differences between Europe and the USA for instance. In Europe, Internet access costs are still very high because the incumbent national telecoms generally still control the networks. In the USA there is more competition for that space. Because of high access costs, there are fewer people online in Europe. Therefore, the penetration is lower and, because of that, the consumption of digital product also is lower. If Europe has an advantage it is because of a more unified mobile environment. A parallel wireless network, driven by the pervasive use of mobile telephony and communication, is leading to the rapid development and deployment of increasingly higher **bandwidth** service. This wireless and therefore mobile broadband network will be the future form of delivery of all media products in the European context.

Contrary to initial beliefs voiced by many new entrants into the digital music space – as well as many media commentators – it requires all parties, starting with the artist talent, labels, intermediaries, distributors, retail and consumers to build and accept new ways of accessing music. A music executive (Koepke 2000) explains that:

> we will continue on our path of building compelling platforms on which artists and music fans can interact, be they on the Web, mobile or other channels. And we will work closely with our existing media and retail partners to add value to their offerings, using the digital space. This is a huge paradigm shift. But in the changes we are undergoing and the challenges we face, our prime goal is to work for our artists and deliver their music and creativity through the new media channels that will continue to develop.

DOLBY ON INTERNET

Thomas Dolby Robertson has a message for record company executives: the Internet is punishing them for 20 years of abusing their fans. 'The record industry increasingly over the years has desensitized us to the reason that we originally got into music in the first place. The music industry is now going to have to own up to the fact that the flocking of people to the Web as a venue for music is really an expression of the fact that the Web ... is a much better venue for that activity than a large chain store in a shopping mall.'

Computerized radio playlists, the packaging of music in 12-song formats that cost US$20, and a lumbering production schedule 'takes away the fans' sense of loyalty and belonging and participation,' said Robertson. With this new distribution alternative, and a more direct relationship with the fans, artists will be able to leverage dramatically different contracts with their labels, Robertson predicted. Instead of the 15 per cent on units sold today, songwriter/performers may one day take 70 to 80 per cent of the revenue. And instead of getting paid within 12 to 18 months, artists will be paid 'instantaneously, or within a few days. It's going to mean a shift in the balance of power,' he said. 'I could see myself five years from now taking bids from a half-dozen different recording companies, see what they could do for me to add value to my music sales.'

Record companies should adapt by emphasizing their talent management and promotion skills, and realizing that the manufacturing and retail side 'will fade, inevitably,' he said. 'What they have to realize really is that this talent business that they're in is something eternally valuable.' Robertson has a more sceptical view of the labels' future. 'The question really is how will the record industry survive?' Robertson said. 'In effect, they've had an unfair advantage over everybody else for the last few decades, and that unfair advantage is very clearly threatened and undermined by what is effectively a much more efficient way of getting music from the musician to the fan.'

Source: Welch 1999

WHY THE MUSIC INDUSTRY?

Within a short period of time, the music industry has transformed itself into an operation which makes use of, and relies heavily on emerging new digital technologies. At a grass roots level, this process began where music is created, in the recording studio, where engineers found themselves parting from **analogue** and moving onto digital transmission. Digitalization has already had a profound effect on the studio recording process, allowing for greater sound manipulation and ease of editing and storage of sounds. Music produced in studios no longer even requires that musicians working on a track ever have to meet. Highly sought after studio musicians often are hired on a contract basis and 'lay down' their contributions in a digital MIDI file in the comfort of their home studio. The MIDI file is then effortlessly sent over the Internet to the producer who then mixes it into the rest of the track to produce a final mix. This form of **'virtual** work' certainly challenges prevailing notions of time and space in relation to employment.

One can note a state of 'digital life' where sampling becomes a 'state of mind' for the creative musician, who often see life as a 'permanent remix', in a constant state of flux. Musicians are now in the process of rethinking the role of 'live music' and are often producing Web sites with a 'creative agenda'. One can also call this 'recombinant' music where the artist takes something old, takes something contemporary, and combines them to make something new. The old 'cut and scratch' production process in the analogue world takes on a larger and new meaning in a digital context.

Already musicians such as Karlheinz Essl (Austria), Steve Gibson (Canada) and Todd Machover (USA) are 'composing in **cyberspace**' in which they use digital technology and the Internet as a new production tool. This can in effect take the form of interactive real-time composition. Several good examples exist of how new digital computer technology changes the field of composition for the composer who is willing to embrace the opportunity. This will surely be an important field of growth. Technology has throughout history changed the relationship between creator, producer, distributor, retailer and consumer.

With increased use of computers and the Internet, creators have found a new outlet from which they can offer even more to their audience, including enhanced CDs and Web sites. The latter has become an important source of information, where one can make use of Real Audio, **MPEG** and QuickTime technologies, and engage in an interactive experience which was once impossible. Record companies have been quick to realize this invaluable resource, as something as simple as promotion, or as complex as a full-staged concert can now be presented on the Web. The leading file format behind the sites is the Moving Picture Experts Group Audio Layer 3 (MP3), which compresses digital music so it can easily be downloaded by **users** via PCs. The MP3 software format – whose name is shortened from an engineering designation known as MPEG-1, Layer 3 – makes it practical to send songs relatively quickly over the Internet. The following will discuss some of the aforementioned technologies, and how they have affected the music industry as a whole.

Like so much else it was only a matter of time before the music industry got online, and since it has, things have changed rapidly coinciding specifically with the development of computers. Computers are changing at an ever increasing rate, and with the average system being upgraded and out-dated every eighteen to thirty months, it is no wonder that the Internet and online services have grown at such an accelerated rate. Today's systems are a far cry from the first PCs, as they now have stereo speakers, built-in CD players, increased memory capability and high resolution monitors that can now compete with most televisions. The average computer is today marketed as an online home **multimedia** entertainment system. All this aside, it still remains that the instant transmission of text, audio and video via the Internet is having a profound effect on how people receive their music and music related information.

The developments mentioned above have had a significant effect on how the public receives its music information, but there have also been steps taken by musicians as to how they now interact with the public. An increasing number of bands today have their own Web sites that can be accessed quite easily by the majority of people who use computers. It is important to note that many of these sites are controlled and maintained by an independent site creator, who often has no connection with the affiliated music label. This often occurs as a result of prioritizing: although many music companies now have impressive Web sites; to create one for each individual artist to their specifications is difficult. Therefore, many times the artists take it upon themselves to ensure that their site becomes an important resource available for their fans. They generally contain various pieces of up-to-date information on the artist, such as tour dates, personal information and band history, lyrics, discography, as well as links to associated sites. In addition,

KORN ON THE NET (1996)

The Net has given a sense of control back to the artist, control which has been lost upon entering into contracts with large record companies, or simply, that which comes with popularity. Epic/Immortal Records signed an alternative band by the name of Korn, a group lucky to get an audience of approximately 50 to 500 at any given show. However, after opening a Korn page on the Sony Web site, which included among other things, daily voice-clips from the lead singer, the band's popularity grew immensely. The Web page was a huge success, and their record sales took off with their CD, *Life is Peachy*, breaking into Billboard's album chart at No. 3, selling 152,000 in its first two weeks. This was one of the first examples of the importance that the Internet can have, not only to the audience but to the musicians as well, opening up doors and increasing their economic potential.

Source: Atwood 1996

they allow for a new level of **interactivity**: that between the musician and the fan. Although this may be obvious, fans are also enabled to interact with each other, as guestbooks and live chat rooms are now becoming more prevalent in various Web sites. Besides artist driven sites, there exists numerous 'fan' sites that often outdo the mainstream company sites in terms of artist adulation. These fan 'virtual communities' are often a rich source of dialogue and information. The Internet has become an invaluable resource for both artist and audience, at both the local and global level.

Music, its production, distribution, regulation and reception, is an essential feature of the **Information Society**. There are today five major music transnationals (known as the Big Five) that control about 80 per cent of the global market share: Sony (Japan), Time Warner (USA), BMG (Germany), Universal Vivendi (France) and EMI (UK) (Burnett 1996, 2002). At the same time there are still thousands of small independent companies. Although they are somewhat at a disadvantage due to their size and lack of notoriety, independent music companies are continually at the forefront of the industry. Experimentation continues to set new standards in the business – this can be seen with the acceptance of such things as the enhanced CD and the Internet. The Big Five have not been quick to follow suit, but slowly realized what indie companies knew for years: technology can be utilized in such a manner to the benefit of all involved; the creator, producer, distributor, retailer and consumer. Many small scale music companies got their start on the Net.

An interesting example of the independent as innovator is the Internet Underground Music Archive (IUMA), one of the pioneers in the online music business which got its start selling the CDs of unsigned bands that were virtually unknown. IUMA helped artists and labels promote and develop themselves for online discovery and depended on the community of artists and listeners coming together and posting information freely. In 1993, Jeff Patterson and Robert Lord, then studying at the University of California, Santa Cruz, wanted to promote their band, The Ugly Mugs. They decided to distribute their music on the newsgroups they frequented to see what would happen. Patterson and Lord then recorded their band's music in MP2 format, translated the file into an ASCII test file, broke that into twenty-six separate pieces and spent about an hour uploading the pieces of music to the Internet using a 14.4 baud **modem**. Immediately the duo began getting **e-mails** from bands wanting them to upload their music. By October, the university granted them **server** space for an **FTP** (File Transfer Protocol) site so they could post those MP2 files instead of the unwieldy ASCII files. A mere three months after creating the Internet Underground Music Archive, the digital music revolution launched in full force. At its peak during 1998 IUMA carried over a thousand bands, drew more than a half a million **hits** a day and brought in nearly $1,000,000 a year in revenues (King 2001).

VIRTUALLY UNREAL (1998)

A Scottish rock band, the Jesus and Mary Chain, played during the 1998 Intel New York Music Festival, and two hours later their live performance of *Virtually Unreal* was on the Internet for the group's fans worldwide to download and listen to on their computers.

Commercially speaking, it was not significant: a technology demonstration by an alternative-rock band with a devoted following but not a mass public. Yet the uploading of *Virtually Unreal* presaged a day when most recorded music would be available as digital information, distributed not on discs and tapes that have to be manufactured and shipped, but as data files that can be zapped instantly across the Internet.

The Jesus and Mary Chain gained valuable publicity from their **World Wide Web** demo. But just as significant, the band and its label, Sub Pop Records, received not a dime from the thousands of fans who downloaded the song off the Internet. No wonder the record industry was worried. It is easy to give music away on the Internet. The question now facing the music business is how to sell recordings as profitable pieces of data.

Emusic acquired the Internet Underground Music Archive in June of 1999 with hopes of commercializing the site into a destination for underground music. After a disappointing fiscal period, Emusic (EMUS) decided not to renew its funding contract with IUMA. Those manoeuvres left IUMA's future in jeopardy and in the prevailing cold venture capital climate for Internet ventures with uncertain revenue streams, IUMA was unable to find additional funding and effectively ceased all new operations. This brought a rather unceremonious end to the Web site widely considered to have started the digital music revolution (King 2001).

INDUSTRY RESPONSE

The mainstream recording industry response to the Internet challenge is best represented by Hilary Rosen, Chief Executive Officer of the Recording Industry Association of America (RIAA) who claims, 'Right now about 95 per cent of the MP3 downloads on the Internet are illegal downloads ... unauthorized use of these MP3 files is really creating a problem for artists in the music community' (CNN 2000b). According to Strauss Zelnick, of BMG Entertainment: 'Piracy is not a way to encourage artistry. People create and they have to be compensated for their creation. Right now, the music available on the Web is largely pirated' (CNN 2000b). This larger problem of general compensation from artist to music corporation to distributor explains why the RIAA has been fighting the spread of digital music on the Internet – and decided to make a public spectacle out of its legal battle with Napster.

For the unsigned or unknown artist, MP3 is creating opportunities. Through Web sites, stars of the future can offer their music for sample or sale to a potentially global audience. MP3.com's CEO Michael Robertson says, 'What they're really doing is trying to use the Internet as a radio, in effect, a hundred-million-person radio as a way for them to broadcast their music and alert new fans to their music' (CNN 2000b). Even among established recording artists, however, there are varying degrees of concern over MP3 and its impact on their livelihoods. Jim Sonefeld, of Hootie and the Blowfish fame, says, 'It can hurt the artist, and it's not just a money issue, it's a control issue . . . being able to control what you put out and market it properly' (CNN 1999). On the other hand, singer/songwriter Jewel takes a more philosophical approach, 'I'm not too worried about it in the long run. I have plenty of money, I'm okay' (CNN 1999).

While critics of the anti-piracy effort argue that the industry is trying to control a fast growing medium that can expose artists to a wider audience, music executives seldom neglect the bottom line – profits. Sony Music CEO Thomas Mottola says: 'Our artists are very enthusiastic about the prospects and what we have to look forward to in opening a wide range of audiences around the world, providing of course the proper protection can be provided' (CNN 2000c).

The Internet poses difficult questions for the retail business. If someday soon you can store all of your music on your hard drive instead of your shelves, what is going to happen to the record stores? While major retailers are reluctant to speak about the digital future, even among MP3 proponents opinions are divided. If you are buying music over the Internet, what will you be buying from the CD retailer? Robertson is confident that record stores are here to stay. 'I don't think the CD retailers go away. I think that if record labels and artists use the Internet effectively, there will actually be a greater demand for CDs' (CNN 2000b). Regardless of who is right, MP3 and its related hardware, are creating a major shift in the music industry. The recording establishment still misses the most important point: the Internet has forever changed music distribution; record companies therefore need to rewrite their business models. 'It's not about "secure digital music" – they are totally misguided,' said an industry critic. RIAA members 'are so focused on "we've got to lock it up" rather than focused on "we've got to open up to the digital age"' (CNN 2000c).

At a recent music industry panel discussion examining the 'MP3 syndrome', one official described the RIAA's efforts as 'killing ants with a hammer,' while others said that artists care more about reaching a broad audience with their music than the short-term worries of record companies. 'I have never met a musician who used [the words] "business" and "model" in the same sentence,' said Gerry Kearby, CEO of Liquid Audio (CNN 2000c).

The Big Five music industry has been involved in a common security project, named the Secure Digital Music Initiative, which aims to make recordings available as pure digital information while letting only the copyright owners choose how the information can be disseminated. It would be, in other words, an attempt by the major recording labels to stake out retail territory in the one part of the music business they do not control, even as their power is being challenged on the Internet by home-recorded musicians, independent labels and Web-savvy music fans.

The labels, of course, are already using the Internet to sell conventional products – CDs, DVDs and cassettes – through online retailers like CDNow, and Amazon.com and their own Web sites. But the Secure Digital Music Initiative is planning for an era when many consumers will be buying music as downloaded computer files rather than pre-recorded discs and tapes. With a uniform standard, embodied in computer codes that all the

---

DAVID BOWIE (1998)

'MPEGs of my music are all over the network,' said the rock songwriter David Bowie. 'Things that are embarrassingly cringe-making, things that I swore never would see the light of day, they're completely available.'

Bowie has founded his own Internet service (www.davidbowie.com), whose members have online access to rare Bowie music and videos. He said that he was now considering making some new music available for downloading as MP3 files, but that he had a recording contract with Virgin Records, which he said was 'ambivalent' about the idea. And Bowie is ambivalent about the industry's Secure Digital Music Initiative. 'I'm not sure about uniform standards,' he said. 'They've never appealed to me. And however much they try and move in that direction, it ain't going to work. Quirkiness and decentralization are what define the Internet, and the idea of trying to formalize it and police it is abhorrent. The Internet is so volatile and idiosyncratic that whoever tries to police it will be beaten.'

Musicians might also choose to make their songs available free or cheap, build fan bases, and then make their money touring or selling merchandise. 'What should we do,' Bowie commented, 'give the music away, and sell the T-shirts? Maybe we'll become salarymen again ... the notion that music could be free is really something we have to contend with.'

Source: www.davidbowie.com

major recording companies would use, consumers could download best-selling music directly through the Internet and play it back using one kind of software. Once the labels agreed on a standard, a fan could jump to a top band's or a label's Web site, bill the purchase through a credit card, and download a song or an album, saving it to the computer's hard drive, recording it onto a CD or transferring it to a memory chip in a portable player like the Rio player. In turn, the recording company would know where the music was sent, could specify whether or how often it could be copied, and could tabulate royalties and sales. But while the major labels hesitated, many of their holdings are already travelling the Internet as files compressed into manageable size via MP3. Independent labels and individual musicians have made their music available in the MP3 format, but the major labels are alarmed by MP3 because the files can be copied without restriction. The vast majority of MP3 songs circulate free of charge. Some musicians encourage this practice; some like *Metallica*, openly oppose it, and others simply tolerate it.

SEEKING CONTROL

The recording companies are intent on developing software coding standards that would specify what consumers can do with the music they download. Some songs may be available to be copied at will, or copied once, or not at all; some may be listened to for a day, or a week, or forever. Other codes would direct royalties to the appropriate recipients – a particularly tricky process when the global Internet meets contracts that change at national borders.

The recording industry has begun selling music CDs designed to make it impossible for people to copy music to their computers, trade song files over the Internet or transfer them to portable MP3 players. This strategy has provoked strong reactions in Europe and America from music lovers who fear that they will be unable to play the CDs on their computers, burn their own CDs to copy music or make MP3 files for their portable players of music that they have legally purchased. The new protected CDs are drawing the wrath of several consumer electronics manufacturers, including Sony Electronics and Philips Electronics, who argue that they cannot guarantee the audio quality of the CDs on their machines.

It is also opposed by manufacturers of portable MP3 devices such as the Diamond's Rio and Apples's iPod who have legal backing ensuring that their devices do not violate copyright law because consumers had a right to 'space shift' music they owned. Politicians such as US Democrat Representative Boucher have also raised concerns that the record companies 'were seeking to use their copyright not just to obtain fair compensation but in effect to exercise complete dominance and total control of the copyrighted work' (Greenfield 2000).

Digital distribution is still impractical for the vast majority of consumers. Conventional home modems cannot download information quickly enough to make the process convenient. But faster broadband computer connections that are already available, particularly on college campuses, make it

PUBLIC ENEMY (1999)

(What follows is a conversation with Chuck D from a public chat session on the Public Enemy Web site that was subsequently printed in *Wired* magazine.)

The Rap group Public Enemy released several new songs on their www.public-enemy.com site in late 1998. The groups record label Def Jam owned by Polygram demanded that they remove the tracks and a legal battle followed. The group's spokesman Chuck D explains some of the thinking behind the strategy. He notes that 'the major labels are like dinosaurs . . . they move slow.' When asked how the Internet will affect the music being made he said, 'there's incredible, diverse talent. But the way radio, retail, and the record companies govern the music is whack – playola, payola, and censorship turns artists into one-track ponies.' When asked about the way business will get done in the future he noted, 'You'll see 3 dollar albums, which artists won't mind if they're getting the money. And the public will ask, "shit, I can get 25 songs off the Net and make my own CD – or have a Real-Player in my car – why the hell should I spend 14 dollars at a store?" . . . the true revenge will come when the major labels start dropping their prices. I can see the public saying, "OK. I could go to the store and pick up the album I want for 5 dollars, but I can get it on the net for fucking 3 dollars."'

Chuck D is optimistic when it comes to the musicians as well. He states, 'it's great for the musician. Instead of just depending on a song and a video, the Net will bring back live performances. Artists will be able to release a song every two weeks, instead of waiting six, seven months for a label to put it out. A band can become like a broadcaster . . . We have our site. We recently launched the Bring the Noise online radio show. Our Rappstation online radio station is coming. And we just started Slam Jazz, the affiliated superinteractive label. It's going to be the label on the Web that people can download music from. We should have a good stable of artists by 2002, and then we'll release singles like crazy. We'll also offer videos that people can burn to disc . . . that's my vision.'

When asked about piracy he said, 'To the pirates, I say the more the merrier. Success comes from the fans first – if someone is going to pirate something of mine, I just have to make sure to do nine or ten new things. I mean you can't download me.'

possible to send and receive music almost instantly. With cable modems as well as high-speed DSL services from some telephone companies, faster broadband connections are becoming available in a growing number of households.

Unauthorized copying is nothing new and has long worried the music business. When cassette tapes became popular, the recording-industry association began lobbying for a royalty on blank tapes, as compensation for the sales believed lost to unauthorized copying. In the United States, the Audio Home Recording Act of 1992 levied a 2 per cent royalty on the wholesale price of digital recorders and a 3 per cent royalty on blank digital tapes and discs. Even with those royalties, the recording companies refused to release pre-recorded tapes in the DAT, or digital audiotape, format, fearing the spread of high-fidelity digital copies. As a result, DAT is used largely by musicians and journalists, not in home audio systems. Labels had refused to release pre-recorded DATs to protect the CD format, which has been a boon for the music business. But for those worried about copying, the CD turned out to be a grand strategic error: every CD is a digital master copy that can be duplicated *ad infinitum*.

Some executives predict that a public already used to this free flow of Internet music may resist the industry's effort to shut it down. 'Why would I buy into a system that gives me less control than I have now with a CD?' noted an industry executive. 'You have to give people more value if you want to charge the same price, or you have to charge a lower price. All the talk about security is nonsense. The major labels are circling the wagons to preserve their current business model, the CD. But scarcity-based models do not work on the Net' (Stroud 2000). Music would not have to be packaged in the conventional forms of albums and singles, but could be in any bundle the musicians choose. And with store shelf space no longer defining the limits of choice, many more selections could find their way to the market at an array of prices.

THE NAPSTERIZATION OF THE INTERNET

On 26 July 2000, the San Francisco District Court ruled that Napster, the Internet-based music sharing software, was, in the words of Judge Marilyn Hall Patel, 'essentially a program to facilitate the **downloading** and uploading of music . . . pirating be damned is the sense one gets' (Grimaldi 2000: A01). Although a final decision regarding the future of Napster is pending, this case has evoked responses from all sides of the issue, claiming that Napster has 'changed the world' (Greenfeld 2000: 62). Whether the software has made the Internet better or worse depends on whom you ask. David Boies, lead attorney for Napster, says that 'this is a new technology that threatens control'. The technology has been called a part of the Internet revolution by mainstream sources such as *Time Magazine* which featured Napster whiz kid Shawn Fanning on its cover. What one can today refer to as the 'Napsterization of the Internet' has a rather long history.

Napster is an example of a Web or network community as conceptualized by Wellman (1999), as being more horizontal and equalitarian as opposed to vertical, stratified relationships. These network communities tend to be narrow, specialized, with not broadly supportive (loosely knit or coupled) ties. They have frequently changing members who are not geographically bound. They are more private than public and usually large in size. There is usually little perception of similarity with the physical characteristics, expressive style, way of life, or historical experiences of others.

With the introduction of the **ARPAnet** in 1971 and the development of the **TCP/IP** protocol in the early 1980s, the first communications services

PRINCE (2000)

Funk and rock star Prince weighed in this week on music-sharing technology issues, calling services like Napster 'exciting' and sharply criticizing the record industry for exploiting artists. 'From the point of view of the music lover, what's going on can only be viewed as an exciting new development in the history of music,' said Prince, whose hits include '1999', 'When Doves Cry', and 'Cream'.

'And fortunately for (the music lover), there does not seem to be anything the old record companies can do about preventing this evolution from happening.' Prince said that Napster is an illustration of 'the growing frustration over how much the record companies control what music people get to hear'.

'Young people ... need to be educated about how the record companies have exploited artists and abused their rights for so long and about the fact that online distribution is turning into a new medium which might enable artists to put an end to this exploitation.'

Prince has long been an outspoken critic of the record industry, stemming in part by a dispute with Warner Brothers over the ownership of his master recordings and the pace at which he was allowed to release albums. During the dispute, he changed his written name to a cryptic, unpronounceable symbol and took to appearing in public with the word 'slave' painted on his face. Prince is one of the higher profile artists to use the Internet to sell music outside traditional channels.

Source: www.prince.org

were developed. These included e-mail, Telnet and FTP. The FTP was used for the direct transfer of **data** between different computers without an intermediary server in the ARPAnet i.e. in the subsequent Internet. This protocol can therefore be seen as the original conceptual form of peer-to-peer technology. There is a major criterion to which technical and social aspects of the development of distributed computer system architectures can be traced back, and that is the shared use of resources of all kinds (sharing).

In today's Internet-based peer-to-peer (P2P) architectures, the shared use of resources refers to disk storage space or files (file sharing), processing power (cycle stealing) and human work or knowledge (**collective intelligence**). Well-known examples include *Gnutella, FreeNet, MojoNation, Kazaa* and *Morpheus* for file sharing; *Popular power, United devices* and *Moneybee* for cycle stealing systems; and *Worldstreet* and *Opencola* for collective intelligence.

The best-known file sharing tool is Napster. Indeed, one might say that the general idea of file sharing on the Internet has been definitively shaped by the exchange of music in MP3 format facilitated by Napster even though it is not a true P2P system, but is based on a central directory containing the data offered by registered users (users make available a portion of their hard disk for this purpose). By entering a search query, the user receives a list of other participants offering the data she is looking for. A direct exchange can then take place. Gnutella, Freenet or MojoNation, on the other hand, are true P2P file sharing systems which, like Napster, were started by individuals or by a group of interested people and do not use a central server with a central directory. In this case, each computer is both a client and a server. Search queries are made directly to another computer which relays the query further to other computers until one is found which can answer the query directly. P2P essentially abandons the networking notions of separate 'clients' and 'servers' and instead allows every networked machine to connect to another machine.

P2P networking and the Napsterization of the Internet are exciting new approaches to building up virtual communities and business-to-business e-commerce platforms using public and private networks. The rapid decommodification of commercial music through Napster, Gnutella and FreeNet also posed a powerful new threat to the music industry. Ian Clarke, founder of FreeNet, a P2P network, commenting on the Napster court case:

> The music industry did not win this. They may have won the battle, but the collateral damage – in terms of fan loyalty, etc. – was substantial, so much that I doubt they'd ever do something like this again . . .
>
> [Napster's demise] was going to happen sooner or later,

Freenet, on the other hand – since it's completely decentralized – it would be very difficult for them to shut us down. That's the idea of peer-to-peer, people communicating with each other. What we see in our culture is the increasing disenfranchisement of the artist and the consumer – the artist is distanced from the consumer.

(Schenker 2000)

PEW STUDY: NAPSTER USE ISN'T STEALING

Napster's main – and some say only – asset was its user base of 30 million people. But a study conducted by the Pew Internet and American Life Project found that a large segment of non-Napster-using Americans might be on the side of the controversial file-trading company. The Pew study, found that 53 per cent of Internet users thought downloading music wasn't stealing.

And though only 40 per cent of the general population – both Internet users and non-Internet users – also felt that it wasn't stealing, that compares favorably to the 35 per cent who felt downloaders were stealing. Twenty-five per cent of respondents didn't feel strongly one way or another.

However, the Pew study points out that 86 per cent of the Internet music listeners were downloading familiar music. But most of the music being downloaded wasn't music that had been previously purchased. In fact, only 28 per cent of people downloading music owned a CD or cassette of the music.

The Recording Industry Association of America has been pressing the point that people increasingly expect to get their music for free on the Internet – and argue that just because consumers don't think they are stealing, doesn't mean that they aren't stealing.

The Pew study gathered information from two separate phone surveys between March and August 2000. The first focused on 238 Internet users in the United States who downloaded music. Its margin of error was plus or minus 7 percentage points. The second survey of 12,751 Internet and non-Internet users had a margin of error of 2.5 percentage points.

Source: King 2001

JUPITER STUDY

Users of Napster software, which allows users to share digital music files, are more likely to buy more records than non-Napster users, according to a study by the research firm Jupiter Communications (JPTR) Inc. 'Because Napster users are music enthusiasts, it's logical to believe that they are more likely ... to increase their music spending in the future,' said Jupiter analyst Aram Sinnreich. 'But when we conducted our consumer survey, ... we still found that Napster usage is one of the strongest determinants of increased music buying.'

The study comes against the backdrop of a war between Napster and the music industry trade group Recording Industry Association of America, which claims that such software are tools to pirate digital music. Among the arguments the RIAA makes is that Napster is responsible for the decline of music sales among college students, who make up a sizable portion of the software's users. 'An inherent flaw in the RIAA's argument against Napster is that the association's supporting research shows a decline in record sales in college areas, with high Napster usage,' Sinnreich said. 'However, the RIAA did not clarify that the most attrition took place before Napster's launch, and the analysis did not account for channel shift to online transactions that would have occurred independent of Napster's existence.'

Instead of resorting to litigation, 'the labels have to get on the ball and start licensing out their catalogs to service providers that are going to provide a legitimate alternative to (Napster),' Sinnreich told Reuters in an interview. 'The labels are absolutely ridiculous to come crying to the courts ... when they haven't put anything out there themselves that consumers can have an alternative to.'

Source: Reuters 2000a

The industrial giants contributing to the international music industry are well represented at court and in the World Intellectual Property Organization, holding out against P2P networking. Meanwhile, many music companies are facing legal challenges of their own, standing accused of anti-competitive behaviour and price-fixing in the world markets for CDs and other commercial music recordings.

In the Napster case, does technology really outstrip the capacity of the legal system to protect property rights in the age of digital reproduction? What new opportunities might be foreclosed by a successful legal challenge to P2P networking? What interests and claims is the music industry defending at court, both in the Napster case and in their defence of business practices and pro-competitive ethics?

'We have recognized for some time the inevitable nexus between public policy and litigation in these online issues', said RIAA Chief Executive Hilary Rosen. 'We really believe this is a public policy debate that has very broad implications' (CNN 2000b). The debates over how to and who can distribute music, videos and other copyrighted works online have risen quickly out of legal and Net circles and into the mainstream, following the success and for now uncertain future status of Napster's music-sharing service.

The RIAA and allies such as the Motion Picture Association of America (MPAA) have consistently won legal battles in court against file-swapping services such as Napster and Scour. But each successive victory has helped galvanize opposition to their actions among an increasingly vocal coalition of free speech advocates, programmers and music and film fans.

Napster itself appealed to its tens of millions of members to call or e-mail their congressional representatives and to join a 'Napster Advocacy Network,' which aims to spread the gospel of legal file-sharing. High-profile intellectual allies – including Stanford University law professor Lawrence Lessig, who came to prominence as a court-appointed 'special master' in the Microsoft antitrust case – aided in the call to action. Lessig mused that as music disappears from Napster 'one song at a time, people will become aware that there is a political battle ... It's time we should be fighting it' (Stroud 2000).

NAPSTER'S SIDE OF THE STORY

May 19, 2000
Web posted at: 1:01 p.m. EDT (1701 GMT)

(FindLaw) – In this commentary, Napster's attorney Laurence Pulgram answers questions raised by the copyright litigation against the Internet music provider.

Q: Metallica argues that, even though Napster has non-infringing uses, most of the MP3 files shared by Napster users are copyright protected. So how can Napster be justified?

A: Let's start with the Supreme Court's decision in the Betamax case. That case rejected the entertainment industry's effort to keep the VCR off the market. The Supreme Court has said that copyright is first and foremost about 'promoting progress' in the arts and sciences; monetary rewards are secondary. Put another way, copyright exists in the United States for the benefit of the public, and the public interest requires that new technologies be made available where they have potential non-infringing uses. That's clearly the case with the peer-to-peer file-sharing breakthrough that Napster created. Let me point out just a few of those non-infringing uses.

First, consider distribution of new bands and new music. Metallica seems happy to pull up the ladder after they reached the top. But the fact is that only a tiny fraction – maybe 2 per cent – of all musicians get recording contracts with the big labels. The rest are out there struggling to build a career. The little guys are competing against huge corporate conglomerates to capture fans, but they don't have the resources to promote themselves on radio, on television or on tour in the current system. Napster gives new artists a way to distribute and promote their music directly to a huge community of fans worldwide. In fact, in just the last few weeks, Napster has had more than 5,000 artists sign up to approve Napster's distribution of their music.

Second, Metallica itself has shown how effective grass-roots promotion can be, if given a chance. Metallica built its name through word-of-mouth, bootlegs and underground tape distribution. So did the Grateful Dead, Phish, Dave Matthews and others. Ironically, Metallica now says it wants Napster to allow fans to share Metallica bootleg recordings, but to prevent fans from sharing Metallica's studio recordings. So Metallica acknowledges Napster's utility for spreading promotional materials. And yet, it seeks to deprive everyone of those opportunities by trying to shut the system down.

Third, what about the rights of fans who have already legally bought a Metallica album, or any other album, and just want to download an MP3 copy to play through a computer or to compile play lists from various CDs? Is Metallica saying those fans don't have the right to download that MP3 copy? The law entitles those fans to make that duplicate for their own non-commercial enjoyment using Napster. These are just a few of the uses of the Napster system that are non-infringing. There's no justification for shutting down Napster and throwing out the baby with the bath water.

Source: CNN.com 2000a

Bertelsmann's CEO Middelhoff said in 20001 that he was confident that many users of the Napster software would be happy to pay for music. An internal survey of 25,000 Napster users conducted by the group showed that 70 per cent would be willing to pay for a subscription service. Middelhoff said the company decided to work with Napster, rather than fight it, because the Internet was changing the music industry's business models. 'The music industry was not ready to handle this new consumer behavior.

The publishers threatened to sue, but you can't sue 100 million customers, because at the same time these customers are heavy buyers of music. They love music', he said. 'We decided to speak to the company (Napster) and develop a legitimate business model, I don't think anyone will say they are against it. If you find the right terms and business model, I don't think anyone will stay out of this peer-to-peer file-sharing network'. The media-publishing industry was already looking beyond the music business for Napster-like services, Middelhoff said. 'File sharing is not just about music, it is also about films and entertainment' (Reuters 2001).

THE MUSIC INDUSTRY'S THREE MISTAKES

The first mistake: the music industry seriously underestimated the profound effect of the Internet and the rapid speed at which it would develop

During the late-1990s, while so many others were succumbing to dotcom hype, the music business resisted any accommodation with the new techno-logy. Its corporate leaders used all of their lobbying power and legal resources to attack the Net. They had the copyright laws strengthened, blocked software development and closed down Web sites. By adopting a 'business as usual' approach the music industry missed a unique window of opportunity to lead music into the digital era.

The second mistake: the music industry chose to see the arrival of the MP3 file format and Napster as a threat instead of an opportunity

Many executives hoped that the digital future implied nothing more serious than producing more sophisticated CD-ROMS or DVDs. They were worried that online distribution systems would wipe out their substantial investments in disc pressing plants. Others feared that a virtual music mar-ketplace would lead to the 'disintermediatization' of the industry. The Net might allow musicians to sell tunes directly to their fans across the world without needing to sign with a major music label.

The third mistake: the music industry decided to see file sharing music fans as criminals instead of as early adaptors and innovators

The failure to create an early virtual marketplace for selling music was a fatal error. Deprived of a legal method of obtaining music over the Net when it became technically possible, people began trading digital copies of their CD and vinyl collections with each other. Sharing music over the Net soon developed into a fun way of meeting people online. Fans could chat about their favourite musicians while giving away songs. This underground scene was given a massive boost by the invention of Napster, which created a virtual meeting-place where people into sharing music files could find each other. From the moment of its release, the popularity of Napster grew exponentially. Early adopters recommended the program to their friends who, in turn, passed on the news. What had begun as a cult quickly crossed over into the mainstream. For the first time, youth was identifying itself not by following particular bands, but by using a specific Net service: Napster.

As noted earlier, the music industry response was to close down fan Web sites, and to aggressively pursue prosecution of any company working with new distribution systems (Napster) or new means of listening to music (Rio). Some artists like Metallica sided with their music labels and argued that 'file trading is theft', thus echoing earlier industry responses to new technology such as 'home recording is theft' which was prevalent during the introduction of cassette tape recorders. Needless to say, this response has probably alienated an entire generation of music fans.

THE GIFT ECONOMY AS A LOOSE WEB

The music industry must find some way of commercializing P2P file-sharing. Even before the Napster case was concluded, the Bertelsmann corporation broke ranks with the other major record companies to buy a stake in Napster. The business plan was that for a small monthly subscription, Napster users would be allowed to break the copyright laws and download Bertelsmann owned music. Soon afterwards, the other transnational music firms announced their own plans for online music services, which became the current *PressPlay* and *MusicNet*. Yet even this compromise may have come too late. Why would anyone pay for music which is easily available for free? The old songs are all available on unencrypted digital formats and the protection on new tracks is quickly cracked. Once they have experienced digital abundance, why would anyone welcome the forced imposition of analogue scarcity upon the Net? Even artists are unhappy as they complain that any PressPlay or MusicNet profits bypass them and go directly to the music labels.

There are alternative economic models that have worked with some success in the past. The Grateful Dead – a late-1960s psychedelic rock band – pioneered one promising way of creating an alternative economic relationship between musicians and their audiences. Although signed to a major label, its members encouraged their fans to make and trade tapes of their live performances. Contrary to free market orthodoxy, these altruistic ethics proved to be financially rewarding. While their contemporaries faded into obscurity or lost all credibility, the Grateful Dead are still worshipped by a devoted community of fans long after the demise of the band's charismatic leader. Any money lost from bootlegs has been more than compensated by increased sales of their commercial recordings and of tickets for their live concerts. The Grateful Dead proved that musicians could earn a good living out of free music (Alderman 2001).

Exchanging music files can be understood as the contemporary equivalent of trading bootleg tapes. Instead of fighting this phenomenon, corporate executives should realize that giving away music can be another way of making money. For instance, a song available for free over the Net could persuade someone to buy a concert ticket or, as long as the sound quality remains superior, to purchase CD or DVD versions. Above all, the music industry must move from selling CD albums to servicing fans. Music fans are probably willing to pay for a more intimate relationship with their idols. New releases, concert tickets, celebrity gossip, chat zones and other features can be made available online for a monthly fee. From being little more than a sideline, fan clubs could become the major source of revenue for the music industry in the future. As one way of making money disappears, another may be opening up (Alderman 2001).

From its earliest days, the Internet was organized around the sharing of information between its users, a loose Web of connection. Despite its recent commercialization, this gift economy remains at the heart of the Web experience. People build their own Web sites, contribute to listservers, send e-mails, take part in chatrooms and find new ways of connecting with each other. If someone asks for some information, there is usually an abundance of people happy to give it to them. As long as the Net was only used by a minority of enthusiasts, the music industry could ignore what was going on in cyberspace. This passive stance was no longer an option when advances in hardware and software meant that large numbers of people started connecting with each other through sharing music files. Meeting through services such as Napster, users could connect in loose Webs of similar music taste groups, or virtual communities based on fandom. In these environments, it was easy to share music files with each other.

The Web gift economy is not just a short-lived phenomenon. One of the main reasons why the Web was invented in the first place was to allow file-sharing between computers in different locations. This concept is at the centre of P2P computing. Contemporary developers are enabling computers, mobile phones, games consoles and all sorts of other devices to interact with each other. The goal is everything linked with everything, and everyone swapping files with everyone. A large amount of current research work is concerned with achieving this 'cross platform' mobility. For example, in the area of network computing, people are pursuing the vision of being able to call up functionality and processing power from anywhere via the Web. In the field of mobile and ubiquitous computing, the aim is to integrate specialized terminal devices as transparently as possible into the Internet. This means 'smart devices' – everyday appliances with built-in processors and sometimes also sensors, as well as 'Internet information appliances' – mobile, cordless networked devices such as mobile phones, PDAs, cameras and 'wearable computers'. The place of music in this 'smart' future remains to be seen.

The broader lessons for the web of entertainment

Three general lessons pertaining to the web of entertainment can be learnt from the stuggle over digital music.

First, what has happened with music may well happen in other content industries as well, as other products become digitized. Content owners must heed the warning from the music industry experience – film, software, games, books, scientific journals – and many other types of content are increasingly widely available online.

What has happened within the music industry is already beginning to spread to Hollywood. With a broadband connection, sharing movies becomes almost as easy as swapping music. Lots of jobs and money could be at risk in Hollywood if the leaders of the movie business repeat the same mistakes made by the CEOs of the music industry.

The second lesson, is that the struggles over protecting intellectual property take many forms and reach into a variety of areas, including battles over technology, standards, industry structure and business models. Entertainment firms will have to accept lower profit margin models for digital sales in order to compete effectively with pirate services.

The third lesson is that among the various struggles, the fight over standards is often the most intense, as it typically has the most far reaching effects, with consequences for artists, producers, publishers and consumers alike, as well as the shape and character of the industry. Keeping this in mind often makes it easier to decode the different agendas and strategies of the many players engaged in the struggle.

CONCLUSION

Here we enter the territory of opposites, contradictions, conflicts and speculation about the digital future. Clearly one can see that 'digital is different' and that one can see digital technology as either a threat or a possibility. Due to technology driven developments such as the Internet we have a new set of relationships between producers, distributors and consumers. In fact the traditional media value production chain has become in a sense a circle. We are also seeing a growing **convergence** of policy domains. This means that it is more important than ever to nurture 'pro-active' policy development as opposed to 'reactive' policy development.

The world of music is an ever changing industry, with music companies striving to reach the next level ahead of their competition, and the musicians themselves embracing new technologies to reach a larger and more diverse audience. All of the key players in the music business will be challenged by technical changes in network technologies and especially by the Internet. Infrastructure may be inhibiting the development of digital distribution, but the music industry may or may not be ready for such innovative developments. Furthermore, existing copyright legislation is believed to be insufficient to protect music companies or recording artists in this new digital arena.

Unlike earlier forms of youth or counterculture rebellion, P2P computing is a direct threat to the economics of the music industry. Despite the rapid changes in musical tastes over the decades, the fundamentals of its business structure have remained the same. Musicians are contracted to make recordings. Music is sold on bits of plastic to consumers. Copyright laws ensure that no one can distribute recordings without paying their owners. Everyone supposedly benefits from this arrangement. Fans are offered a wide choice of many different types of music. Musicians are able to earn a living – and a few can become rich beyond their dreams. Small companies can survive by finding new artists and selling niche styles of music. Transnational corporations can own profitable music companies as part of their media empires. Having a strong track record of co-opting successive cultural revolutions, this business structure appeared to be firmly in place. It took the arrival of P2P computing and companies like Napster to prove otherwise.

The next wave of file sharing could well be via instant messaging, where file sharing and instant messaging morph into one function. The newest versions of MSN Messenger, Yahoo! Messenger and AOL Instant Messenger all have functions to send files, a process that is faster than with P2P programs such as *Kazaa* and *Morpheus*. What this means is that in effect the very mainstream industry has embraced file sharing, thus making it the very essence of the present Web experience.

At the same time it is important to remember that we live in a world where five transnational music companies control the global flow of music. The trend towards corporate concentration, conglomeration and hypercommercialism is the same across the entire media and entertainment industry. In the field of music at least, if we do not allow for hackers, pirates, experimenters and innovators, people willing to push the technology to the edge, then the industry as we know it today may very well become irrelevant and fade away.

CONCLUSION

UNIFYING THE WEB into a simple medium is fraught with inconsistencies and exceptions to a degree that is unparalleled in past media. Researchers have been more successful at laying claim to the idea of 'television', where its intrinsic modality was evident. McLuhan could essentialize the experience of these media into hot and cool metaphors. Or Williams could comfortably claim that television was all about 'programme flow' (1974); but the Web makes such claims to an essential nature ludicrous. As much as we might crave for this overarching understanding, we actually have to develop concepts that acknowledge that at the core of the Web is simultaneous dispersion and connection. This book has worked from this dual premise and has attempted to develop two key concepts through looking at the Web from various vantage points that come closest to the modality of the Web and the experiences it engenders. We have called these two concepts that have helped us unpack the regularities of the Webscape the **loose Web** and the **Cultural Production Thesis**. The best way to summarize these concepts that stitch together the approaches we have presented here is to talk about what way our *use* of the Web has been routinized. How has the Web has been integrated into our everyday lives? Even as we think through this process of use, it is important to realize that this use is certainly not universal but an experience of the richest fifth of the world; nonetheless, we can gain a great deal from observing how youth in particular appropriate Web culture, make it normal and ordinary, and transform it into part of the way they make sense of their world. What follows is a description of watching one of our teenage daughters on the Web:

> After school, the networked computer becomes the centrepiece
> of her home life. Once logged on, the Web disperses into a

series of windows of activity. Two chat programs are immediately started, one from AOL and the second from MSN which allow her to intersect with two different groups of friends that are in fact dispersed in two different parts of the globe. She is comfortable opening up other chatrooms from the same programs that of course adds to the complexity of her engagement, but seems incredibly normal and mundane to her eyes. As the questions and responses carry on in each chatroom, she has learnt to develop a sophisticated shorthand that speeds up the exchanges and maintains the connection to others. In another window that lurks in the background she has music she has downloaded – the selections are a combination of those sent to her via e-mail from her friends and those she has taken through visiting Web sites. In an even further recessed window, her homework on the Renaissance sits as a Microsoft Word file. Sometimes through questioning her friends from school she moves to search further information about Machiavelli and Florence. And through another Internet Explorer window she is looking for new images that someone from the chatroom has said are worth displaying as her screen saver. The conversation advances and she realizes that there are three choices of activities for the weekend: a film, going skating or going bowling. She moves to the movie database and gets the movie times for the local Cineplex and then opens yet another window to search for the phone number and addresses of bowling alleys and skating arenas that are close via the online white and yellow pages. The pictures have now downloaded for her desktop and she has decided they do not suit and has opened up a drawing program to manipulate them into her own style of image. At the behest of a friend online she ensures that the television is turned on as JaRule performs and she goes to Muchmusicusa Web site where further background information is provided along with the possibility of chatting with the star. She suddenly realizes that she has let her homework on Machiavelli go idle and she prints out an Introduction to his life. Throughout all these other activities she maintains her participation in several chatrooms and checks her e-mail for downloads and correspondences from her mother . . .

From the range of activities described above we can see the way the Web operates through use. It provides the avenues for connection in its networked structure. The forms of connection and communication with others are often highly interpersonal, whether in the form of **e-mail** or chat. Rubbing shoulders with this form of connection is that the Web is also operating as a source of authoritative and relatively anonymously delivered **information**. We have used the idea of the loose Web to explain these different functions of the Web: in terms of **user** identity, the user is simultaneously known and involved in private and perhaps intimate conversations as well as an anonymous searcher. The Web must be thought of elastically in its ability to constitute both kinds of registers of engagement of the user. That elasticity has to be understood as evidence of the loose Web – it is a site for the constitution of public and private identities as well as public and private forms of presentation.

On another plane, the user described above is attached to the economic dimensions of the Web. Entities such as Microsoft with their contested bundling of their **browser** with their operating system and their connection to content providers such as MSNBC are attempting to engulf the Web with certain imperatives that are coming from a commercial ethos. Indeed, any popular Web site alighted upon by a user is also encumbered with advertising banners and pop-up pages entreating the user to change direction and move into a buying state of mind. The very use of Internet Explorer incorporates the user into a particular capitalist reading of the Web. Nonetheless, the user can find a wealth of information that has been developed and made available for free that partially counters the commercialization of the Web. The loose Web expresses this competing game of the Web where neither the commercial parameters nor the freeware and **shareware** approach completely dominate. As we have indicated the Web is in some ways the **new agora**, where multi-purposes are active and soliciting on the Web, each vying for attention. A new version of politics as much as a new version of shopping is emerging from the loose Web.

Compounding this elastic dialectic is that the anonymity of the user of the Web is a mirage. Information about users can be collected and actions can be reconstructed. The loose Web has the capacity for increased surveillance of its users that can feed into the commercial imperatives. The sheer volume of activity however is the insurance of relative freedom of access and movement on the Web.

From still another angle, the Web expresses the possibilities and challenges of the digitalization of culture. Ownership and property rights are much more difficult to maintain when the product is infinitely reproducible without a loss of quality. The **virtual** nature of cultural forms such as film and music is further highlighted and problematized when distributed via the Web. The loose Web identifies the unregulatability inherent in its architecture and the nature of the **digital** material floating around the **Internet** in packets. Every **firewall** can somehow be cracked with new codes. The loose Web thus loosens the governing structures of our culture industries and new techniques of protection of intellectual property are being formulated to counteract these Web effects.

Because of this loose nature of the Web, the user is a much more active player in what the Web actually constitutes. In other words, users through their **interactivity** produce the Web. The Web is individualized on the desktop computer. News is transformed, reused and re-sent by users. The Web therefore is an incredible location of cultural production.

The success of the Web as a cultural phenomenon is dependent on its difference from television and film precisely because of its accessibility to actually produce new content. The millions of personal Web sites are a testament to the persistent will to production, the desire to remake and restate the world for others to peruse in contemporary culture. As much as the Web is a location for the professionalization of Web looks and designs and as much as there are efforts to hierarchize the Web with sophisticated commercially constituted Web sites, one of the most interesting dimensions of the Web is the persistent presence of the personal Web site which can expand into some hybrid form as a portal dedicated to an interest area. From interactivity and play on the Web to actual Web site development and proselytizing, these are the elements of what we have called the Cultural Production Thesis.

The forms of cultural production are not always clearly delineated in Web culture. For instance, news has transformed into a phenomenon we have called **informational news**: it relies on the user's searching, selecting and hierarchizing for the rarely-finished-product called the story. Journalists by necessity perform a fundamentally different task in the relationship to reporting events for the online world. What we have uncovered is a general shift in the site of production where news becomes a subset of information and it is neither professionally produced nor user-produced but a blended phenomenon. Similarly, in the field of entertainment where digital files can be passed freely from person to person via the Internet, the product can be restructured for different uses. Images can be retooled as backgrounds for desktops or screensavers; music can be altered and made into yet another personalized version of a popular song and writing can be a collaborative process of hyperlinking among a number of sites.

From these two vantage points, the conceptualization of the loose Web and the understanding of the Web as an expression of the Cultural Production Thesis, we have developed a particular and extended reading of the Web. What this work underlines is the need for more research on the users of the Web and greater study of the way that this particular media form is engaged with by those users. It is hoped that this book will establish some of the groundwork for this kind of research and investigation of the Web.

GLOSSARY

active link   Highlighted text on a Web page that connects the user to another Web page.

ADSL   Asymmetrical digital subscriber loop. A digital connection into the home at the end of the telephone line.

Advanced Research Project Agency (ARPAnet)   Agency established to build the advanced system to interconnect computers.

analogue   Through direct and continuing creation or transmission of natural signals, for instance vibration in the air.

applet   Application associated with Java that animates Web graphics.

audience-commodity   The buying and selling of audiences has been the economic mainstay of the commercial television industry and has now migrated to the Web. Audiences are bought by advertisers who share the space with the content provider who attracts the audience in the first place. It is the basis of the free-lunch system of media.

authoring   The action of writing and producing an online document.

avatar   A word adopted by computer users to denote the digital manifestation that humans take on when entering virtual worlds.

B2B Internet   Refers to business to business trade via the Internet.

B2C Internet   Refers to business to consumer commerce via the Internet.

bandwidth   The amount of data that can be electronically transmitted all at once through a communication path, such as a communication line.

banner advertisement   The earliest and most prevalent form of online advertising. Banners are typically about $6\frac{1}{2}$ inches wide by about 1 inch high (468×60 pixel).

bit   Binary digit: smallest unit of information in digital data (a 1 or a 0). Series of eight bits is a byte.

bookmarking   The methods of saving the URLs of frequently visited sites so addresses do not have to be entered each time before accessing the sites.

broadband/wideband   Property of a connection channel offering high frequency space for fast transmission, generally 1 million bits per seconds (1MB/s) or more. High/quality moving pictures require 2MB/s.

browser   A program such as Netscape Navigator or Internet Explorer that allows a person to browse the World Wide Web by navigating from site to site using hypertext protocols.

CERN   An acronym that stands for *Conseil Européen pour le Recherche Nucleaire* a research laboratory based in Geneva that pioneered the development of the World Wide Web along with Tim Berners-Lee.

chat forum   Online discussion group used for exchanging live, real-time messages.

click-through rates   A pricing structure for banner advertisements based on the number of visitors who click through from and to the advertiser's homepage.

client computer   The computer from which original messages or requests for information are sent.

collective intelligence   A reading by Pierre Levy of the networked and information-rich world as exemplary of an increasingly connected body of knowledge and application of that knowledge.

communication (social)   Transfer and/or exchange of symbolic information by senders with interpretation of a meaningful context and with attention to the presence of receivers.

communication mode   Way of communication using particular signs or symbols (words, images, speech acts, gestures, formulas, etc.). Alternative terms: symbol systems and sign systems. Examples: linguistic, iconic, music, gestural.

communication network   Network, the main function of which is to supply facilities of communication. The most important information traffic patterns are allocution and conversation.

compression   The condensing of data files into a smaller size for faster transmission through the Internet.

computer mediated communication (CMC)   A generic term used to describe the full range of communication that now occurs through computers.

convergence   The coming together of many forms of media, such as television programming on the Web, or Internet delivery by cable television companies.

cookies   A device that tracks a user's Web travels and saves online visitor information sometimes without the user's knowledge or permission to create personal files that companies use to customize their Web pages to target individuals.

Cultural Production Thesis   An interpretation of the contemporary Web which identifies that one of the central tropes of the Web is that it enacts, enables and articulates the will and desire to produce.

cybercast   The delivery of radio or television programmes over the Web.

cyberculture theory   An emerging area of study that focuses on the transformation of identity in an increasingly virtual world. Drawing on poststructuralism, gender studies and postmodernism this critical reading of culture, subjectivity and technology has generated and utilized such concepts as 'post-gender' (Haraway 1991), 'virtual persona' (Turkle) and cyborg (Haraway 1991) to describe the possibilities and constraints around new media and culture.

cybernetics   A theory for the study of communication and control in machines and organisms. Related to the development of systems theory and in its modern usage usually attributed to the work of Norbert Wiener but also extended by the Palo Alto School and in particular Gregory Bateson.

cyberspace   Term coined by the science fiction writer William Gibson to describe the 'consensual hallucination' of people working in computer networks adopted by network users as a (vague) expression for the common virtual or abstract space created and experienced in computer networks.

cyborg   A merging of human and machine. A term that is used to describe the coming together of technology and what it means to be human.

A common science fiction trope that deals with the threatening triumph of the machine over the human. Also seen as an emancipatory contemporary condition by writers like Haraway (1991) who imagine that the cyborg represents the possibility of moving beyond gender identity through technological form.

data   Numerical, alphabetical and other notational signs or symbols rendered in bits and bytes and serving as the raw material for information.

database   Systemically composed and retrievable file of data in a computer (network).

digital   Through the creation, transmission or simulation of artificial signs in the form of binary digits (ones and zeros).

digital divide   A term employed to describe the gap between the information-rich and the information-poor. The digital divide is emerging through the new economy leaving new international divisions as well as clear economic disparities within countries.

domain name system (DNS)   Rules for structuring Internet addresses in the following way: username@host.subdomain.

downloading   To copy data from one location to another. It is often used to describe the process of copying a file from an online service to one's own computer.

electronic billboard   Central file or medium storing and forwarding message of electronic mail to be retrieved at any time; also called bulletin board system (BBS).

electronic commerce   Formal transaction of buying and selling goods and services on proprietary or open networks like the Internet.

electronic mail (e-mail)   Conversation with (mainly) messages of text, asynchronously sent and received in computer networks and stored in an electronic mail box on a computer (server).

encryption   Encoding of messages to protect them from unwanted access; to be decoded for reception by a legitimate user.

ethernet   Coined by XeroxPARC researcher Robert Metcalfe to describe a cabled connection between computers. Ethernet refers to a faster and direct connection to the Internet than conventional phone lines. It allows transmission by two or more systems to send information simultaneously.

firewall   Online security system that keeps confidential data from unauthorized individuals by separating it from public information.

FTP (file transfer protocol)   The standard Internet protocol for copying files between computers.

gatekeepers   Newsroom executive or any person or group who decides which new items or information should be presented to the public.

globalization   A contested designation of the changes wrought by capitalism that has been reconfigured under the new transnational flows of information.

global village   A term coined by Marshall McLuhan to describe how the new technologies of communication provided a different form of connection that resembled the village. It remains a celebrated term in discourses on both the Internet and its relationship to globalization.

gopher   A system of networked links between computers that predated the Web, where links were presented as a hierarchically structured list of files. Developed and distributed from the University of Minnesota where the gopher is their official mascot.

graphic internet stage   A description of the dominance of text and graphics on the Web, particularly in the period from 1993 to 1998.

graphic user interface (GUI)   A program designed to make the use of the computer easier and to alleviate the user from learning the original coding and commands of a program.

handle   The name used to identify oneself in various online services.

HDSL   High bit-rate digital subscriber line.

hits   A counting designation which identifies the number of users that have alighted on a particular site. It is significant in the development of advertising on the Web and calibrating its value for the advertiser.

hot link   Highlighted area on a Web page that doubles as a hypertext link to another site or document within the same site.

HTML (Hypertext Markup Language)   A computer language made up of a set of symbols or codes that tells the Web browser how to display a Web page's words and images, and how to link between pages and documents.

http (Hypertext Transfer Protocol) Set of rules for transferring hypertext (World Wide Web) documents. All Web addresses begin with http://

hybrid media Combination of heterogeneous media, not actually belonging to one another.

hypertext/hypermedia Text and other contents edited and to be received and read in a non-linear way, jumping from one source, page, image, etc., to another; typical way to design and consume Web content.

icons Small representative images that link one domain of a computer to another that became the basis for hyperlinks between computers.

ideology of technology/ideology of information technology A fundamental societal and normalized belief in the power of technology to lead to societal betterment which leads society to focus on implementation issues not public debate about their value.

information Data and other signals interpreted by humans and animals with sufficient capacities of perception and cognition.

information society Society in which information has become the dominant source of productivity, wealth, employment and power.

information superhighway Project future communication network(s) with a broadband capacity high enough to integrate current networks of tele, data, and mass communication.

informational news A term that describes the transformation of journalism and news in Web culture where there is a greater involvement of the user and news hierarchies are in flux. News has become a subset of a wider search for information by Web users.

initial public offering (IPO) The technique for new start-up companies to officially list their companies on a stock exchange. It is a process of capitalization for companies which not only gives them access to new sources of funds to expand the business but also a public guage of the relative worth of the company. Some of the most phenomenal transformations in value of any stock offering were with Internet IPOs in the late 1990s.

interactivity A term used to describe interaction between parties where both are sources and receivers of information via a communication medium such as telephone or the Internet. Sequence of action and reaction.

Internet Global connection of hundreds of thousands of public and private computer networks by means of public exchanges, that is nodes, gateways and computer centres using the TCP/IP protocol.

Internet investment bubble The collapse of the NASDAQ stockmarket where on 21 April 2000, the stock exchange lost 25 per cent of its value. In the subsequent weeks thousands of Internet-related companies declared bankruptcy and disappeared.

Internet protocol (IP)   A set of rules that tell routers how to reassemble and address electronic data packets for transmission to the proper server and then to the client computer.

Internet relay chat (IRC)   A type of chat software that must be installed to access a chat forum. The software is usually downloadable free of charge.

Internet service provider (ISP)   Company that provides Internet access for a fee.

Intranet   A network using Internet software that transmits property and open information among computers housed within an entity such as a corporation. Intranets are mainly used to share company information and computing resources among employees.

ISDN   Integrated service digital network: narrowband, digital network offering integrated services of (mainly) digital telephony (e.g. telephony), data communication (file transfer) and relatively fast Internet connections, to be used alongside each other as the network is based on two lines to the subscriber; with improving capacity one gets broadband ISDN (B-ISDN).

Java   A computer programming language based on FORTRAN C++ that allows animated gifs and other movement on Web pages to contain programming algorithms that manipulate and manage data.

killer application   A form of software or use of the Web that leads millions to pay or subscribe to a particular service.

library/directory Web site   Information storage areas that can be accessed by online users.

listserv   An electronic mail box/discussion for subscribed users.

loose-audience   A term to describe the different temporal relationship users have to a particular Web site compared to television viewers. Although a site may have a large number of visitors, the 'audience' is individuated in its connection and further differentiated in how it might use the various parts of a site.

lurker   A chatroom participant who does not converse and only watches the interplay of other chatroom members.

menus   A dominant organizing pattern of Web pages, where links within and outside of a Web site are categorized and listed for the user.

modem   Modulator and demodulator: a device connecting a digital computer to analogue media like the traditional telephone.

MOOs (multi user domain-object oriented)   Topic specific MUDs.

MPEG (motion picture experts group)   A standard for compressing video images developed by the Motion Picture Experts Group.

MUDs (multi-user domains or multi-user dungeons)   Very popular interaction and online games where participants are involved in fantasy adventures that they help create.

multicasting   A system for sending an audio file to multiple receivers simultaneously.

multimedia   Used with two meanings: (1) a connection or a system of a number of devices (media); (2) a single device integrating several functions formerly used separately, like a multimedia PC (computer, VCR, audio, photo-editing and telephone in a single machine).

multitasking   The practice of using the Web at the same time while performing other computer tasks.

narrowcasting   Cable television delivery of topic-specific shows that appeal to small but loyal audiences.

NASDAQ   The stock exchange most associated with technology, electronic commerce, and Web-based corporations working to raise capital funds. NASDAQ which stands for the National Association of Securities Dealers Automated Quotation System is located in New York.

navigation   The process of moving from one site to another through the Web. This is normally done by following links. Various features of a browser also make navigation possible by keeping a history of the sites which the user has visited.

network   A hardware/software system that allows two or more computers to be connected so they share resources.

network society   Society in which social and media are shaping its prime mode of organization and most important structures.

New agora   A metaphor to describe how the Internet economy has developed: replicating marketplaces and squares, the Web and the Internet represent a new space where commerce, culture, class and politics collide in new and interesting ways.

new economy   Both a journalistic and governmental way to express the shift in the contemporary economy towards information and away from the industrial.

niche audience   A group of people who share an interest in a specific and narrow interest, such as Hawaiian music.

niche marketing   Directing marketing efforts towards a niche audience.

packet-switched network   The basic framework of the Internet that takes bundles of data and breaks them up into small packets or chunks that travel through the network independently.

pay-per-view   Commercial supply of television and video material, paid for by the piece, whole program or unit of time: also see video/audio on demand.

pixels   Tiny dots of colours that form the image on a Web page. Computer monitors display 72 pixels per inch, so one inch equals 72 pixels or dots per inch (dpi).

promotional aesthetic   A presentation of a cultural form through providing incomplete elements that are constructed to heighten the desire to want more. It is a dominant part of television and film, and has enveloped much of the Web's construction of content and its connection to advertising.

push technology Special online software that delivers Web information, initiated by an information provider rather than by a user.

robot A software program that automatically finds, identifies, and indexes information for online databases.

routers Powerful computers that link networks together on the Internet.

search engines Searching tools that find and retrieve information from the Web.

semiotics/semiology The study of signs and signification whatever their form and origin.

servers Powerful computers that provide continuous access to the Internet.

set-top boxes Systems such as Web TV, that transmit the Web over standard television sets.

shareware movement Copyrighted software distributed through an honour system: if you use the software and like it there is the expectation that some fee will be passed back to its creator.

slide show A technique to connect a series of images related to an event or person on a particular Web site where the user moves through the images in sequence.

smart technologies Machines that appear to 'think' and interact through cybernetic feedback loops.

spamming The unauthorized e-mail transmission of advertising messages.

streaming Technology that sends data through the Internet in a continuous flow so that information is displayed on a user's computer before the entire file has finished downloading.

subjectivity A term that has been used to conceptualize the constructed nature of identity that underlines that identity is not innate but constituted by one's cultural environment. In media studies, subjectivity often deals with how a text 'hails' or interpellates its audience and thereby attempts to position the audience's identity.

T1 line T1 is the fastest telephone trunk line commonly used to connect networks to the Internet. ADSL and HDSL technologies are implemented on T1 transmission links.

tags HTML labels that tell the Web browser how to display the text. Each tag consists of a left angle bracket (<), followed by the name of the tag and closed by a corresponding right angle bracket (>). Tags are usually paired and the ending tag is the same as the starting tag except the slash (/) precedes the text within the brackets. For example, to centre the word *title*, the HTML tags would be used as follows: <center>title</center>.

TCP/IP Network protocol based on packet switching, most often used in narrowband networks like the Internet.

technological determinism A conceptual understanding that social change is fundamentally shaped by the technology employed in a given culture.

telnet A terminal emulation protocol used when logging into other computer systems on the Internet.

TIMES An acronym used to describe the interrelated economic sectors of Telecommunication, Internet, Multimedia, E-commerce, Software and Security.

transmission control protocol (TCP/IP) Rules that define how computers made by different manufactures and running different software communicate with each other on the Internet.

uniform resource locator (URL) Set of codes that specify the location of files on Web servers. A URL includes the type of resources being accessed, the address of the server, and the location of the file. The syntax is scheme://host.domain/path/filename, where scheme is one of:

File: a file on your local system or a file on an anonymous FTP server

http: a file on a World Wide Web server

gopher: a file on a Gopher server

WAIS: a file on a WAIS server

News: a Usenet Newsgroup

telnet: a connection to a TELNET-based service.

Usenet newsgroup A conferencing bulletin board system that serves as a discussion and information exchange forum on specific topics.

user A metaphor that differentiates people's engagement with the Web from their status as viewers, listeners, readers and audience members of other media.

virtual Not tied to a particular place and time and not directly to a physical reality.

virtual reality media Multimedia switched in parallel creating three dimensional artificial environment to be perceived and experienced with a plurality of senses and offering the opportunity to interact with this simulated and pre-programmed environment.

virus A computer program that replicates on computer systems by incorporating itself into shared programs. Viruses range from harmless pranks that merely display an annoying message to programs that can destroy files or disable a computer altogether.

VRML (virtual reality modeling language) A computer language used to describe three-dimensional images; it allows a user to interact with image by viewing, moving or rotating it.

Webcams A simple video camera that sits next to your computer monitor. It is designed to send live and recorded video as well as still pictures over the Net to one or more users.

Webcasting   Broadcasting information and television channels on the Internet (e.g. receiving TV on Multimedia PC).

Web culture   The manner in which the Web represents, enacts, and supports the network society and how its users construct a space that exemplifies the fragmentation of the postmodern and the flows of information that loosely underwrite a sense of dispersed globalization and identity.

Weblog (Blogger)   A Web site (or section of a Web site) where users can post a chronological, up-to-date e-journal entry of their thoughts.

Webportal   Opening menu of an Internet access or service provider or a search engine offering a variety of daily services (news, entertainment, shopping, etc.).

Web radio   Radio transmitted over the Internet.

WebRing   A concept (or service) of linking together groups of Web sites that have the same theme.

Web-TV   Broadcasting Internet sources/sites on a television using a set-up box as a switch between a telephone or cable TV line and a television device offering interactive services from the Internet; one of the steps on the way to interactive television. It is now a trademark of Microsoft.

World Wide Web (WWW)   Collection of graphically designed Internet sites and pages mainly using HTML, that presents information in text, graphic, video and audio formats.

wysiwyg   An acronym that refers to software that eliminates the presence of codes so that the user for instance making a Web site sees what you see is what you get.

WEB THEORY TIMELINE
(1990 TO 2001)

A TIMELINE HIGHLIGHTING some of the key events and technologies which helped shape the Web.

1990

Major Events
- Tim Berners-Lee at CERN, Geneva implements a hypertext system to provide efficient information access to the members of the international physics community.
- Electronic Frontier Foundation (EFF) is founded.

Major Technology
- Archie released at McGill University.

1991

Major Events
- US High Performance Computing Act (Gore 1) establishes the National Research and Education Network (NREN). The purpose of this network is to conduct high speed networking research.
- NSFNET traffic passes 1 trillion bytes/month and 10 billion packets/month.

Major Technologies
- World Wide Web (WWW) released by CERN.
- Gopher released by the University of Minnesota.

1992

Major Events
- Internet Society (ISOC) is chartered.
- Number of hosts breaks 1,000,000.
- First MBONE audio multicast (March) and video multicast (November).
- The term 'surfing the Internet' is coined by Jean Armour Polly.

Major Technology
- Veronica, a search tool, is released by University of Nevada.

1993

Major Events
- US White House comes online (http://www.whitehouse.gov/): President Bill Clinton: president@whitehouse.gov.
- Internet Talk Radio begins broadcasting.
- United Nations (UN) comes online.
- US National Information Infrastructure Act.
- Businesses and media begin taking notice of the Internet.

Major Technologies
- Marc Andreessen, NCSA and the University of Illinois develops a graphical user interface to the WWW, called 'Mosaic for X'.
- WWW experiences a 634 per cent growth rate of service traffic. Gopher's growth is 997 per cent.

1994

Major Events
- ARPAnet/Internet celebrates twenty-fifth anniversary.
- Hundreds of thousands of new hosts were added to the Internet during this time period.
- Virtual shopping malls arrive on the Internet.
- NSFNET traffic passes 10 trillion bytes/month.
- First Virtual, the first cyberbank, opens up for business.
- The first banner ads appear on hotwired.com in October.
- Trans-European Research and Education Network Association (TERENA) is formed by the merger of RARE and EARN, with representatives from thirty-eight countries as well as CERN and ECMWF (October).

Top 10 Domains by Host #
- .com, .edu, .uk, .gov, .de, .ca, .mil, .au, .org, .net.

Major Technologies
- WWW edges out telnet to become second most popular service on the Net (behind ftp-data) based on percentage of packets and bytes traffic distribution on NSFNET.

1995

Major Events
- NSFNET reverts back to a research network. Main US backbone traffic now routed through interconnected network providers.
- Radio HK, the first commercial 24 hr Internet-only radio station starts broadcasting.
- Traditional online dial-up systems (CompuServe, America Online, Prodigy) begin to provide Internet access.
- Thousands in Minneapolis-St Paul (USA) lose Net access after transients start a bonfire under a bridge at the University of Minnesota causing fibre-optic cables to melt (30 July).
- A number of Net-related companies go public, with Netscape registering the third largest ever NASDAQ IPO share value (9 August).

Top 10 Domains by Host #
- .com, .edu, .net, .gov, .mil, .org, .de, .uk, .ca, .au.

Major Technologies
- Search engines.
- Sun launches JAVA.
- RealAudio, an audio streaming technology.
- WWW surpasses ftp-data in March as the service with greatest traffic on NSFNET based on packet count, and in April based on byte count.

Major Hacks
- The Spot (June 12), Hackers Movie Page (12 August).

1996

Major Events
- WIPO meeting produces WIPO copyright treaty.
- The controversial US Communications Decency Act (CDA) becomes law in the US in order to prohibit distribution of indecent materials over the Net. A few months later a three-judge panel imposes an injunction against its enforcement. Supreme Court unanimously rules most of it unconstitutional in 1997.
- Various ISPs suffer extended service outages, bringing into question whether they will be able to handle the growing number of users. AOL (19 hours), Netcom (13 hours), AT&T WorldNet (28 hours – e-mail only).
- Domain name tv.com sold to CNET for US$15,000.
- The Internet Ad Hoc Committee announces plans to add 7 new generic Top Level Domains: .firm, .store, .web, .arts, .rec, .info, .nom. The IAHC plan also calls for a competing group of domain registrars worldwide.
- The WWW browser war, fought primarily between Netscape and Microsoft, has rushed in a new age in software development, whereby new

releases are made quarterly with the help of Internet users eager to test upcoming (beta) versions.

- Restrictions on Internet use around the world:
    China: requires users and ISPs to register with the police.
    Germany: cuts off access to some newsgroups carried on CompuServe.
    Saudi Arabia: confines Internet access to universities and hospitals.
    Singapore: requires political and religious content providers to register with the state.
    New Zealand: classifies computer disks as 'publications' that can be censored
    source: Human Rights Watch.

Top 10 Domains by Host #
- .com, .edu, .net, .uk, .de, .jp, .us, .mil, .ca, .au.

Major Hacks
- US Department of Justice (17 August), CIA (19 September), US Air Force (29 December), UK Labour Party (6 December).

Major Technologies
- Search engines, JAVA, Internet Phone, Virtual environments (VRML), Collaborative tools, Internet appliance (Network Computer).

1997

Major Events
- Domain name business.com sold for US$150,000.

Top 10 Domains by Host #
- .com, .edu, .net, .jp, .uk, .de, .us, .au, .ca, .mil.

Major Hacks
- Indonesian Government (19 January, 10 February., 24 April, 30 June, 22 November), NASA (5 March), UK Conservative Party (27 April), Spice Girls (14 November).

Major Technologies
- Push, Multicasting.

1998

Major Events
- Dotcom boom takes off.
- Web size: estimates range between 275 (Digital) and 320 (NEC) million pages.
- Network Solutions registers its two millionth domain on 4 May.
- Compaq pays US$3.3million for altavista.com.

- ABCNews.com accidentally posts test US election returns one day early (2 November).
- US DoC enters into an agreement with the Internet Corporation for Assigned Names and Numbers (ICANN) to establish a process for transitioning DNS from US Government management to industry (25 November).
- Digital Millennium Copyright Act implements WIPO treaty under US law.

Major Bandwidth Generators
- Winter Olympics (February), World Cup (June–July), Starr Report (11 September).

Top 10 Domains by Host #
- .com, .net, .edu, .mil, .jp, .us, .uk, .de, .ca, .au.

Major Hacks
- US Department of Commerce (20 February), *New York Times* (13 September), China Society for Human Rights Studies (26 October), UNICEF (7 January).

Major Technologies
- E-Commerce, E-Auctions, Portals, XML, Open source software.

1999

Major Events
- First Internet Bank of Indiana, the first full-service bank available only on the Net, opens for business on 22 February.
- IBM becomes the first Corporate partner to be approved for Internet2 access.
- MCI/Worldcom, the vBNS provider for NSF, begins upgrading the US backbone to 2.5GBps.
- A forged Web page made to look like a Bloomberg financial news story raised shares of a small technology company by 31 per cent on 7 April.
- First large-scale Cyberwar takes place simultaneously with the war in Serbia/Kosovo.
- The Web becomes the focal point of British politics as a list of MI6 agents is released on a UK Web site. Though forced to remove the list from the site, it was too late as the list had already been replicated across the Net (15 May).
- business.com is sold for US$7.5million (it was purchased in 1997 for US$150,000 (30 November).

Top 10 Domains by Host #
- .com, .net, .edu, .jp, .uk, .mil, .us, .de, .ca, .au.

Major Hacks
- Star Wars (8 January), E-Bay (13 March), US Senate (27 May), Microsoft (26 October).

Major Technologies
- E-Trade, Online Banking, MP3.

Major Viruses
- Melissa (March), ExploreZip (June).

Major Lawsuit
- Microsoft.

2000

Major Events
- Dotcom crash begins (April).
- Black Friday, 21 April, NASDAQ loses 25 per cent of its value.
- Web size estimates by NEC-RI and Inktomi surpass 1 billion indexable pages.
- ICANN selects new TLDs: .aero, .biz, .coop, .info, .museum, .name, .pro (16 November).
- The European Commission contracts with a consortium of thirty national research networks for the development of Géant, Europe's new gigabit research network meant to enhance the current capability provided by TEN-155 (6 November).

Major Hacks
- RSA Security (February), Apache (May), Western Union (September), Microsoft (October).

Major Technologies
- Napster, Embedded Computing.

Major Virus
- Love Letter (May).

Major Lawsuit
- Napster.

2001

Major Events
- The first live distributed musical – *The Technophobe & The Madman* – over Internet2 networks debuts on 20 February.
- VeriSign extends its multilingual domain testbed to encompass various

European languages (26 February), and later the full Unicode character set (5 April) opening up most of the world's languages.
- Radio stations broadcasting over the Web go silent over royalty disputes (10 April).
- Napster is embroiled in litigation and is eventually forced to suspend service.
- European Council finalizes an international cybercrime treaty and adopts it on 9 November. This is the first treaty addressing criminal offences committed over the Internet.
- .biz and .info are added to the root server on 27 June with registrations beginning in July.
- Code Red worm and Sircam virus infiltrate thousands of web servers and e-mail accounts, respectively, causing a spike in Internet bandwidth usage and security breaches (July).
- A fire in a train tunnel running through Baltimore, Maryland seriously damages various fibre-optic cable bundles used by backbone providers, disrupting Internet traffic in the Mid-Atlantic states and creating a ripple effect across the US (18 July).
- GEANT, the pan-European Gigabit Research and Education Network, becomes operational (23 October).
- First uncompressed real-time gigabit HDTV transmission across a wide-area IP network takes place on Internet2 (12 November).

Major Viruses
- Code Red (July), Nimda (September), SirCam (July), BadTrans (April, November).

Major Technologies
- Grid Computing, P2P, Wireless devices.

Source: This timeline builds upon some of the material contained in Hobbes' *Internet Timeline*, *Pros Online – Internet History*, *What is the Internet?*, *History of the Internet* and *WWW: View from Internet Valley* and a variety of newspaper articles and books.

BIBLIOGRAPHY

Abercrombie N. and Longhurst B. (1998) *Audiences: A Sociological Theory of Performance and Imagination*, London; Thousand Oaks, CA: Sage.

ActivMedia Research (2000) 'Real numbers behind Net profits 2000', Online. Available http://www.activmediaresearch.com/real_numbers_2000.html

Alderman, J. (2001) *Sonic Boom: Napster, P2P and the Battle for the Future of Music*, London: Fourth Estate.

Alford, W. (1995) *To Steal a Book is an Elegant Offense*, Stanford, CA: Stanford University Press.

Allen, R. (1990) 'User models: theory, method and practice', *International Journal of Man Machine Studies* 3: 511–43.

Ang, I. (1991) *Desperately Seeking the Audience*, London: Routledge.

Attali, J. (1985) *Noise: The Political Economy of Music*, Minneapolis: University of Minnesota Press.

Atwood, R. (1996) 'The net grows', *Internet World*, September 10: 23.

Australia Government (1994) *Networking Australia's Future*.

Barlow, J.P. (1993) 'Putting old wine into new bottles: the economy of ideas', *Wired* 2 (5): 1 Online. Available HTTP: www.hotwired.com/wired/2.03/features/economy.ideas.html

Bateson, G. (1972) *Steps to an Ecology of Mind: Collected Essays in Anthropology, Psychiatry, Evolution, and Epistemology*, San Francisco: Chandler Publishing.

Baym, N. (2000) *Tune In, Log On*, London: Sage.

Baym, N., Zhang, Y.B. and Lin, M.C. (2001) *Is the Internet Really Any Different? Social Interactions Across Media*, presented at the International Communication Association, Washington DC, May 25.

Bell, D. (1973) *The Coming of Post-Industrial Society*, New York: Basic Books.

Bellis, M. (2002) 'Remote controls', available online: http://inventors.about.com/gi/dynamic/offsite.htm?site=http://www.ideafinder.com/history/inventions/story061.htm

Benedikt, M. (ed.) (1991) *Cyberspace: First Steps*, Cambridge, MA.: MIT Press.

Benjamin, W. (1968) *Illuminations*, edited and with an introduction by Hannah Arendt; translated by Harry Zohn, New York: Schocken Books.

Berger, P. and Luckmann, T. (1967) *The Social Construction of Reality*, New York: Doubleday.

Bergman, M. (2000) 'The deep Web: surfacing hidden value' accessed at Bright-planet.com, available at http://brightplanet.com/deepcontent/tutorials/DeepWeb/index.asp

Berman, M. (1993) 'Today's world news – creating a desktop news delivery system', *Proceedings of the 14th National Online News Meeting*, 33–8.

Berners-Lee, T. (1999) *Weaving The Web*, London: Orion Business Books.

Best, K. (2002) 'Networking culture: the contemporary cultural politics of com-puter-networked communication in relation to democratic organising', unpublished PhD dissertation, Royal Melbourne Institute of Technology (RMIT).

Bijker, W.E., Hughes, T.P. and Pinch, T. (1987) *The Social Construction of Techno-logical Systems: New Directions in the Sociology and History of Technology*, Cam-bridge, MA: MIT Press.

Biskupic, J. (2002) 'Online, the line on porn is more difficult to draw', *USA Today*, May 14:2.

Blumler, J.E. and Katz, E. (eds) (1974) *The Uses of Mass Communications*, London: Sage.

Briggs, F. (1981) 'Throughout analysis and results', *Proceedings of the 8th Annual Symposium on Computer Architecture*, pp. 31–6.

Brook, J. and Boal, I.A. (1995) *Resisting the Virtual Life: The Culture and Politics of Information*, San Francisco, CA: City Lights Books.

Bruckman, A. (1992) *Identity Workshop: Emergent Social and Psychological Phenom-ena in Text-Based Virtual Reality*, Online, available ftp://ftp.media.mit.edu/pub/asb/papers/identity-workshop.ps

—— (1993) 'Gender swapping on the Internet', *Proceedings of INET 93* San Francisco, CA, August 17–20. ftp://media.mit.edu/pub/asb/papers/gender-swapping.txt

Bruns, A. (2002) 'Resource centre sites: the new gatekeepers of the Web?', unpub-lished PhD dissertation, University of Queensland.

Burnett, R. (1996) *The Global Jukebox: The International Music Industry*, London: Routledge.

—— (1997) 'Media and information technology: the blindspot of media and com-munication research?', *Nordicom Review* 18 (2): 83–9.

—— (2002) 'A look inside the global music industry: explaining Swedish music export success'. Presented at Media in Transition 2 conference, MIT, Cam-bridge, MA, May 11.

Burnstein, D. and Kline, D. (1995) *Road Warriors: Dreams and Nightmares Along the Information Highway*, New York: Dutton.

Business Wire (2001) 'Alexa research finds "sex" popular on the Web', *Business Wire*, February 14.

Canada Government (1996) *Connection, Community, Content: The Challenge of the Information Highway* and *Building the Information Society: Moving Canada into the 21st Century.*

Castells, M. (1996) *The Rise of the Network Society, The Information Age: Economy, Society and Culture*, Volume I. Cambridge, MA; Oxford, UK: Blackwell.

—— (1997) *The Power of Identity, The Information Age: Economy, Society and Culture*, Volume II, Cambridge, MA; Oxford, UK: Blackwell.

—— (1998) *End of Millenium, The Information Age: Economy, Society and Culture*, Volume III. Cambridge, MA; Oxford, UK: Blackwell.

CNN.com (1999) Record labels force artists into fight for survival, April 27, 1999, Web posted at 4:30 p.m. EDT.

—— (2000a) Napster's side of the story, May 19, 2000, Web posted at: 1:01 p.m. EDT.

—— (2000b) Judge nixes Napster: record industry wins round in copyright infringement suit over music swapping, July 26, 2000, Web posted at 11:26 p.m. EDT.

—— (2000c) Napster shutdown seen as potential boon for competitors. July 27, 2000. Web posted at: 5:50 a.m. EDT.

Chesher, C. (1996) 'CD-ROM's identity crisis', *Media International Australia*, No. 81, August: 27–33.

Cheung, C. (2000) 'A home on the Web: presentations of self on personal home-pages', in D. Guantlett, *Web Studies: Rewiring Media Studies for the Digitial Age*, London: Arnold.

Creative Coalition Incentive (1996) 'Growth of the copyright industry'. http://www.iipa.com/pdf/1996_EXEC_SUMMARY.pdf

Cronin, B. and Davenport, E. (2001) 'E-Rogenous zones: positioning pornography in the digital economy.' *The Information Society* 17: 33–48.

Cubitt, S. (1998) *Digital Aesthetics*, London: Sage.

Cutler, N.E. and Danowski, J.A. (1985) Process gratification vs. content gratification in mass communication behavior: a cohort analysis of age changes in political and information-seeking, presented at the Fifteenth Annual Conference of the Pacific Chapter of the American Association for Public Opinion Research.

Cyveillance (2000) 'Sizing the Internet' White Paper, July online and accessed at http://www.cyveillance.com/web/corporate/white_papers.htm, July: accessed May 26 2002.

Davis, E. (1998) *Techgnosis*, New York: Harmony Books.

December, J. (1996) 'Units of analysis for internet communication', *Journal of Computer Mediated Communication* 1: 4. http://shum.cc.huji.ac.il/jcmc/vol1/issue4/december.html

DeFleur, M.L. and Ball-Rokeach, S.J. (1989) *Theories of Mass Communication 5th edn*, New York: Longman.

Deleuze, G. and Guattari, F. (1987) *A Thousand Plateaus: Capitalism and Schizophrenia*, translated by B. Massumi, Minneapolis: University of Minnesota Press.

Denmark Ministery of Research and Information (1995) *From Vision to Action. Info-Society 2000.*

Dery, M. (ed.) (1994) *Flame Wars*, Durham, NC: Duke University Press.

Dimmick, J., Kline, S.L. and Stafford, L. (2000) 'The gratification niches of personal e-mail and the telephone: competition, displacement and complementarity', *Communication Research* 27 (2): 227–48.

Dominick, J. (1999) 'Who do you think you are? Personal home pages and self-presentation on the World Wide Web', *Journalism and Mass Communication Quarterly* 76: 646–58.

Douglas, S. (1987) *Inventing American Broadcasting*, New York: Johns Hopkins University Press.

Dreyfus, H.L. (1979) *What Computers Can't Do*, New York: Harper & Row.

Drucker, P. (1994) *Post-Capitalist Society*, New York: Harper Business.

Dusseldorp, M. van, Scullion, R. and Bierhoff, J. (1999) *The Future of the Printed Press – Challenges in a Digital World*, Maastricht: European Journalism Centre.

Dyer-Witheford, N. (1999) *Cyber-Marx: Cycles and Circuits of Struggle in High-Technology Capitalism*, Urbana, Chicago: University of Illinois Press.

Economist. (1996) 'The property of mind', July 27: 1 http://www.economist.com/issue/27-07-96/wbsfl.html

Ellis, C.A., Gibbs, S.J. and Rein, G.L. (1993) 'Groupware: some issues and experiences', in R. Baecker (ed.) *Readings in Groupware and Computer–Supported Cooperative Work: Assisting Human–Human Collaboration*, San Mateo, CA: Morgan Kaufmann.

Ellul, J. (1965) *The Technological Society*, translated by John Wilkinson, New York: Knopf.

Enzenberger, H.M. (1974) *The Consciousness Industry: On Literature, Politics and the Media*, New York: Seabury Press.

European Commission (EC) (1994) Bangemann Task Force Report, *Europe and the Global Information Society.*

European Union (EU) (2001) TIMES Sector Jobs Statistics, Brussels.

Fallons, J. (1997) 'The Net as savior', http://hotwired.lycos.com/synapse/hotseat/97/36/transcript2a.html

Family Research Council (2000) 'Zogby/Focus Survey Reveals Shocking Internet Sex Statistics', *Family Research Council: Legal Facts*, 2 (20): March 30.

Fischer, C. (1992) *America Calling: A Social History of the Telephone to 1940*, Berkeley, CA: University of California Press.

Fiske, J. (1989) *Understanding Popular Culture*, Boston: Unwin Hyman.

—— (1994) *Media Matters: Everyday Culture and Political Change*, Minneapolis: University of Minnesota Press.

Fitzsimon, M. and McGill, L. (1995) 'The citizen as media critic', *Media Studies Journal* 9 (2): 91–101.

Foltz, P.W. and Dumais, S.T. (1992) 'Personalized information delivery: an analysis of information filtering methods', *Communications of the ACM* 35 (12): 51–60.

Frow, J. (1996) 'Information as gift and commodity', *New Left Review* 219: 89–108.

Galison, P. (1994) 'The ontology of the enemy: Norbert Wiener and the cybernetic vision', *Critical Inquiry* 21: 228–66.

Gardner, E. (2002) 'Online journalism's canary in a coalmine', *USC Annenberg Online Journalism Review*, May 14 http://www.ojr.org/ojr/business/ 1017777059.php

Garfinkel, H. (1984) *Studies in Ethnomethodology*, Cambridge, UK: Polity Press (see also Prentice-Hall 1967).

Gates, B. (1996) *The Road Ahead*, New York: Penguin.

Gauntlett, D. (ed.) (2000) *Web Studies*, London: Arnold.

Gibson, W. (1984) *Neuromancer*, New York: Bantam Books.

Gilder, G. (1994) *Life After Television*, New York: W.W. Norton.

Godwin, M. (1997a) www.hotwired.com/wired/3.08/departments/cyber.rights. html.

—— (1997b) 'Copyright Crisis', *Internet World* 3: 102.

Goffman, E. (1959) *Presentation of Self in Everyday Life*, New York: Anchor Books.

—— (1967) *Interaction Ritual*, New York: Anchor Books.

—— (1971) *Relations in Public*, New York: Basic Books.

Goodwin, A. (1992) *Dancing in the Distraction Factory: Music, Television and Popular Culture*, Minneapolis: University of Minnesota Press.

Graham, E. (1999) 'Cyborgs or goddesses? Becoming devine in a cyberfeminist age', *Information, Communication & Society* 2 (4): 419–38.

Graham, J. (2002) 'Thrill of hunt lures Google competitors', *USA Today* May 13: 4D.

Green E. and Adam A. (1998) 'On-line leisure: gender, and ICTs in the home'. *Information Communication and Society* 1 (3): Autumn: 291–312.

—— (eds) (2001) *Virtual Gender: Technology, Consumption, and Identity*, New York: Routledge.

Green, L. (1996) 'Technology and conversation: construction and destruction of community', *Australian Journal of Communication*, 23 (3): 54–67.

Greenfeld, K.T. (2000) 'Meet the napster', *Time Magazine*, October 2: 60–8.

Grimaldi, J. (2000) 'Napster ordered to shut down: piracy of music judge says', *The Washington Post* July 27: A01.

Gumpert, G. (1987) *Talking Tombstones and Other Tales of the Media Age*, New York: Oxford University Press.

Habermas, J. (1975) *Legitimation Crisis*, Boston: Beacon Press.

—— (1984) *The Theory of Communicative Action*, Boston: Beacon Press.

Hall, S. (1973) 'The determination of news photographs', in S. Cohen and J. Young (eds) *The Manufacture of News*, London: Hutchinson, 176–90.

Haraway, D. (1991) *Simians, Cyborgs and Women: The Reinvention of Nature*, New York: Routledge.

Hartley, J. (1996) *Popular Reality: Journalism, Modernity, Popular Culture*, London: Edward Arnold.

Hauben, R. and Hauben, M. (1995) 'Netizens and the wonderful world of the Net: an anthology', available from http://www.columbia.edu/~hauben/project_book.html

Hayles, N.K. (1999a) *How We Became Post-Human: Virtual Bodies in Cybernetics, Literature and Informatics*, Chicago: University of Chicago Press.

—— (1999b) 'The condition of virtuality' in P. Lunenfeld (ed.) *The Digital Dialectic: New Essays on New Media*, Cambridge MA: MIT Press, pp. 69–94.

Heilbroner, R. (1992) *Twenty-First Century Capitalism*, Ontario: Anansi Press.

Herman, E. (1996) 'The propaganda model revisited', *Monthly Review*, July 1996: 23–4.

Herman, A. and Swiss, T. (eds) (2000) *The World Wide Web and Contemporary Cultural Theory*, New York: Routledge.

Horkheimer, M. and Adorno, T.A. (1987) *The Dialectic of Enlightenment*, New York: Continuum.

Hugo, V. (1978) *Notre Dame of Paris*, London: Penguin Books.

Huyssens, A. (1986) *After the Great Divide: Modernism, Mass Culture, Postmodernism*, Bloomington: Indiana University Press.

Industry Canada (1994) *The Canadian Information Highway: Building Canada's Information and Communications Infrastructure*, Ottawa: Industry Canada.

Information Highway Advisory Council (IHAC) (1994) *Providing New Dimensions for Learning*, Ottawa: Creativity and Entrepreneurship.

Innis, H.A. (1940) *The Cod Fisheries; The History of an International Economy*, New Haven: Yale University Press

—— (1950) *Empire and Communications*, London: Oxford University Press.

—— (1951) *The Bias of Communication*, Toronto: University of Toronto Press.

—— (1956) *The Fur Trade in Canada: An Introduction to Canadian Economy History*, Toronto: University of Toronto Press.

Internet Indicators (2000) 'Measuring the Internet economy', The Center for Research in Electronic Commerce, Graduate School of Business, University of Texas at Austin located online at http://www.internetindicators.com/archives.html, accessed July 23, 2000.

Internet Society (2002) 'All about the Internet', online at http://www.isoc.org/internet/history/index.shtml, accessed May 25, 2002

Japanese Government (1994) *Reforms Towards the Intellectually Creative Society of the 21st Century*.

Jones, S.G. (ed.) (1995) *CyberSociety: Computer-mediated Communication and Community*, Thousand Oaks, CA: Sage.

—— (ed.) (1997) *Virtual Culture: Identity and Communication in Cybersociety*, London: Sage Publications.

Joyce, M. (1987) *Afternoon, A Story* [CD], Watertown, MA: Eastgate Systems.

Katz, J.E. and Aspden, P. (1997) 'A nation of strangers?', *Communications of the ACM* 40, 12: 81–6.

Katz, E., Blumler, J.G. and Gurevitch, M. (1974) 'Utilization of mass communication by the individual', in J.G. Blumler and E. Katz (eds) *The Uses of Mass*

Communications: Current Perspectives on Gratification Research, London: Sage, 19–32.

Kaye, B. and Medoff, M. (1999) *The World Wide Web*, London: Mayfield.

—— (2001) *Just a Click Away: Advertising on the Internet*, Boston: Allyn and Bacon.

King, B. (2000) Napster CEO Gets Intellectual, *Hotwired*, October 2, 2000, 3:00 a.m. PDT.

—— (2001) Music archive going silent, *Hotwired*, February 9, 2001, 2:00 a.m. PST.

Kitzmann, A. (2003) (forthcoming) *Saved From Oblivion*, New York: Peter Lang.

Klein, N. (2000) *No Logo*, Toronto: Knopf Canada.

Knopf, H.P. (1996) 'Copyright zealots are the real threat to the Net', *The Globe and Mail* January 5: 62.

Koepke, N. (2000) Sony music executive plug in Europe, April 2.

Kraut, R., Patterson, M., Lundmark, V., Kiesler, S., Mukhopadhyay, T. and Scherlis, W. (1998) 'Internet paradox: a social technology that reduces social involvement and psychological well-being?', *American Psychologist* 53 (9): 1017–31.

Kuhn, T. (1970) *The Structure of Scientific Revolutions*, Chicago: University of Chicago Press.

Landauer, T. (1995) *The Trouble With Computers: Usefulness, Usability and Productivity*, Cambridge, MA: MIT Press.

Landow, G.P. (1992) *Hypertext: The Convergence of Contemporary Critical Theory and Technology*, Baltimore: Johns Hopkins University Press.

—— (ed.) (1994) *Hyper/Text/Theory*, London: Johns Hopkins University Press.

LaRose, R., Eastin, M.S. and Gregg, J. (2001) 'Reformulating the Internet paradox: social cognitive explanations of Internet use and depression', *Journal of Online Behavior* 1 (29): available at www.behavior.net/JOB/v1n1/paradox.html

Lasch, C. (1995) *The Revolt of the Elites and the Betrayal of Democracy*, New York: W.W. Norton and Company.

Lasswell, H. (1971) *Propaganda Technique in World War I*, Cambridge, MA: MIT Press.

Latour, B. (1987) *Science in Action*, Cambridge, MA: Harvard University Press.

Leiss, W., Kline, S. and Jhally, S. (1990) *Social Communication in Advertising: Persons, Products and Images of Well Being*, Scarborough, ON: Nelson Canada.

Lessard, D. (2002) *pcbiography*, available at http://www.pcbiography.net/ (May 2002).

Lessig, L. (2001) *The Future of Ideas*, New York: Random House.

—— (1999) *Code and Other Laws of Cyberspace*, New York: Basic Books.

Levinson, P. (1999) *Digital McLuhan: A Guide to the Information Millennium*, New York: Routledge.

Levy, M.R. and Windahl, S. (1985) 'The concept of audience activity', in K. Rosengren *et al.* (eds) *Media Gratifications Research*, Belmont, CA: Sage, 109–22.

Levy, P. (1997) *Collective Intelligence: Mankind's Emerging World in Cyberspace*, translated by Robert Bononno, New York: Plenum.

Lieb, C. (1998) 'News filters as layers', Proceedings of the 19th National Online News Meeting, 62–6.

Linder, L. (1999) *Public Access Television: America's Electronic Soapbox*, Westport, CT: Praeger.

Lippman, W. (1992) *Public Opinion*, New York: Macmillan.

Littlejohn, S.W. (1996) *Theories of Human Communication 5th edn*, Belmont, CA: Wadsworth.

McChesney, R. (1990) 'The battle for the US airways, 1928–1935', *Journal of Communication* 40 (4): autumn.

—— (1999) *Rich Media, Poor Democracy: Communication Politics in Dubious Times*, Urbana, IL: University of Illinois Press.

—— (2000) 'So much for the magic of technology and the free market', in A. Herman and T. Swiss (eds) *The World Wide Web and Contemporary Cultural Theory*, New York: Routledge, 5–35.

McLuhan, M. (1962) *The Gutenburg Galaxy*, Toronto: University of Toronto Press.

—— (1965) *Understanding Media: The Extensions of Man*, New York: McGraw Hill.

McNamara, T. (2000) 'Defining the blurry line between commerce and content', *Columbia Journalism Review*, July–August, 31.

McQuail, D. (1992) *Media Performance*, London: Sage.

—— (1994) *Mass Communication Theory, 3rd edn*, London: Sage.

Marvin, C. (1998) *When Old Technologies Were New*, New York: Oxford University Press.

Manjoo, F. (2001). 'Peer-to-peering into the future', *Hotwired*, February 15, 2001, 2:00 a.m.

Markus, M. (1990). 'Towards a "critical mass" theory of interactive media', in J. Fulk and C.W. Steinfield (eds) *Org and Communication Technology*, Belmont, CA: Sage, 194–218.

Marcuse, H. (1964) *One Dimensional Man: Studies in the Ideology of Advanced Industrial Society*, Boston: Beacon Press.

Marshall, P.D. (1997) 'The commodity and the Internet: interactivity and the generation of the audience commodity', *Media International Australia*, February: 51–62.

—— (1998) 'Thinking through new', *M/C: A Journal of Media and Culture* 1, (1), http://www.uq.edu.au/mc/9807/think.html (July 23, 1998).

—— (2000) 'The mediation is the message: the legacy of McLuhan for the digital era?', *Media International Australia* 94: February, 29–37.

—— (2002) 'New media hierarchies: rethinking media through access, excess, exclusion', in M. Wark, *Thinking Media*, Sydney: Pluto Press.

Marx, Karl (1978) 'The German ideology', in R.C. Tucker, *The Marx-Engels Reader*, 2nd edn, New York: W.W. Norton & Co.

Meyrowitz, J. (1985) *No Sense of Place: The Impact of Electronic Media on Social Behavior*, New York, NY: Oxford University Press.

Middelhoff, T. (2000) 'Let's journey into the digital everyday life of music', Keynote opening of the PopKomm conference, August 18, Cologne.

Miller, D.L. (1973) *George Herbert Mead: Self, Language and the World*, Texas: University of Texas Press.

Mitchell,W.J. (1995) *City of Bits: Space, Place, and the Infobahn*, Cambridge, MA: MIT Press.

Modleski, T. (1982) *Loving with a Vengeance: Mass-produced Fantasies for Women*, Hamden, CT: Archon.

Morley, D. (1986) *Family Television: Cultural Power and Domestic Leisure*, London: Comedia.

Morris, M. and Ogan, C. (1996) 'The Internet as Mass Medium', *Journal of Computer Mediated Communication* 1: 4, available from http://shum.cc.huji.ac.il/jcmc/vol1/issue4/morris.html

Moulthrop, S. (1994) 'Rhizome and resistance: hypertext and the dreams of a new culture', in G.P. Landow (ed.) *Hyper/Text/Theory*, London: Johns Hopkins University Press.

Mumford, L. (1963) *Technics and Civilization*, New York: Harcourt, Brace & World.

Naisbitt, J. (1982) *Megatrends*, New York: Warner Books.

NASDAQ (2001) 'NASDAQ Newsroom' available at http://www.nasdaqnews.com/ (May 25, 2002)

National Research Council, USA (2000) *The Digital Dilemma: Intellectual Property in the Information Age*, Committee on intellectual property rights and the emerging information infrastucture, Washington DC.

Nava, M. (1989) 'Consumerism and its contradictions', *Cultural Studies*, 1.2.

Negroponte, N. (1995) *Being Digital*, London: Hodder and Stoughton.

Nie, N.H. and Erbring, L. (2000) *Internet and Society: A Preliminary Report*, Palo Alto, CA: Stanford Institute for the Quantitative Study of Society, available www.stanford.edu/group/siqss

Nelson, T. (1987) *Computer Lib/Dream Machines*, revised edn, Redmond, Washington: Tempus Books of Microsoft Press.

Nielsen Netratings (2000) available: http://www.netratings.com

Nix, J. (1998) 'Bertelsmann to sell books on the Internet', *Variety* March 2–8: 7.

NUA Internet Surveys (2000), available http://www.nua.ie/surveys/ (June 9, 2000).

Organization for Economic Cooperation and Development (OECD) (1989) Information Technology and New Growth Opportunities, Information Computer Communications Policy, 19, Paris.

—— (1992) Information Networks and New Technologies: Opportunities and Policy Implications for the 1990s, Information Computer Communications Policy, 30, Paris.

Palmgreen, P. and Rayburn, J.D. (1994) 'An expectancy-value approach to media gratifications', in K.E. Rosengren, L.A. Wenner and P. Palmgreen (eds) *Media Gratifications Research: Current Perspectives*, Thousand Oaks, CA: Sage, 171–93.

Papacharissi, Z. (2001) 'The utility of personal World Wide Web home pages', presented at the International Communication Associatation, Washington DC, May 25.

Paterson, H. (1996) 'Computer mediated groups: a study of culture in Usenet', unpublished PhD dissertation, Texas A&M University.

Pavlik, J.V. (1996) *New Media Technology: Cultural and Commercial Perspectives*, Boston, MA: Allyn and Bacon.

Pew Internet and American Life Project (2000) *Tracking Online Life: How Women Use the Internet to Cultivate Relationships with Family and Friends*, Washington DC, available www.pewinternet.org

Poole, S. (2000) *Trigger Happy: The Inner-life of Videogames*, London: Fourth Estate.

Poster, M. (1990) *The Mode of Information: Poststructuralism and Context*, Chicago: University of Chicago Press.

Prodigy.com (2000) 'Small biz Websites on the rise, yet many owners slow to embrace the Internet', available http://www.prodigy.com/pcom/prodigy_business/business_content.html (April 12, 2000)

Putnam, R. (2000) *Bowling Alone*, New York: Simon and Schuster.

Rafaeli, S. and Sudweeks, F. (1994) 'ProjectH overview: a quantitative Study of computer-mediated communication', Technical Report, University of Minnesota, ftp://ftp.arch.su.edu.au/pub/projectH/papers/techreport.txt

—— (1995) 'Interactivity on the Nets', in S. Rafaeli, F. Sudweeks and M. McLaughlin (eds) *In Network and Netplay: Virtual Groups on the Internet*, Cambridge, MA: AAAI/MIT Press. ftp://ftp.arch.su.edu.au/pub/projectH/papers/netint.ps

Reid, E. (1991) 'Electropolis: communication and community on internet relay chat', unpublished Honours thesis, University of Melbourne. ftp://ftp.parc.xerox.com/pub/MOO/papers/electropolis.

—— (1994) 'Cultural formations in text-based virtual realities', unpublished Master's thesis, University of Melbourne. ftp://ftp.parc.xerox.com/pub/MOO/papers/CulturalFormations.ps

Reuters.com (2000a) 'Study: Napster increases music sales', July 21, 2000, 6:20 a.m. PDT.

—— (2000b) 'Prince really digs his Napster', August 9, 2000, 2:20 p.m. PDT.

—— (2001) 'Start paying for Napster in June', January 29, 2001, 7:00 a.m. PST.

Rheingold, H. (1993) *The Virtual Community: Homesteading on the Electronic Frontier*, Reading, MA: Addison-Wesley.

Rogers, E.M. (1986) *Communication Technology: The New Media in Society*, New York: The Free Press.

Rosoff, M. (1999) 'Sex on the Web: an inside look at the Net porn industry', *CNET.com*, accessed http://home.cnet.com/internet/0-3805-7-280110.html (September 1999).

Rubin, A.M. (1983) 'Television uses and gratifications: the interaction of viewing patterns and motivations', *Journal of Broadcasting* 27 (1): 37–51.

—— (1984) 'Ritualized and instrumental television viewing', *Journal of Communication* 34 (3): 67–77.

Rubin, A.M., Perse, E.M. and Powell, R.A. (1985) 'Loneliness, parasocial interaction, and local television news viewing', *Human Communication Research*
12 (2): 155–80.

Samoriski, J. (2002) *Issues in Cyberspace*, New York: Allyn and Bacon.

Samuelson, P. (1997) 'Big media beaten back', *Wired* 3: 61.

Sanford, G (1996–2002) 'Apple history', accessed online at: http://www.apple-
history.com/history.html (October 25, 2001).

Schenker, J. (2000) 'The Infoanarchist', *Time* July 17: 42.

Schmidt, A. (2000) 'Bertelsmann keynote speech', *Plug in Europe*, April 2.

Schudson, M. (1995) *The power of News*, Cambridge, MA: Harvard University Press.

Schutz, A. (1970) *On Phenomenology and Social Relations*, Chicago: University of
Chicago Press.

Shank, G. (1993) 'Abductive multiloguing: the Semiotic dynamics of navigating
the Net', *The Arachnet Electronic Journal on Virtual Culture* 1, 1.
www.unikoeln.de/themen/cmc/text/shank.93a.txt

Shattuc, J. (1997) *The Talking Cure: TV Talk Shows and Women*, New York: Routledge.

Shields, R. (ed.) (1996) *Cultures of Internet: Virtual Spaces, Real Histories, Living
Bodies*, London: Sage.

Singapore Government (1996) *IT 2000:Vision of an Intelligent Island*.

Slevin, J. (2000) *The Internet and Society*, London: Polity Press.

Smith, M.J. (1998) 'E-merging strategies of identity: the rhetorical construction of
self in personal Web sites', unpublished doctoral dissertation, Ohio University.

Smith, M. and Kollock, P. (eds) (1998) *Communities in Cyberspace*, London: Routledge.

Smythe, D. (1981) *Dependency Road: Communications, Capitalism, Consciousness
and Canada*, Norwood, NJ: Ablex Publishers.

Spears, R. and Lea, M. (1994) 'Panacea or panopticon? The hidden power in
computer-mediated communication', *Communication Research* 21 (4):
427–59.

Stafford, L., Kline, S.L. and Dimmick, J. (1999) 'Home e-mail: relational maintenance and gratification opportunities', *Journal of Broadcasting and Electronic
Media* 43: 659–69.

Stone, A.R. (1996) *The War of Desire and Technology at the End of the Mechanical
Age*, Cambridge, MA: MIT Press.

Stranahan, P. (1999) 'Personal computers: history and development', *Jones Telecommunications and Multimedia Encyclopedia*, http://www.digitalcentury.com/
encyclo/update/pc_hd.html

Stroud, M. (2000) 'A music industry death knell?' *Hotwired*, January 11, 2000,
3:00 a.m.

Sundar, S.S. and Nass, C. (1996) 'Source effects in users' perception of online
news', paper presented to the Communication and Technology Division at
the 46th annual conference of the International Communication Association,
Chicago, IL.

Sveningsson, M. (2001) *Creating a Sense of Community: Experiences from a Swedish Web Chat*, Linkoping: Linkoping University Press.

Sweden IT Commission (1994) *Information Technology: Wings to Human Ability*, Stockholm: SOU.

Teilhard de Chardin, P. (1965) *The Phenomenon of Man*, (translated by Bernard Wall), New York: Harper & Row.

Tetzlaff, D. (2000) 'Yo-ho-ho and a server of Warez', in A. Herman and T. Swiss (eds) *The World Wide Web and Contemporary Cultural Theory*, New York, Routledge, 99–126.

Toffler, A. (1970) *Future Shock*, New York: Random House.

—— (1980) *The Third Wave*, New York: Morrow.

Touraine, A. (1971) *The Post-Industrial Society; Tomorrow's Social History: Classes, Conflicts and Culture in the Programmed Society*, translated by Leonard F.X. Mayhew, New York: Random House.

Tuchman, G. (1978) *Making News: A Study in the Construction of Reality*, New York: Free Press.

Turkle, S. (1985) *The Second Self*, New York: Simon & Schuster.

—— (1995) *Life on the Screen: Identity in the Age of the Internet*, New York: Simon & Schuster.

—— (1996) 'Who am we?', *Wired* 4 (1): 48.

UCLA Internet Report (2000) 'Surveying the digital future', UCLA Center for Communication Policy, available at www.ccp.ucla.edu

Upsdell, C. (2002) 'Browser news', online at http://www.upsdell.com/BrowserNews/stat.htm, accessed May 25, 2002.

US Government (1995a) The Working Group on Intellectual Property Rights. Intellectual Property and the National Information Infrastructure, White Paper, Washington, DC.

—— (1995b) NII Copyright Protection Act of 1995, Washington, DC.

—— (1999) The digital Millennium copyright act (DMCA), Washington, DC.

US Government Department Of Energy (1993) National information infrastructure – agenda for action, Washington, DC.

Van Dijk, J. (1999) *The Network Society*, Sage: London.

Volovic, T. (1995) 'Encounters on-line', *Media Studies Journal* 9 (2): 113–21.

Wall Street Research Net (2000) 'Internet.com's Internet stock list', accessed at http://www.wrsn.com/apps/internetstocklist/(July 23, 2000).

Wark, M. (1994) *Virtual Geography*, Bloomington: Indiana University Press.

Watters, C.R., Shepherd, M.A. and Burkowski, F.J. (1998) 'Electronic news delivery project', *Journal of the American Society for Information Science* 49 (2): 134–50.

Wayner, P. (2000) *Free for All: How Linux and the Free Software Movement Undercut the High-Tech Titans*, New York: Harper Business.

Webster, F. and Robins, K. (1999) *Times of the Technoculture*, London: Routledge.

Welch, M. (1999) 'Dolby says it's payback time', *Hotwired*, September 9, 1999, 3:00 a.m. PDT.

Wellman, B. (ed.) (1999) *Networks in the Global Village*, Boulder, CO: Westview Press.

Wellman, B. and Hampton, K. (1999) 'Living networked in a wired world', *Contemporary Sociology* 28, 6.

Wenner, L.A. (1985) 'The nature of news gratifications', in K.E. Rosengren, L.A. Wenner and P. Palmgreen (eds) *Media Gratifications Research: Current Perspectives*, Thousand Oaks, CA: Sage, 171–93

White, H., McConnell, E., Clipp, E., Bynum, L., Teague, C., Navas, L., Craven, S. and Halbrecht, H. (1999) 'Surfing the net in later life: a review of the literature and pilot study of computer use and quality of life', *The Journal of Applied Gerontology* 18 (3): 358–78.

White, P.B. (1996) 'Online services: the emerging battle for transactional space', *Media International Australia*, 79: 4–11.

Wiener, N. (1948) *Cybernetics; Or, Control and Communication in the Animal and the Machine*, New York: Wiley.

Winn, M. (1977) *The Plug-in Drug*, New York: Viking Press.

Winner, L. (1977) *Autonomous Technology: Technics as Out-of-Control in Political Thought*, Cambridge, MA: MIT Press.

Winston, B. (1998) *Media Technology and Society – A History*, London: Routledge.

Williams, F., Rice, R.E. and Rogers, E.M. (1988) *Research Methods and the New Media*, New York: The Free Press.

Williams, Raymond (1965) *The Long Revolution*, Harmondsworth: Penguin.

—— (1974) *Television, Technology and Cultural Form*, London: Fontana.

—— (1989) *What I Came to Say*, London: Hutchison Radius.

Wolff, K.H. (1950) *The Sociology of Georg Simmel*, New York: The Free Press.

World Lingo (2002) 'World Language Statistics', online at http://www.worldlingo.com/resources/language_statistics.html, accessed on May 25, 2002.

Wynn, E. and Katz, J. (1998) 'Hyperbole over cyberspace: self-presentation and social boundaries in Internet home pages and discourse', *The Information Society* 13 (4): 297–328.

Yahoo! (2001) 'The history of Yahoo! How it all started', online at http://docs.yahoo.com/info/misc/history.html, accessed on April 10, 2002.

Youngs, G. (2001) 'The political economy of time in the Internet era: feminist perspectives and challenges', *Information Communication and Society* 4 (1): 14–33.

Zakon, R.H. (2002) 'Hobbes Internet timeline', online at http://www.zakon.org/robert/internet/timeline/, accessed May 25, 2002.

WEB SITE RESOURCES

THE FOLLOWING IS a list of sites that may be useful to engage in some of the themes presented in each of the chapters. General resources, updates and new developments of sites related to the concepts developed in the book are available on the book's Web site: www.webtheory.nu

Chapter 1

Tallest building/skyscraper debate:

http://www.xs4all.nl/%7Ehnetten/tallest.html

Innis – a biographical essay:

http://www.mala.bc.ca/~soules/paradox/innis.htm

McLuhan – from his original institutional home at the University of Toronto:

http://www.mcluhan.utoronto.ca/mm.html

Mumford – an homage to Lewis Mumford:

http://bluehawk.monmouth.edu/~library/mumford.html

The MIT Media Lab – the institutional home of Nicholas Negroponte:

http://www.media.mit.edu/

An interesting site developed by Daniel Chandler on technological determinism:

http://www.aber.ac.uk/media/Documents/tecdet/tecdet.html

The best historical timeline for the Internet is Hobbes':

http://www.zakon.org/robert/internet/timeline/

Chapter 2

Cybernetics can be explored through the following site developed by F. Heylighen:

http://www.google.com/search?hl=en&ie=UTF8&oe=UTF8&q
=cybernetics

The interactive Bonzi purple ape can be found at:

http://www.bonzi.com/bonzibuddy/bonzibuddyfreehom.asp

Mindy McAdams has developed an approach called *cybermedia*:

http://www.well.com/user/mmcadams/cyber.main.html

Chapter 3

A massive selection of emoticons and acronyms can be found at:

www.pb.org/emoticon and www.pb.org/acronym

Chapter 4

A resource centre for Cyberculture Studies:

http://www.com.washington.edu/rccs/

Sarah Zupko's site is also useful to find resources on the links between popular culture, cultural studies, and new media studies:

http://www.popcultures.com/

A provocative article on cyberfeminism by Rosa Braidotti:

http://www.let.uu.nl/womens_studies/rosi/cyberfem.htm

A massive amount of research has been generated by the Pew Internet and American Life Study:

http://www.pewinternet.org/

An interesting article on Enzensberger by James Poniewozik:

http://www.salon.com/media/1999/01/cov_27mediab.html

Chapter 5

A site devoted to locations that discuss and present Web design:

http://www.digitalthread.com/

The Webby Awards homepage:

http://www.Webbyawards.com/main/

Although filled with advertisements, one of the best locations to look at html tutorials to learn to make Web pages:

http://www.htmlgoodies.com/

An example of sophisticated and interlinked movie promotional site: Spider-Man the official movie Web site:

http://www.spiderman.sonypictures.com/

Chapter 6

The famous efforts of Salon.com are worthy of a study of how the Internet is trying to create new content and a form of commercial publication:

http://www.salon.com/

To understand the ebbs and flows of the advertising value of Web sites, Nielsens' Netratings site is important:

http://www.netratings.com/

Other services that survey the Net are NUA:

http://www.nua.ie/surveys/index.cgi

and Jupiter Mediametrix

http://www.jmm.com/

Major amounts of electronic commerce research is generated by the University of Texas Center for the Study of Electronic Commerce:

http://www.internetindicators.com

The continuing play of NASDAQ can be perused via:

http://www.nasdaq.com/

A site devoted to linking to hacker-related sites:

http://www.livinginternet.com/?i/ia_hackers_sites.htm

Chapter 7

World Intellectual Property Organization:

www.wipo.org

Electronic Frontier Foundation:

www.eff.org

Chapter 8

One of the leaders in meshing their televised news with their online news is CNN:

http://www.cnn.com/

Metro remains an example of a paper that has taken on the ethos of informational news look in a paper:

http://www.metro.lu/

Alternative and mainstream media are linked and debated through the mediachannel site:

http://www.mediachannel.org/

Equally alternative and connected to the issues around globalization is znet:

http://www.zmag.org/

Some national television broadcasters:

ABC USA: www.abc.com
CBS USA: www.cbs.com
NBC USA: www.nbc.com
Fox USA: www.foxnetwork.com
CBC Canada: www.cbc.com
SVT Sweden: www.svt.se
BBC UK: www.bbc.com

Newspapers

New York Times: www.nytimes.com
San José Mercury News: www.sjmercury.com
Washington Post: www.washingtonpost.com
USA Today: www.usatoday.com
Guardian: www.guardian.co.uk

Academic efforts to create online journals that cross over into the popular can be seen through *M/C* and *M/C* Reviews: http://www.media-culture.org.au/

Online journalism Review site from the Annenberg School of Communication at USC:

   http://www.ojr.org/ojr/page_one/index.php

Chapter 9

BMG music: www.bmg.com
EMI music: www.emigroup.com
Sony music: www.sonymusic.com
Warner Music group: www.warnermusic.com
Universal Music group: www.umusic.com
Internet Underground Music Archive: www.iuma.com
MP3: www.mp3.com
IFPI: www.ifpi.org
Pressplay: www.pressplay.com
Musicnet: www.musicnet.com
Recording Industry Association of America: www.riaa.com
Motion Picture Association of America: http://www.mpaa.org
Napster: www.napster.com
Gnutella: www.gnutella.com
Kazaa: www.kazaa.com
FreeNet, the free network project: http://freenetproject.org

Web Theory site: www.Webtheory.nu
(links, general resources, teaching aides, power point slides, discussion)

INDEX